# North Korea

## the Bradt Travel Guide

**Robert Willoughby**

edition
2

www.bradtguides.com

Bradt Travel Guides Ltd, UK
The Globe Pequot Press Inc, USA

KEY
Capital city
Main city
Main town
Airport
Mountain
Main road
Railway
Ferry
International boundary

CHINA

NORTH KOREA

Sonbong
Rajin
Rason Free
Enterprise Zone
CHONGJIN
Mt Chilbo
KILJU
TANCHON
Musan
Sinpo
Mt Paektu
HYESAN
HAMHUNG
Mt Paektu
page 197
KANGGYE
Huichon
Mt Myohyang
Kaechon
Myohyangsan
page 157
PAKCHON
SINUIJU
DANDONG

West Sea of Korea

East Sea of Korea

Japan (Korean use only)

Russia-China-Paektu

Hyundai-Asan

Land crossing (road)

Lake Sijung
page 165

Inner Kumgang
page 168

Kaesong to Panmunjom
page 133

SOUTH KOREA

SEOUL

Kaesong

De-militarised Zone (DMZ)

Mt Kumgang

Kosong

WONSAN

PHYONGSONG

PYONGYANG

SARIWON

Pyongsan

Haeju

Nampo

Mt Kuwol

Pyongyang — Grand Monument,
May Day stadium, Moran Hill
page 93

Yellow Sea

West Sea of Korea

N

Bradt

50km

50 miles

0

0

# North Korea
# Don't
# miss...

**Monuments**
Juche Tower
(NB) page 112

**Pyongyang**
The capital shrouded in
early morning mist
(NB) page 93

**Palaces**
Kumsusan Memorial
Palace, Kim Il Sung's
home in life and
death
(NB) page 111

**Spectacular
scenery**
The volcanic
mountain Mt Paektu
(JTB/Alamy) page 197

**Beaches**
Between Wonsan
and Mount Kumgang
(RT) page 164 & 166

*above* **The Monument to the Three Charters of National Reunification**
(KT) page 115

*centre* **The hammer, sickle and writing brush form the Workers' Party Monument**
(NB) page 114

*below* **Men of the Korean People's Army**
(NB) page 55

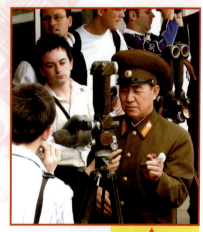

## AUTHOR

**Robert Willoughby** was born in London where he is based as a freelance journalist and author. Realising conventional university would be the death of him, he went to work selling ice-cream in Chicago for a summer and in 1995 was smitten with the absolute thrill and education of living and working abroad – something he also thinks he inherited from his father. He qualified as a TEFL teacher and started an Open University degree, while working in Moscow and Hanoi and travelling across southeast Asia before moving to Beijing, where he moved into journalism. In late 2001 he crossed the final frontier into North Korea, then returned to London to hire out his soul reporting commodity markets in order to buy a place in Deptford. As well as the truly pioneering Bradt *Guide to North Korea*, he co-wrote the best-selling *Rough Guide to Conspiracy Theories* and is currently working on a book on the rise of the global neo-Stasi state, as well as a novel.

## CONTRIBUTOR

**Robin Paxton**, a journalist formerly based in Singapore and now in Moscow, contributed sections on the parts of the DPRK other travellers haven't reached, which in this volume consists of the East Coast to Tanchon. Robin Paxton can be contacted at robinpen@hotmail.com

### FEEDBACK REQUEST

Every effort has been made to ensure that the details contained within this book are as accurate and up to date as possible. Inevitably, however, things move on. Any information regarding such changes, or relating to your experiences in North Korea – good or bad – would be very gratefully received. Such feedback is priceless when compiling further editions, and in ensuring pleasant stays for future visitors. Either email the author direct (e *robertwiloughby@yahoo.co.uk*) or contact Bradt (*23 High Street, Chalfont St Peter, Bucks SL9 9QE, England;* e *info@bradtguides.com*).

## PUBLISHER'S FOREWORD

The first Bradt travel guide was written in 1974 by George and Hilary Bradt on a river barge floating down a tributary of the Amazon. In the 1980s and '90s the focus shifted away from hiking to broader-based guides to new destinations – usually the first to be published on these places. In the 21st century Bradt continues to publish these ground-breaking guides, along with others to established holiday destinations, incorporating in-depth information on culture and natural history alongside the nuts and bolts of where to stay and what to see.

Bradt authors support responsible travel, with advice not only on minimum impact but also on how to give something back through local charities. Thus a true synergy is achieved between the traveller and local communities.

\* \* \*

We're incredibly proud to be publishing this second edition of *North Korea*. It just goes to show travellers are continuing to visit this strictly controlled country without letting red tape hinder its merits. A feedback letter we received from a reader sums up its importance perfectly: 'I found [this guide] very useful to have with me. And I was not the only one: on the train back from Pyongyang we shared a compartment with the Indian ambassador for North Korea. He was surprised to discover we had a guidebook about the country; he didn't know it existed. He spent most of the journey writing down notes from the guidebook!'

**Second edition January 2008**
First published 2003

Bradt Travel Guides Ltd, 23 High Street, Chalfont St Peter, Bucks SL9 9QE, England.
www.bradtguides.com
Published in the USA by The Globe Pequot Press Inc, 246 Goose Lane,
PO Box 480, Guilford, Connecticut 06475-0480

Text copyright © 2008 Robert Willoughby
Maps copyright © 2008 Bradt Travel Guides Ltd
Illustrations copyright © 2008 Individual photographers and illustrators

ISBN-10: 1 84162 219 2   ISBN-13: 978 1 84162 219 4
British Library Cataloguing in Publication Data
A catalogue record for this book is available from the British Library

**Photographers** JTB Photocommunications/Alamy (JTB/Alamy), Nick Bonner (NB), Robin Tudge (RT), Sian Pritchard-Jones (SPJ)
*Front cover* Korean dancers (The Photolibrary Wales/Alamy)
*Back cover* Propaganda poster (NB), Ryugyong Tower Hotel (KT)
*Title page* Guryeong Shingeysa Temple (SPJ), Performers at May Day Stadium (NB), Sunset over Grand People's Study House, Pyongyang (NB)
**Illustrations** Robin Tudge
**Maps** Alan Whitaker, Steve Munns

Typeset from the author's disc by Wakewing
Printed and bound in India at Nutech Photolithographer, New Delhi

# Acknowledgements

For both editions, it has been rarely possible to gather information by straightforward question and answer; I've often felt I had to master the black arts of inference, deduction and logic puzzles.

However, the help and encouragement from the following people really changed writing and later updating this book from a laborious task of accumulating and assessing a million post-it notes into a labour of love, and it has been amazing how one contact has led to another, because everybody with anything to do with the DPRK knows everybody else, making for a richly diverse crowd yet peculiarly exclusive for it.

For me, all are united by a common enthusiasm to share their knowledge and experiences of that country. By plane, fax, phone and email, online, in print and in the pub I have many great people who all proved invaluable one way or another in producing this book, and I haven't been able to include countless people in agencies and embassies.

This book could not have been written without the following. First, foremost, for information, contacts, nitty detail et al, I have to thank the ebullient Nick Bonner, whose knowledge and infectious enthusiasm he so generously imparted. I must also thank Robin Paxton for his section on the northern parts of the DPRK.

In both London and Pyongyang, Dr Jim Hoare and Susan Pares donated their time and knowledge of the DPRK from decades of working with and in the country, giving angles and insights ranging from Pyongyang's place in history to where's good to eat in the early evening.

A great many thanks are also due to Roger Barrett for his support, information and introductions, enthusiasm, for imparting his pioneering spirit, and for the maps he loaned and contacts shared. Also I have to thank Keith Bennett, who smoothed off a surprising number of corners in the original draft and made invaluable insights.

I also have to thank Jon Cannon for so enthusiastically sharing his views and experiences of the DPRK and giving gen about the view of the DPRK from China, especially from Dandong, and how to go about various capers and trips on the Chinese side of the fence.

In addition for the second edition, Simon Cockerell and Hannah Fairclough of Koryo Tours, and Carl Meadows of Regent Holidays have been of greatly appreciated assistance in answering my multiple enquiries and numerous follow-up pedantries as well as sharing their own insights and asides. Jos Emmerik and Kees van Galen of VNL Travel also provided nitty bits and pointers.

As for the first edition, which remains the bulk of the book, I still have to thank Neil Taylor, then of Regent, who saw what needed clarifying and suggested further leads and fill outs. Thanks also to Pyongyang resident Joanne Richardson and frequent Pyongyang visitor Paul White for their snippets of life in the city, for which I also thank Bryan Schmuland for his additions about travelling along China's border. I must also thank Dermot Boyd-Hudson, primarily for his help on explaining and understanding Juche; Dr Philip Edwards, Hall Healy and Angela Choe for their help with the wildlife and DMZ peace park project; and Guy Horne for his Pyongyang Marathon information. Andrea Godfrey and Rachel Russell brought forth further information and other assistance, and Veronica Malykh and Richard Hunt used their skills to attain those itsy bits just beyond my linguistic reach. Many thanks to Steve and Rowena Samuels for housing me in Beijing during my last DPRK foray, as they had done the time before that, too. Peter Hare and Tiffany You helped organise the first DPRK visit and Michelle Gamelin was invaluably generous for lending her Beijing flat for a summer.

Amanda Cooper and Chris Bland read the finished manuscript and gave very valuable comments and questions, Colin Tudge also gave good advice, and thanks also to Matt Milton and Jerry Goodman for commenting on the original. I must also thank Laetitia Antonowicz for her unending support and asking the right questions when and where I couldn't throughout the writing of the book, especially those five days when the wheels came off the whole adventure. James McConnachie, who tipped me off about Bradt and commented on the texts. Everyone at Bradt. Thanks to my Ma for putting me up, and putting up with me while I wrote the first edition book during the nuclear winter of my earning ability, and to all my friends and family who listened to me talk of little else until spring finally arrived, and to Robin Tudge, whose help can't be put into words.

# Foreword

The Democratic People's Republic of Korea, generally known as North Korea, is by no means an ordinary tourist destination. Not only has its government been traditionally wary of the outside world but the long-lasting state of tension on the Korean peninsula has tended to put off visitors. Yet the country has much to offer. There are spectacular mountain scenes, fast-flowing rivers, waterfalls and fine beaches. The sea is clear and unpolluted. Whatever view one may have of the country's political system, the monuments and vistas of Pyongyang, the capital, are like no others in the world.

All of this is covered in Robert Willoughby's most welcome guidebook, which should meet the needs both of the visitor and of the growing number of longer-term foreign residents. Hitherto, it has been hard to find an adequate guidebook to North Korea. At best, the country has attracted a chapter or two tacked onto much fuller accounts of the Republic of Korea or South Korea. It is true that, once in North Korea, the visitor may find quite good locally produced guidebooks. But even the best of these assume that all visitors will be part of a guided tour, with no free time. They are far from comprehensive and usually fail to deal with practical matters such as where to eat or how to get around. And they are not always available, even in the bigger hotel bookshops. So to have gathered together in one place both descriptive and practical information is a great benefit. In addition, the reader will find sufficient background material to make any visit enjoyable and more rewarding.

Unless there is some major change in the country's circumstances, visiting North Korea will always be something for only a few. Those few will in future have the benefit of this useful and informative work.

J E Hoare
Chargé d'Affaires, British Embassy, Pyongyang 2001–02

# Contents

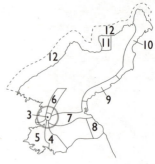

## LIST OF MAPS

*Moranbong Park,*
*Pyongyang*

# Introduction

The first time I flew from Beijing to Pyongyang, in the late 1990s, I became aware of going somewhere else, somewhere different, before even getting on the plane. The plane, a compact Air Koryo Ilyushin-62 with an unusually well-glazed cockpit, sat parked at the farthest, darkest end of a Beijing terminal wing. It didn't look like a Boeing or Airbus or anything built to fly this last decade; it had engines at the back and a particular swoop to its design. The Koreans waiting to board wore quality suits of sombre-coloured cloth of an oddly uniform, timelessly stylish cut. They talked to each other, not on mobiles, and not to me. I did speak to the other foreigners, all strangers to one another but bound by the common interest and thrill of having any business in North Korea.

Boarding the plane, I saw that in the interior, the colours, shapes, seats, knobs and dials were all stylish in a conservative, '70s kind of way. The in-flight magazine and free copy of the *Pyongyang Times* newspaper wrote of the brilliance and world-encompassing influence of people and ideas I hadn't heard of, with current affairs dominated by wars and empires I thought were finished 50 years ago. The air hostess wheeled the drinks trolley along, laden with beer, cider and mineral water, all of North Korean brands, none that I recognised.

Pyongyang airport looked like any other, except for Kim Il Sung's portrait hanging over it. I and the other passengers went through passport control, with the passport officer notably high up in his cubicle. The other side, everyone was met by a driver and car. No throng of taxi men hassling and haggling, no buses. No advertising! I and some other strangers who quickly befriended one another on our joint adventure (of being in North Korea) were whisked away in a large car, with driver and guide, around empty hills, through road checkpoints dotted along empty roads. Everything seemed straight out of the opening scenes in Tintin's *Destination Moon*.

Soon, a clean, tall city unfolded before us, and unfold is the word. Many cities unravel, their layouts like random bits of string flung in a box, but Pyongyang unfolds, vistas and boulevards of buildings with sharp lines panning out so neatly as definable sections on a vast plan of the city. We arrived at the hotel, a soaring metallic gantry tower on an island, and entered its cavernous foyer, with its steel-frame roof and a glass elevator zooming up and down through it. Here I met everyone I'd met waiting for the plane. You're here too? My my! This wasn't Tintin, but Orwell, and any second, Bond. A Korean Blofeld would appear in the lift, guffawing over the tannoy, 'Ho ho ho! So, Mr Willoughby… or should I say, Mr. Smith?' whereupon the roof would open like a massive steel flower and we would all disappear in a shower of sparks and rocket fumes.

It's easy for the imagination to run riot about North Korea. I first got interested in the place while working in China, itself a country abounding in frontiers for foreigners convinced they're the first to set foot anywhere. It was at Beijing's airport that I noticed flights to Pyongyang on the departures board. So there was a way into the land on the edge of the world, that small pocket of mountains that the Western press was forever wailing to be a worry and a menace, this secretive, hermetic state referred to as Stalinist on the good days, that final bastion of high ideals and base deeds. I got my chance to go as part of a larger delegation, and whilst I remember every single moment, the trip as a whole confirmed some rumours and debunked other myths. A lot of things I had read about the place before going didn't seem true while there, or was I being brilliantly hoodwinked? I realised I didn't really know anything at all worth knowing. So when the grapevine sent a memo that Bradt wanted someone to write a guidebook about North Korea, I jumped at the chance, to find out as much for myself as to try and flash a bit of torchlight into this dark corner of the world.

That said, it hasn't been easy to research. A massive amount of the information in print is incomplete and out of date, and it's an uphill climb to stay on top of recent changes. In the country, a lot of basic information about places, like opening times, prices and phone numbers, was refused. I learnt this was because if the person I was asking actually knew, and I was definitely asking the right person, they still wouldn't tell me because they didn't feel entitled to tell me. It was not up to them to decide what I could and couldn't be told, and that rule applies to everything. On a wider note, there are few objective sources about the country, and literature ranges between the extremes of veneration and vitriol.

I've tried to write this book as much for those people who go in with a guide (mainly tourists) as for those who live there or are visitors for other reasons. There are omissions of basic information and broad issues. On the first point, for tourists, questions about times, prices and numbers are largely irrelevant because they're with guides at all times and their itineraries are planned so that museums and whatnot can be opened especially for one tour group. Non-tourists are still barred from visiting grand public buildings or museums without guides to take them round, which must be arranged, but parks, the right restaurants and shops can all be visited relatively freely, as can a few outlying temples and museums in outer places – but don't rely on just turning up. As for broader issues, remember that this guide is only useful in the country if it's allowed in, so what I haven't explicitly written about I've included links to; just consider who writes what and for what reason.

I promise I've done my best to provide as much information as possible; to anyone who can plug the obvious gaps, snippets of prices, numbers, times, who can prove something is wrong or something is no longer true, I and Bradt will be exceedingly grateful for your input.

Keep your eyes and mind open, smiles wide and hands waving high – when not shaking the hands of Koreans.

# Part One

## GENERAL INFORMATION

## NORTH KOREA AT A GLANCE

**Location** Northeast Asia: China and Russia along northern borders; South Korea (the Republic of Korea, ROK) to south; Japan east across the Sea of Japan

**Area** 120,540km²

**Climate** Long, cold winters; short, hot, humid and rainy summers

**Population** 22,225,000

**Capital** Pyongyang

**Main towns** Kaesong, Wonsan, Hamhung, Nampo, Chongjin, Kangye, Sinuiju

**Currency** Won (1 won = 100 chon)

**Official language** Korean

**Religion** Atheist

**Ethnic divisions** Racially homogeneous; there is a small Chinese community and a few ethnic Japanese.

**Type of government** Authoritarian socialist dictatorship

**International telephone code** +850

**Time** GMT +9

**Weights and measures** Metric

**Electricity** 220v, 60Hz

**Flag** Three horizontal bands blue–red–blue with thin white lines dividing them; off-centre-left of the red band is a white circle with a red, five-pointed star.

# Background Information

## GEOGRAPHY

The Korean peninsula protrudes about 1,000km southwards from northeast Asia, a mountainous outcrop centred squarely between China, Russia and Japan, the last cupping the peninsula in shelter from the Pacific. The peninsula runs from 43° 00' north, south down to the sea at 33° 06' north, and its 222,209 km² area was, up to 1945, a landmass of one homogeneous people in one country: Korea. However, since that time, this country has been bitterly divided into north (the Democratic People's Republic of Korea, DPRK) and south (Republic of Korea, ROK) along a wavy border around the 38th line of latitude. A 238km-long demarcation line snakes from the east to the west coast, coated by a 4km-thick band of restricted military activity, namely the De-Militarised Zone or DMZ. But maps from both sides show the DMZ as a faint detail across one country; Pyongyang, the only capital on northern maps, is marked as a village on southern maps that claim the capital as Seoul. This can be confusing, for at least in northern publications, figures exclusively for the northern area slip amid figures for the whole peninsula. For example, the figure for Korea's borders totalling 1,369km in the Korean International Travel Company's 'Korea's Tourist Map' excludes the DMZ and the same book states Korea's total area as 222,209.31km², not mentioning that the DPRK is only 120,540km² of that (CIA Factbook). For this section, all figures pertain to the DPRK unless stated for the peninsula.

Besides the DMZ, the DPRK has a 1,425km-long northern border with China and a 19km one with Russia. Both borders are 'natural'. The Chinese border follows the 803km River Amnok (or Yalu by its Chinese name) southwest between Sinuiju and Dandong cities to the West Sea and the 548km Tuman River that flows northeast to the Korean East Sea (also called the Sea of Japan), the Tuman's final section comprising the Russian border at Rajin-Songbon. These rivers source approximately two-thirds north along the Chinese border at the vast volcanic Lake Chon on Mt Paektu. From the lake's opposing shores Chinese and Koreans holler at one another in this forum amid a formidable range of mountains, so Korea's northern border is a natural border of igneous walls and river-sized moats.

The DPRK has the monopoly on the peninsula's mountains, which with highlands constitute 80% of the DPRK's land area. Mt Paektu is the peninsula's highest at 2,750m. The DPRK has over 50 mountains above 2,000m, many grouped in the Hamgyong range that tapers into the wedge shape of the country's northeast. In the DPRK's north are the higher and drier hills and plains spiked with needle-leaf and spruce trees. Only faint traces of farmland tuck into the gaps between the hills. The lowland, fertile plains in the southwest and scattered along the island-free east coast hold most of the arable land (and most of the country's 22.2 million people), tended by the orderly groups of houses that are the collectivised or co-operative farms. These neat one-storey brick houses with traditional roofs, or multi-storey concrete cubes, stand in the centre of vast

3

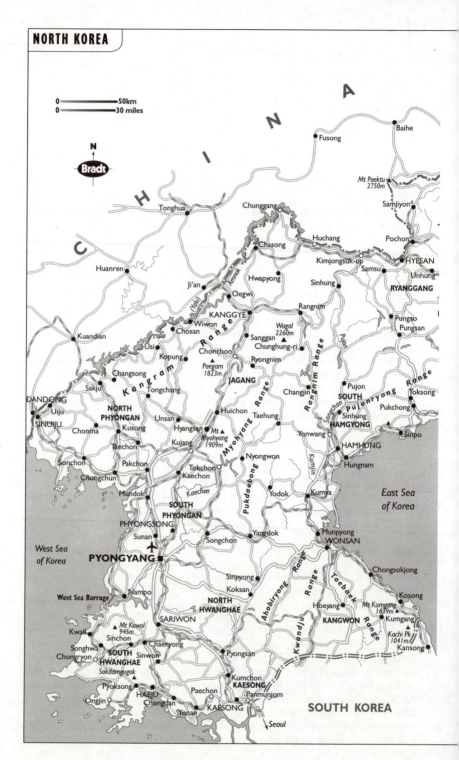

**NORTH KOREA**

0 ———— 50km
0 ———— 30 miles

N

**Bradt**

CHINA

Fusong

Baihe

Tonghua

Chunggang

Mt Paektu
2750m

Chasong

Samjiyon

Huchang

Pochon

Kimjongsuk-up

HYESAN

Huanren

Hwapyong

Samsu

Unhung

Ji'an

Oegwi

Sinhung

**RYANGGANG**

(Yalu)

KANGGYE

Rangnim

Kuandian

Wiwon

Pungso

Chosan

Sanggan

Wagal
2260m

Pungsan

Usi

Chonchon

Chunghung-ri

Kopung

Ryongnim

Changsong

Paegam
1823m

**JAGANG**

Pujon

Sakju

Tongchang

Changjin

**SOUTH**

Toksong

DANDONG

Pujon

Uiju

NORTH
PHYONGAN

Unsan

Huichon

Taehung

Sinhung

Pukchong

SINUIJU

Chonma

Kusong

Hyangsan

Mt
Myohyang
1909m

Yonwang

**HAMGYONG**

Sinpo

Taechon

Kujang

HAMHUNG

Sonchon

Pakchon

Nyongwon

Hungnam

Chongchun

Tokchon

Kaechon

Mundok

Kaechon

Yodok

Kumya

*East Sea
of Korea*

**SOUTH
PHYONGAN**

**PHYONGSONG**

Sunan

Songchon

Yangdok

Munpyong

**WONSAN**

*West Sea
of Korea*

**PYONGYANG**

Chongsokjong

Sinpyong

Nampo

Koksan

Hoeyang

Kosong

West Sea Barrage

**NORTH
HWANGHAE**

Mt Kumgang
1639m

Kumgang

**KANGWON**

Mt Kuwol
945m

SARIWON

Kachi Pk
1041m

Kwail

Sinchon

Chaeryong

Pyongsan

Kansong

Songhwa

Sinwon

Chongryon

**SOUTH
HWANGHAE**

Sokdamgugok

Kumchon

**KAESONG**

Pyoksong

Paechon

Panmunjom

Ongjin

**HAEJU**

Chongdan

**KAESONG**

Yonan

**SOUTH KOREA**

Seoul

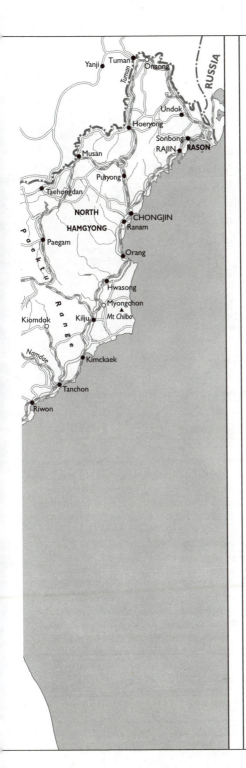

## KEY TO NORTH KOREAN NAMES

| | |
|---|---|
| 안주 | Anju |
| 칠보산 | Chilbo san |
| 청진 | Chongjin |
| 해주 | Haeju |
| 함흥 | Hamhung |
| 회령 | Hoeryong |
| 회양 | Hoeyang |
| 희천 | Huichon |
| 흥남 | Hungnam |
| 향산 | Hyangsan |
| 혜산 | Hyesan |
| 개성 | Kaesong |
| 강계 | Kanggye |
| 고성 | Kosong |
| 금강산 | Kumgang san |
| 구월산 | Kuwol san |
| 과일 | Kwail |
| 만포 | Manpo |
| 문덕 | Mundok |
| 묘향산 | Myohyang san |
| 남포 | Nampo |
| 온정 | Onjong |
| 온성 | Onsong |
| 백두산 | Paektusan |
| 박천 | Pakchon |
| 판문점 | Panmunjom |
| 보천 | Pochon |
| 평성 | Pyongsong |
| 평양 | Pyongyang |
| 라진 | Rajin |
| 라진-선봉 | Rajin-Sonbong |
| 라선 | Rason |
| 리원 | Riwon |
| 삼지연 | Samjiyon |
| 사리원 | Sariwon |
| 신의주 | Sinuiju |
| 선봉 | Sonbong |
| 순천 | Sunchon |
| 태천 | Taechon |
| 단천 | Tanchon |
| 덕성 | Toksong |
| 의주 | Uiju |
| 원산 | Wonsan |

KEY TO PROVINCES
자강 Jagang
개성 Kaesong
강원 Kangwon
함경 북도 North Hamgyong
함경 남도 South Hamgyong
황해 북도 North Hwanghae
황해 남도 South Hwanghae
평안 북도 North Phyongan
평안 남도 South Phyongan
평양 Pyongyang
량강 Ryanggang

paddyfields that roll floor-flat to the horizon. The elaborate hillside terracing seen in southern Asia isn't here, as the water in these thin, muddy strips would quickly freeze in winter and destroy the paddies' delicate structure. Instead, the hillsides are covered with maize, as is every spare strip of earth; in the cities as out in the country, maize protrudes from every orifice. Rice and maize are harvested around October, so spring is for the secondary crops of barley, wheat and potatoes. Soya beans, eggplant, red peppers and ginseng are also important.

The seasonal droughts and floods that have always blighted the peninsula's agriculture have worsened partly through extensive deforestation of the lowlands' mixed forests of pine and broad leaf, oak and birch. Afforestation is visible in many of the DPRK's nine provinces (Kangwon, Jagang, Ryanggang, North & South Pyongan, North & South Hamgyong, North & South Hwanghae), and around its four 'special cities' (Pyongyang, Nampo, Rajin-Sonbong, Kaesong) that are under central authority. Under the ground, the country's mineral wealth includes soft coal, copper, tungsten, gold and uranium. Place names are suffixed by what the feature is, like Panmun-ri (*ri* = town, *si* = city), Taedong-gang (*gang* = river), Pothong-dong (*dong* = district), Kumgang-san (*san* = mountain), Moranbong (*bong* = hill).

## CLIMATE

The DPRK's warm, temperate climate divides into four seasons, spring (March to May), summer (June to August), autumn (September to November) and winter.

The seasons are dry except the monsoon-like rainy season of summer; that over half of Pyongyang's 916mm of annual precipitation falls in July and August is very typical. Typhoons also tour the peninsula's coasts, causing floods and wind damage The southeast coastal region is the wettest, with Wonsan averaging 1,400mm in annual rainfall. Westerly winds from the Asian landmass make winters cold and dry, getting colder and drier the further north you go. High humidity besides, the DPRK's July temperatures can run up to 25°C in the southwest round Nampo to Pyongyang, while winter in the capital plumbs to –8°C and atop Mt Paektu plummets below –20°C.

## HISTORY

A stock phrase found everywhere in Korean literature is '5,000 years of Korean history'. It comes from the following tale:

> In the beginning, there was the God Hwan In and his son Hwan Ung, who wanted to govern the earth's people. His father consented and sent him earthwards into the Korean peninsula where he established agriculture and the laws of humanity. A bear and a tiger prayed to Ung to be human. Ung gave them garlic and cloves and told them to avoid sunlight for 100 days. The bear succeeded and transformed into a woman, and later married Ung. In 2,333BC they had a son, Tangun Wanggom, who set up his capital at Pyongyang and called his kingdom Choson (Morning Freshness). So was born Korea, and they ruled for a millennium and a half. This story denotes a Chinese influence: 'Morning Freshness' indicates the peninsula's location relative to ancient China, east where the sun rises, while Wang in Chinese means 'king'.

The more modern alternative history of Korea begins with the first human habitation originating from east and northeast Asia. Remains of 'Ryonggok man' of some 400,000 years age have been found near Pyongyang, as have the remains of man from 40,000 years ago. Culture sites date back to 30000BC, with evidence of ancient Mongolian and Manchurian tribes.

From 6000BC 'combed' pottery and other evidence in unearthed villages suggests sedentary agricultural lives, with domesticated farm animals and huts sunk into the earth. The first dolmens appear from 3000BC, large graves of slabs of stone laid flat across upright stones, possibly also used for ritual sacrifice, with agricultural stone implements found buried around them. Bronze mirrors and daggers date from 1500BC, and mirrors, knives, bells and other ceremonial trinkets with heavy Chinese influence in their design have also been found.

Early records say that by 300BC there were five tribes controlling distinct areas of the Korean peninsula and the adjacent mainland. The largest, most powerful tribe was the Choson, with its capital Wang-hsien-ch'eng near today's Pyongyang. Trade was conducted with the Chinese state of Yan, one of many Chinese warring states, and it was a Yan warlord that took over the Choson. Over a century, Choson expanded from around the Taedong northwards, to the east coast and south to the Han River, building forts all the way.

In China the Han were ascendant and wanted to up the ante from simple trade with the peninsula, preferring tribute and subservience. In 109BC, Han Emperor Wu sent land and sea forces to destroy the Choson, attacking Wang-hsien-ch'eng, and sweeping the peninsula, leaving only the southernmost area free. Wu's gains were absorbed into the Han empire and, combined with Manchurian areas beyond the Yalu and Tuman rivers, were divided into four 'commanderies' under Chinese administration. The biggest commandery, with a population of 400,000, was Lo-lang (with Pyongyang the capital).

Rice cultivation was introduced, mainly in the south, and a greater variety of sophisticated tools and weapons in iron and bronze was imported. Chinese officials' tombs, large mounds dotted around modern Pyongyang, have contained many sophisticated paintings and artefacts from Han culture.

Chinese rule continued uncertainly for four centuries. Individual tribes could be brought to order, their chieftains sometimes given 'official' status and the bronze seals to prove it as their tribes were exploited for labour and goods. There was generally more subservience than outright resistance, and the tribes were controllable while they were divided and in the vicinity of any commandery barracks. But the hardy Koguryo people, hunters and warriors, were spread across the mountains of northern Korea and eastern Manchuria. Their numerous tribes combined under one 'king' who was thus empowered to resist commandery rule and invade Chinese and northeast Korean regions for food, materials and slaves.

By 37BC, the Koguryo had developed a powerful state, with influence from far into Manchuria to the southern Han River. Dynastical and barbarian invasions debilitated China's grip and the weakened commanderies fell prone to tribal resistance by the 3rd century AD. Tribes in the peninsula's south combined and fought the southern Tai-Feng commandery. Both the Lo-Lang and Tai-Feng were cut off when China imploded, and the Koguryo absorbed the Lo-Lang in 313. Meanwhile, two states were forming from the tribes in the peninsula's deepest south. Paekche in the southwest combined from Ma Han tribes, and soon after the Koguryo victory, Paekche abolished Tai-Feng. Southeast, Chin Han tribes united to create the Silla state. Wedged between Silla and Paekche lay the Pyon Han states dominated by Japan (also called Kaya), but it was Silla, Paekche and Koguryo that formed the seven-hundred-year 'Three Kingdoms Period'.

**ANCIENT STATES: THE THREE KINGDOMS PERIOD** The Koguryo was the biggest of the three kingdoms, covering the peninsula's northern half and beyond the rivers Yalu and Tuman. Its expansion west into China halted when the Yen warrior-state raided and ransacked Koguryo in the mid-4th century. So, for easier pickings, Koguryo forces went south, jabbing and clawing territory from Silla and Paekche. Tens of thousands of Koguryo's population were conquered people, including many former officials of Lo-Lang, so a strong, military-based government was needed to run the expanding Koguryo. A large fort in Koguryo's capital Pyongyang (since 427) was among many built, while victims of Koguryo's military defeats or surrenders were executed. From Pyongyang the king ruled, served by administrative and military officials. These posts superseded the tribe-chieftain ties, but as the chieftains became Koguryo nobility, they took the top jobs anyway. Their sons were schooled to head this administration with an education derived from Confucian teachings from China, to collect regular tax in grain from the peasants and labour from the slaves and to codify the nation's laws written in the adopted Chinese written language.

Using Chinese written language made China's literary texts accessible, as well as the Confucian philosophy and the full workings of the remnant political structures. From China also came Buddhism in the 4th century AD, with all its glories of architecture and arts. China also continued in its position as a regional player to ally with as the three kingdoms warred among themselves. Hence Chinese culture permeated the three kingdoms throughout their existence.

Paekche's Sino connections saw it more imbued with Buddhism earlier than the other kingdoms. Paekche's foreign policy was, like Silla's and Koguryo's, a continual series of alliances made to attack or defend the aggressor of the day, but Paekche endured more unwelcome interest from the other two. From the mid-4th to the late 7th century, Koguryo forces compressed Paekche into the peninsula's corner, the Puyo royal family taking the capital south from Hansong to Ungjin to Sabi, leaving behind slain troops and offering tributes of live slaves to appease Koguryo. Apart from sheer size, one problem was that the Puyo, outsiders to the area, were lording over Paekche's indigenous Ma Han, who had unfortunately been suppressed very effectively under commandery rule. The administration was not based on any great loyalty nor had they learned much from Chinese ways of governance. Paekche's main asset was the peninsula's best agricultural land, which the kingdom's slaves cultivated well, but the land was all the more alluring to jealous neighbours.

Silla was the kingdom with the smallest population and land and was clamped between Koguryo and Kaya. From its tribes, the Silla had developed governance from a council of tribal chieftains, a hwabaek that discussed great matters of state. Conquered tribes were not made hwabaek, that was only for the victors who chose their joint leader. Therein began the division of power based on clan, developing into a multi-layered social structure of rights and privileges based on kinship, rank and status, ascribed through a hereditary caste system, the bone-rank system. The ruling royal clan was the songgol rank (the top) and affiliates of the chingol ranks. Regulations dictated the size of one's house and stables, cut of dress and cloth used, and other distinctive ornamentation. This regimented caste system would continue throughout the Silla's existence.

Silla also developed an administrative system of state based on Chinese practice, with the monarch overseeing numerous controlling boards with their own remits over finance, war, personnel, etc. This centralised government drew taxes, labour and troops from the local level through an administrative chain breaking the country down into province, district and county levels. This efficient form of governance, with a stable royal household at its heart, was able to organise Silla's warring so effectively that it averted being totally lost to its neighbours. In the early 600s, the Tang of China were able to refocus on the peninsula, and when taking on Koguryo, Silla took its chance to ally with the Tang and quash conclusively the Koguryo and Paekche threats.

Paekche collapsed, and in 668 Korguryo was pacified. However, the Tang emperor's version of peace was Tang hegemony, something that the Silla hadn't fought long and hard for; it wasn't to be robbed of the spoils this way. Remaining Korguryo aristocrats and their forces were generously welcomed by the Silla in a new front to oust the Tang. A reformed alliance of Silla, Paekche and Korguryo forces, each in distinctive uniforms, set off north, countering Tang attacks with their own crippling assaults, and by the late 670s, the Tang were out.

**Unified Silla ... and Palhae** The Silla dominated from the Taedong southwards, but Koguryo's aristocracy were not spent as a group capable of command and rule. With the Malgal tribes, the state of Palhae was formed straddling the Yalu River, so had sea access on both sides, into the Yellow Sea and the Sea of Japan, and as such could forge substantial trade links with the Chinese and Japanese. It thus grew westwards and northwards, placing its capital in Dunhua in today's Jilin Province. For two centuries the state existed and traded, reaching 2,000km across, until the unity of the tribes succumbed to the nuances of internal conflict that makes tribes tribal, and the state couldn't resist the encroaching Qidan in the 10th century.

Meanwhile, the Silla ran their kingdom for many fortuitous years, albeit with a good deal of Chinese influence politically and culturally. A half-century after the Tang were ousted, Chinese suzerainty over the peninsula was re-established. Silla students had already been sent to study Tang governance administration, bringing back further developments on the ethics of Confucianism and its wisdom on the structures and working relations of administration.

Chinese culture permeated Korea through trade, and was carried on through Korean trade into Japan. Trade with China developed links as far away as Iran, and India became a mine of knowledge for Silla's burgeoning love of Buddhism. Buddhism became the national religion and was lavished with gifts of land, slaves and money in the hope that it would protect the state in return. Woodcut prints of the Buddhist scriptures were housed in magnificent temples built in the royal city and taken cross country high into the fabulous mountain temples and monasteries. A rising tide of literary works from this time was permeated with Buddhist thoughts, and the importing of the religion also imported its associated literature, architecture and paintings that spread across the new territories in what is now considered a golden age of arts.

Silla's territory and population had both more than trebled in size, with the territory then redistributed amongst the nobles of the victorious side and magnanimously given back to the surrendering tribal chiefs; those chiefs who had professional skills and scholarly understanding were employed in government. As such, the 8th century was marked by relative peace in the kingdom, affording the government much time and prosperity to promote advancements in the arts and sciences. Departments of medicine, mathematics and astronomy were established, as was a department of translation for the Silla's growing trade network. Goods from textiles, furs, pottery and instruments to advanced iron weapons, silver and gold jewellery were exported.

The capital Kjongju grew to over a million in population with streets 10km in length, with dozens of immense private estates, palaces, monasteries and government buildings, staffed by a ruling class whose provincial lands were tilled by slaves. The Tang had carted off 200,000 into slavery, and slavery continued under the Silla. In the counties, many peasants had their own life-tenancies on land but were still subject to tax and labour service, kept account of on continually updated registers. These dues were collected and concentrated in the provincial capitals delegated to run the regions outside the capital, and became concentrations of power away from the Silla court.

The capital and county distinction grew as the families of the elite moved to the capital, and the Silla kings became more autocratic and determined to distinguish between themselves and their underlings. The hwabaek was finally replaced by Chinese administration, and by the late 700s, civil examinations allowed a few commoners to attain position through ability, threatening the aristocrats' long-standing system of position through birth.

For the aristocracy however, their own allegiance of bone-clan kin-ties to the dynasty became of less value than material wealth, and with peace and prosperity came decadence. Provincial revolts broke out with increasing frequency, starting in King Hyegong's reign (765–79) which ended in his assassination. A succession of coups and massacres marred the reigns of the next 20 kings in the 150 years from 784, marking the Silla's accelerating decline. While the aristocrats connived and conspired, the people on their lands tired of their toils and rising taxation and left, roaming the counties as destitute migrants, forming their own popular rebellions or turning to banditry. A plague of banditry inland accompanied a plague of piracy that afflicted Korea's coasts, exacerbating regional instabilities, so inciting more power struggles which were ever more focused on the throne. The bandits themselves accrued land and slaves and became powerful factions in their own right, such that one bandit, Kungbok, became a king-maker, helping Kim Ujing take the throne, though Kungbok himself was killed in 846 for his own connivance for the throne.

As the Sillan state began to break down in the late 800s and early 900s Paekche re-emerged, and a formidable general called Wang Kon from the former Koguryo region led from 918 a new state around the Taedong, later called Koryo. These states formed with the Silla the 'Later Three Kingdoms' Period' marked by intense inter-state warfare, from which the Koryo came out supreme.

**Koryo** Wang Kon, crowned King Taejo in 935, welcomed the fallen Sillan king and his nobles into his court, giving them land and positions in government. Over the next couple of decades, from his new Songak capital (today's Kaesong) near to the troublesome northern border, he launched a systematic offensive of gifts and privileges to bring the provincial barons on side, tipping the balance in Wang Kon's favour in bringing to heel the castle towns that defied the Silla. Land, privileges and later caste titles rewarded those helping to found Koryo (the word from which Korea derives) and entice those reluctant to submit. Regional leaders gave familial 'hostages' or kin to the court to ensure loyalty, and Koryo soon spanned all the peninsula up to the Yalu's mouth, from whence its border stretched across to near today's Wonsan. This fortified border was supported by two provinces under military command, connected to Kaesong and the other provinces through new roads and a postal system.

King Taejo's successors developed new government boards, and expanded government-owned factories of raw materials. The career-routes into government were subject to more civil-service examinations taken by students of new Confucian academies, meaning more 'commoners' could attain positions of power and privilege. Privilege principally was the dispensation of land to officials (that returned to the state upon their death), and so the divine rights of the old aristocracy were eroded. Nonetheless, Koryo's social structure was still as regimented as its predecessors and ancestry counted for a great deal, as one new government board dealt with genealogical records. At the top were the royal caste, then the military and civil officials' class, called the yangban. Below them were more grades of profession, down to the yangmin, or commoners of peasants, and below them, the 'untouchables'. At least eight generations clean of untouchable status had to be proved by would-be officials.

Buddhism was further encouraged with lavish gifts of land, slaves and tax exemptions, until the temples and monasteries became grand concentrations of wealth within a tight hierarchical structure of considerable political and economic power, and its leaders of high aristocratic stock. Monasteries provided welfare for the poor and usurious loans for others, and it was a Buddhist monk that persuaded his brother King Sukchong (1082–96) to scrap barter for a standard coinage. Wood-block printing also revived with a great number of Chinese texts.

On that subject, foreign affairs were as usual dominated by events in China. To be safe, from 1033 a grand wall was built connecting the dozen fortified towns along Koryo's northern border. Following centuries of paying tribute to whichever dynasty held the other side of the wall seemed a sure route to peace, with just a few incursions from the Sung, the Jurchen, the Liao and the Chin.

Then in the early 13th century, the Mongols (also known as the Yuan) came. They'd stormed out of the Gobi Desert, smashed the Chin from power, taking China, Manchuria, then looked south onto the peninsula. Years of battling the Jurchen hadn't prepared the Koryo armies for the Mongols, who washed over the country in a tide of blood. The only glimmer of fortune in these years of ravaging was that the Mongols were poor navy men. This allowed the Koryo court, with the Choe family at the front, to take every official and jewel their boats could carry and sail into safe exile on Kanghwa Island. There they lived and prospered for nearly three decades, while the mainland people were enslaved or just massacred. The court used this unreal time to build great palaces and pavilions and recarve the wood blocks for the Tripitika that were burnt in the Mongol invasion. Only in

1258 did the Choe realise that their great service to Buddha wasn't going to remove the Mongols. A little bloody coup won a new leader, who led the return to the mainland, and through apology, tribute, marriage and familial hostage-taking by the Mongols, re-established Koryo as a Mongol vassal state.

Now, through the Mongols, Koryo could prove its heartfelt loyalty to its rulers by pouring all its resources into invading Japan. In 1274 and 1281, hundreds of thousands of soldiers and hundreds of ships and crews were put up for two massive invasions of Japan. Neither succeeded. Notwithstanding the huge economic drain this had on the peninsula, the frustrated Mongols sucked Koryo even drier. Koryo came under complete Mongol control through marriage and appropriation, and for a century, anything the Mongols wanted, they took. The Mongols were not totally parasitical and were partly responsible for the influx of neo-Confucian texts, and the Confucian study of King Chungson (1309–13) at the Mongol capital. This would spell the end of Buddhism's dominance.

For Buddhism was not protecting the state. By the mid-14th century, Japanese pirates, or Wako, were touring and pillaging Koryo shores. In the 14th century, the Mongols were losing control of China as the Ming resurged from the south towards Korea. The Koryo court buckled under factional fights and usurpations, while one general, Ri Songgye, made a name for himself battling the Wako. Sent by pro-Mongol King U to fight the Ming, Ri Songgye considered fighting the Ming to be a futile exercise. Indeed, he decided instead that they would surely be an improvement on the Mongols. So Ri turned his forces on U and deposed him in 1389. An efficient purge followed and, with Ming relations affirmed, Ri Songgye became undisputed Ri Taejo, in 1392.

## Ri (also known as the Chosen or Yi) 1392–1910

Ri Taejo moved the capital from Kaesong to the city of Hanyang, renaming it Seoul, or 'capital'. Holders of large estates loyal to the previous dynasty were dispossessed and their lands given to Ri followers. In 1390 Ri had all the old land registry records burnt, creating a clean slate for him to distribute lands as he liked. However, as under the Koryo, dual governance came through military and civil officials, staffed at the top by Yangban. As under the Koryo, society was rigidly structured, with royal caste, yangban of 'merit' and 'minor merit' in a pyramid of power, then numerous sub-strata of professions and yangmin commoners, and at the bottom the untouchables (including now sorcerers and actors!).

During the reigns of Taejo, Taejong and Sejong, Korea expanded northwards until all the area south of the Yalu and Tuman rivers was theirs, and was populated by southern migrants. The population increased as fast as new land was brought under cultivation and reclaimed.

Foreign policy was sadae or 'serving the great' as in continuing to pay tribute to the Ming Emperor of China. With the Mongol shackles thrown off, and no distracting Ming–Mongol warring, the Ri could deal with the pirates by sending boats to destroy their ships and settlements. By 1420 the threat was curtailed. Then the forts and outposts of the northern frontier could be bolstered.

The capital was fortified and built up. With peace came greater scholarship and the sowon schools of Confucianism, needed for the examination system, flourished about the country. The hangul alphabet was completed in the mid-1440s, along with movable print-type. Korean and Chinese influences led to a rebirth of the arts and sciences, with advancements from arms to poetry.

Although Buddhism again had a hand in the arts, the power of the monasteries was curbed. Over the centuries the monasteries had acquired huge tracts of land and through tax exemption had the wealth to defend them, depriving others to their inevitable discontent. The monks were perceived to have become too powerful, too corrupt and were too collusive with suspicious elements, so they were evicted from the court and cities and stripped of their wealth, albeit slowly, so as not to provoke insurrection. King Taejo finished their tax exemption; King Taejong limited their ownership of land and slaves, which his successor King Sejong reduced further. King Sejo (1455–68) was a practising Buddhist and he supported a brief revival, but his successors were mainly Confucianist.

Copper-type cast printing allowed Confucian texts to be spread amongst the new Confucian schools set up in the prefectures and counties, and the schools achieved a similar build-up of power and privileges that the Buddhists were stripped of. The schools' alumni formed groups for mutual advancement and further ensnaring of the youth. They competed, of course, at court for power and offices, as did the members of the royal families, so all Ri dynasty officials were Confucian scholars.

But their professed veneration of learning and authority was not manifest from the late 1400s, and departments of differing Confucian doctrine stifled their monarchs' wishes so they could concentrate on settling their own scores. The zealous reformers of the Sallim school, a puritan lot, incurred much resentment. To be fired was to get off lightly. Four bloody purges of the 'literati' occurred from 1498 to 1545, so bitter that the bones of dead scholars were dug up and scattered. The ruler Yonsangun was deposed by his own officials in the first purges and the battles became aristocratic feuds, which would mar the functioning of the court thereafter.

These feuds did not affect society as a whole. The comprehensive genealogical records founded under the Koryo were continued. There was a degree of social fluidity, slaves did become tenant farmers as yangban fell earthwards. Some records were lost, some burnt, some doctored as fallen yangban sold their status, but the class system remained largely intact, and Korea had slaves until the 19th century. The real threat instead came from beyond Korea's shores.

**JAPAN AND THE IMJIN WAR** The anti-pirate war and the success in holding off the Mongols made for about two centuries of peace for Korea. Trade routes were established with the Ming and Japan, whose people were allowed to set up trading settlements in the south of the peninsula.

Feudal infighting in Japan in the 15th century meant piracy resumed as Japan's worst export. The Ashikaga military government curtailed piracy and peaceful trade was set up in the late 1400s. But from the mid-1500s the Wako resumed piracy as the Ashikaga declined, now in greater force and sacking whole cities. A new leader, Hideyoshi Toyotomi, brought order and restored peaceful trade with Korea, but this wasn't all he had in mind, for Hideyoshi's imperial plans stretched to India. Korea, of course, was the most convenient land route into China, and Hideyoshi set about persuading the Ri from 1587 to join him against Ming China before taking on all Asia. But the only coherent response from the Ri court, torn between tribute-loyalty to the Ming, profiting from Hideyoshi's scheme and aversion to any involvement, was 'probably not'. Hideyoshi responded by invading Korea in the fourth month of 1592. Within a month, his 158,000-strong force had taken the capital.

Unfortunately, the good years had allowed the Ri military to stagnate. The court fled to the Yalu and tremulously persuaded the Ming that these invaders were dangerous. A Ming army attacked down to Pyongyang but was repelled, only for another force to charge Kaesong in early 1593. Meanwhile, however much face the Ri had lost on land they won back at sea under the brilliant admiral Ri Sunsin, with his cannon-firing, iron-decked 'turtle boats' that sunk Hideyoshi's supply ships. Hideyoshi's debilitated land forces were then kept pinned down by Korean guerrilla attacks. Hideyoshi sued for peace.

It was a lull. Many Japanese stayed on in Korea, eking a living amid the post-battle chaos until Hideyoshi attacked again with 140,000 troops in 1597. Toughened Chinese and Korean forces were ready, and, aided by winter, held up Hideyoshi's forces until he declared on his deathbed in 1598 that this time enough really was enough.

Japan's forces returned home reasonably unscathed with the priceless booty of many skilled artisans. The Toyotomi family were replaced by the Tokugawam, who resumed simple trade as before, after a few thousand captives were negotiated back to the Koreans. On the peninsula, the wars' taxation and devastation compounded the peninsula's material exhaustion. Local rebellions during the conflict preceded passionate factional fighting at court in a series of coups in the 1600s, including the Injo faction of 1624 that briefly installed a new royal family.

Further north, the war had emptied the coffers of the Ming, who faced growing threats from the Manchus in northeast Asia. Ming–Manchu fights stumbled into Korea until the Manchus stood victorious on Korea's borders with Ming China shoved westwards. Now the Manchus demanded suzerainty: the Koreans were to be the Manchus' 'younger brother'. Refusal was met with a punitive invasion in 1627. Still, Korea conspired to have the Ming return, until the Manchus, styling themselves as the Qing, rumbled the plan and invaded Korea again in late 1637. Korea's misery would only cease, seethed the Manchus, upon payment of food, troops and the handing over of 'hostage' envoys. They did, and relative peace was Korea's prize for 200 years.

Not in the court. The literati purges had opened a can of worms. Ancestor worship, the importance of filial piety, familial and old clan ties, sowon alumni and regional relationships meant that the fights of the forebears were carried on by their successors. From the 1550s until the late 1700s, factions fought and splintered into 'westerners', 'northerners', 'greater' and 'lesser northerners', 'southerners', and so on and on, in a maelstrom of fights, coups and burning buildings.

So no-one really saw the real aliens turn up in the 1700s. There had been some bitty contacts with Europeans. Jesuits reached Japan in the late 1500s. Some Dutch washed ashore in 1627, and one became prominent in the Korean army for his cannon-casting skills. Yet in practical terms, Korea's foreign relations had only ever involved jostling between China and Japan.

Meanwhile, European missionaries had been spreading the Gospel across Asia, and Catholic missionaries had had great success in China by the 1790s. From the late 18th century the Catholic Church was spying Korea as the next great congregation. A Chinese priest smuggled himself into Seoul and began converting peasants by the thousand. Bad enough, but Catholicism forbade ancestral worship and therefore threatened the ruling family's legitimacy. News filtered to the court of the Peking government's sufferance of Christian subterfuge, and Korea's Christians were thus pre-emptively persecuted. In 1801 court official Hwang Sa Yong appealed to Peking's French bishop to send in armies to purge the Korean government of its anti-Catholicism, but the message was intercepted. The court's suspicions were proved, and they were mightily alarmed by the extent of these Catholics' reach and conspiring. The mass 'martyring' of Catholics ensued.

**THE GREAT POWERS COME...** The Western nations in the 19th century, mainly the French, Russians, British and Americans, wanted the locals converted to Christ because Christians were easier to trade with than the average Asian. Lone trade ships began arriving, with an English merchant ship anchoring off the Chongchung Province coast in 1832. More and more came and prospected but more often than not returned empty-handed, having been (usually) politely turned away by the Koreans.

These foreign powers were not used to being rebuffed, however politely. China's ports were jemmied for trade following the Opium War in 1842, and Japan's doors were blown open in 1854. Korea had no right not to trade with the West, and if it couldn't be reasoned with, then it would be forced. The occasional trading ships off Korea's coast started sporting more arms. Solitary French, Russian and British warships began hailing more frequently off the coasts.

By the 1860s, King Kojong was a minor and the country was under the regent Taewongun, who concentrated on rebuilding the country's fortifications and reformed the military. The Ri worried that these increasingly aggressive Western traders were the external force of destruction, while Western religion would destroy Korea from within. The country wasn't doing well. A ruinous drought from 1812 had apparently killed millions. Rice riots occurred in Seoul in 1833. The Tonghak 'religion' fused Eastern and Western religions, yet promoted the interests of the poor and not the usual deference to the rich. Its creator Choe Cheu was executed for 'confusing society' in 1862, but his death apparently sparked uprisings by destitute farmers of all classes in the southern provinces. Many merchants and officials were killed before this burgeoning insurrection was put down. More unrest followed in 1864, so all in all the Ri were in less genial mood to receive anyone.

Russian pressure to trade was aggressive, but the French priests' offers to mediate with them in 1866 made the Taewongun suspect a broader foreign plot, and so interrogated and executed nine priests before a bloody purge of tens of thousands of converts. The French took great exception to their priests falling to the sword, and their navy invaded Kanghwa Island in retaliation, but were routed by Korean forces. That year, the armed American missionary trader *General Sherman* arrived in Pyongyang, but was beached and burnt in the shallow waters of the Taedong River. A punitive occupation by American forces of Kanghwa Island in 1871 was as successful as the French occupation. American Admiral Rogers was dispatched to organise the protection of US vessels from Korean 'tiger hunters' along Korea's shores, but Taewongun took heart: his reforms had enabled his country to repel all boarders.

There were other tacky incursions. In 1867, a priest, a German and an American adventurer, bent on raiding royal tombs, sailed from Shanghai to extort concessions from the king for trade and missionary work. Another rumour that circulated Beijing's diplomatic circle was that Korea was volunteering to help expel all foreigners from China. Bolstered by military success, the Taewongun kept Korea closed and belligerent. He believed battle to be the only language these barbarians understood and had stelae erected round the country to remind the people how awful foreigners were and the fate of collaborators.

**THE JAPANESE** But since the 1860s Meiji restoration, the imperial Japanese government had reformed itself and the economy along Western lines. Convinced that Korea could learn from these Western ideas, Japanese emissaries were repeatedly sent to persuade Korea to open up and expand their trade links along more Western lines. King Kojong, enthroned since coming of age in 1873, was as suspicious of outsiders as his father Taewongun. Nor were his courtiers interested in reforms that would put them out of work. They were convinced that these Japanese were simply Eastern conveyors of Western subversion, using trickery to smokescreen more base motives. In 1875, the Japanese warship Unyo sailing off Kanghwa Island was shelled by Korean land-batteries. The incident proved to the Koreans they were right, as did subsequent events. The Japanese retaliated to this ill-mannered action with an armed expedition to Korea, demanding unprecedented trade concessions. These included residence rights in three Korean ports and a legation in Seoul, in the 1876 Treaty of Kanghwa. The treaty also secured 'independence' for Korea from China. This gun-muzzle diplomacy secured a major foothold in what was a long, profitable relationship for Japan, with Korean rice poured out to Japan as Japanese goods and ideas poured in.

It only led to more factionalism in the court. Queen Min and her family favoured Japanese-style reform, but Taewongun still skulked in the court's shadows and, as some feared, reforms disposed and made malcontents of government and army men alike, who flocked to Taewongun's conspiring. In 1882, they rebelled against the queen, killing her, her family and ministers, burnt down the Japanese legation and caused its minister and staff to flee to sea in a junk. Only the intervention of the Qing (also called the Manchus), seeing a way to reassert themselves over Korea, saved the day for King Kojong, sending 2,000 troops to Seoul, suppressing the rebellion, and restoring the Min. Even more joyously, the 'slain' queen was actually alive and well for an impersonator had taken the blade for her.

Brilliantly, the Qing intervention protected Japanese subjects in China's empire, as agreed by the two countries in 1871; so Korea was back under Chinese suzerainty. Nevertheless, the Chinese pressed for greater Korean relations with the outside, arguing this was inevitable and a mix of competing influences would prevent any one foreign nation from dominating, ie: Japan. Commercial treaties quickly ensued with the US, Germany, UK, France, Russia and Italy, with investment inflows (into mining, railways, universities and hospitals) and Western-style banking, customs and communications in post and telegraph being set up.

At the court, the arguments over how to secure Korea's future became more twisted and no less cloak-and-dagger. It divided into the pro-Chinese conservatives and pro-Japanese modernisers. The latter advocated ending Korea's vassal status to China, for how could Korea be the equal of any outside power otherwise, and to this end wanted the country to industrialise. Distracted Chinese military forces led to the modernisers attempting a Japanese-supported coup in 1884, similar in reach and domestic bloodiness as the 1882 incident, and as successful. Again, the Japanese legation was burnt; again, Japanese nationals were killed.

Perhaps now Japan's ambitions had finally been thwarted, the Chinese could prevail in this ding-dong battle for control. Yet into the power vacuum came the Russians, their empire heading south from Siberia and their envoys busy in Korea laying diplomatic and commercial foundations. The only imperial power to stop them was the British, by blocking a Russian sea-route. The British were less interested in taking the region but determined to check Russia's empire. Korea was saved, except for the obviousness of how little control Korea had over its own destiny.

Korea's diplomatic strategy involved many foreign powers cancelling out each other's aims, but economic forces were undermining this power-balance trick. Taxation for the court's expenditure increased to help sustain the unwieldy bureaucracy, procure foreign arms and establish diplomatic missions in those countries whose cheap goods flooded the country and destroyed the local cottage industries. This trade demanded money, not barter, and farmers became tied into exporting their grain to where most of the imports originated: Japan.

Peasants lost their subsistence living to usury and penury as the state's taxes escalated. Uprisings and banditry grew. Yangban joined forces with peasants and in the southwest the Tonghak resurrected, beginning a serious rebellion in February 1894. Japan ignored Korean claims about dealing with the crisis and, with the Taewongun in tow, sent troops in July 1894, sinking the Chinese fleet on the way to driving the Chinese army from Korea altogether.

The Japanese brought reform. Amongst many points they made the Yangban and commoners equal before the law; abolished slavery; abolished the practice of whole families being punished for the crimes of one member; and standardised the currency.

Russia, France and Germany became concerned about anyone except themselves controlling the region. Their 'Three Powers Intervention' demanded from Japan swingeing concessions in Korea (and further north saw China smashed open for the last time). Not outdone, the pro-Japanese faction in the Korean court launched their own coup against the now pro-Russian Queen Min, killing her and sending the king to hide in the Russian legation for a year, before the coup collapsed and the Japanese found themselves being driven out yet again in early 1895.

In a flamboyant, fanciful assertion of Korean sovereignty, King Kojong then pronounced himself the emperor of Taehan Cheguk, Empire of the Han, with envoys sent out from the nation with its own flag and anthem and now the equal of China and Japan. But Kojong's confidence in his empire was demonstrated by his move into the Kyongun palace with its escape doors into each of the surrounding foreign legations.

A more realistic attempt to galvanise independence for Korea came with So Chaep Il (also called Philip Jaisohn), a Korean educated in the US who founded the Independence Club, believing that Korea's structure and fate should be decided by Koreans, with a new covenant of civil rights and independence. Students, intellectuals, workers, urban dwellers and government officials of all ranks rallied to the cause. The court aligned with those profiting from the unbalanced trade regime to form the Imperial Association, and following pitched battles with the Independence Club, had the latter outlawed. The only reform was the modernising of the army.

The last gasps of Korea for Koreans were drowned out as the century turned, for Russia, the UK, Japan and others around whipped up a tornado of treaties, diplomatic and military manoeuvres, checking, bluffing, suspecting and counter-checking each others' imperial plans into east Asia. China's implosion changed it from player to prey. Finally, tiring of the frenetic hoo-ha, Russia and Japan decided all-out war would reach a conclusion of sorts. Japan set troops in Incheon in February 1904 that lead to a Korean–Japanese protocol, with the Japanese guaranteed real powers. They then launched off to fight Russia and won. The Russians left Korea, and the Japanese were back, minus the Chinese, minus the Russians, in force, in charge, with the papers to prove it. It was conclusive indeed.

Shortly after, Japan and Korea signed a treaty of protection. A Japanese resident-general was installed in Seoul to direct the country's foreign affairs as an *in situ* extension of the Tokyo Foreign Office, directing Korea for Japan's ends, to 'protect' Korea against further foreign interference. The diplomatic agencies of those other countries that battled to be in Korea were abolished along with 'Korea's' foreign policy. Indeed, to all geopolitical purposes, Korea, having lost its autonomous national entity, no longer existed at all. Reforms, laws, appointment of officials all required the resident-general's approval. The king was forced to abdicate; the army was disbanded; the administration of justice and prisons came unto Japanese hands, as did the police. Ownership of the land, particularly by the peasants, was difficult to prove to the Japanese authorities taking it over en masse, and resistance was met with execution.

Resistance groups, poorly armed and poorly led, sprung up across the country, carrying out guerrilla attacks on Japanese positions, but the guerrillas' dispersal and the randomness of their attacks achieved nothing but the accelerated drafting in of more Japanese forces of repression. There were, though, thousands of recorded disturbances by individuals and crowds demanding independence. Two of the most spectacular included two Koreans assassinating the Resident-General Ito

Hirobumi at Harbin railway station in October 1909, and in December, the pro-Japanese Prime Minister Ri Wanyong was stabbed. But these only served to convince the Japanese that total domination was necessary. In August 1910 the protectorate was formalised in a treaty of annexation, with the Korean government dissolved two months later, all political organisations banned, and all foreign intervention finished. Korea was gone.

## Korea under the Japanese
The Japanese were the masters of the region. They'd taken Manchuria, flattened the Chinese, ousted the Russians from the region in presence and power, and booted all Western interests from Korea, with the exception of Christian churches and hospitals. Korea was to be Japanese by all measures, so they banned Korean-language newspapers and any 'large' meetings of Koreans.

The resident-general was replaced by a governor-general, a retired Japanese admiral or general appointed by the emperor, to whom the governor-general answered and no-one else. With this autonomy the governor-general could appoint the provincial governors, senior judicial members and high civil-service positions, ostensibly to be shared between Koreans and Japanese. But in practice all those jobs with any seniority went to the Japanese. Grass-roots control came through the ever-increasing police force that had numerous summary powers from flogging and fining to imprisonment. The fact that educators and non-military officials wore Japanese-style uniforms and swords proved beyond doubt the nature of Japan's rule.

Now that the Koreans and their culture mattered little beyond how they could best serve Japan, the colonisers set about reforming the country's economy. From 1912, a comprehensive land registration programme was carried out over six years, establishing nationwide the rights (and restrictions) of the nation's farmers. Many Yangban peasants lost their pre-existent claims, were ruined or made de facto registered tenant farmers on enlarged estates that were therefore taxable by the authorities, and regularly were.

Japan's own industrialisation needed increased Korean rice production to allow its cities to swell with factory workers (Japan suffered rice riots in 1918). Investment from the landlords and Japan's ministries poured into agriculture to increase rice output, and rice exports to Japan indeed went up significantly. However, the exports outweighed actual production gains, and the Koreans were forced to import millet.

Investment went into new planting techniques, irrigation and crop varieties but mainly into the use of chemical fertilisers, the production of which underpinned Korea's own industrialisation. Chemical plants for fertilisers were powered by Japanese-built hydro-electric systems. Mining was another industry that benefited from Japanese investment, producing the raw ores for Japan's manufacturing industries and steel mills, and manufacturing plants came on stream, connected by a vast road and rail network. Most of the industrial growth, operated by the cheap labour of former farmers, was concentrated in the peninsula's north as the south held more and better-quality farming land.

In 1931, a bomb of unknown origin blew up the Japanese railway near China's Shenyang in the 'Manchurian Incident' (otherwise known as the 'Mukden Incident', Shenyang having been renamed by Japan), that pretexted the Japanese military occupation of southern Manchuria. Hence Japan's political economy was galvanised from the pit of the global depression for more vigorous imperial adventures in China and the Pacific. Investment poured into Korea. Chemicals and food processing became the major industries, accounting for over half of the yen value of Korea's output, with their own spin-offs in affiliated industries. Iron and steel output increased dramatically, as did ceramics and light industries, like machine tools. The peninsula was being built as a great staging-post for Japan's Asian empire, and road and rail links were built to the Korean coast closest to Japan and out into the Asian mainland. Well-designed, well-plumbed cities housed Korea's burgeoning industrial workforce, some of whose children received schooling in the practical disciplines of maths, basic sciences and engineering.

But the best schools were for the children of the Japanese plant owners, managers and the imperial administrators who inhabited the best-built parts of town. Proportionally, three times as many Japanese as Korean children and youth went to school (and with no higher education for the latter). Korean students were taught a history that emphasised how Korea and Japan were historically joined at the hip. Anyway, all schooling was in Japanese, as was usually the press; colonial attitudes to Korean newspapers never quite reached tolerance.

In February 1936, those in the Tokyo government advocating a more moderate foreign policy were literally cut down and killed by fanatical army officers. By early 1937, it wasn't enough for Koreans to serve in Japan's war factories (although by 1945 two million Korean men were working in mainland Japan); they were to be needed for the front lines too. Korean women were rounded up and forced into work for the Japanese armed forces as 'comfort women', an outrageously effete euphemism for enslaved prostitution. The population was imbued with Japanese culture under the 'Transformation into Imperial Subjects' policy, from swearing the oath of loyalty to Japan's emperor to saluting the flag. Korean names were replaced with Japanese ones. Shinto shrines and ceremonies were brought to all Korean communities and families. Korea was the front-line state for Japan's imperial plans, not just a route into the Asian mainland but a supplier of food, workers, war materials and (subservient) spiritual brethren.

**Resistance and war** Soon after the Western powers' eviction from the region as the century had turned, they were diverted away from Korea's annexation by their upcoming (first) world war. Hundreds of thousands of Koreans took flight into Russia, America and China. But those that stayed hadn't trusted those fickle foreigners anyway, and the idea of a Korean nation, itself only realised through contact with the outside world, wasn't to be buried by any colonialists.

In the 1910s, the Japanese authorities so keenly sensed any whiff of rebellion that many Koreans were imprisoned, tortured and killed on suspicion of crimes they hadn't even considered. Incidents were just that, isolated expression of malcontent while no coherent resistance formed, although Japan's land and administrative reforms dispossessed, displaced and ruined Koreans from every social strata.

All the Koreans needed was a rallying call, which came in early 1919. Intellectuals, Yangban, professionals and students joined together in signing a 'Declaration of Independence'. They were hoping to catch the eye of the Western powers emerging from war and use US President Woodrow Wilson's spirit of independence, but the Korean delegation to Versailles was ignored. Still the declaration was proclaimed in Seoul on 1 March, two days before the funeral of former King Kojong. Japanese police arrested the leaders, but a crowd gathered, grew restless and shouted Manse! (10,000 years, so Long Live Korea!). They were fired upon by military police, the army and the navy, but Korean turnout reached the thousands. Two months of demonstrations followed and a million people joined the Samil or 'March 1 Movement' on the streets, demanding independence, wrecking colonial buildings and fighting the army hand-to-hand.

The international attention this gained focused less on Korea's independence movement and more on the savagery used in suppressing it, and the only concessions were a few Korean-language newspapers and limited opportunities in education.

Nevertheless, 1 March had demonstrated the huge, latent sense of Korean nationalism, there to be tapped. The anti-Japanese guerrillas, beaten into the Manchurian hinterland (where future leader Kim Il Sung's forebears had fled), were invigorated in their struggle. In Shanghai, a self-declared Provisional government was set up by Syngman Rhee, a Korean imprisoned by the Japanese before escaping to study in the US. Shanghai was also home to a Korean Communist Party, set up in opposition to the Provisional Government-in-exile, but it was not the only political party to take that name. Socialist societies were founded in Seoul and Tokyo, and in 1925 the Korean Communist Party was founded in Korea, using the anniversary of Emperor Sunjong's death to attempt another 'March 1-style' movement. Russia was by then part of a fully fledged communist empire, the Soviet Union, and would later be central to Korea's development and division.

For now, however, the Sunjong rally illustrates that Korean political resistance, full of vigour, was confused. Factions across the political spectrum reached for any symbol of Korean nationalism. The Japanese were, in contrast, eerily singular in their purpose of suppressing insurrection. However, despite mass arrests, imprisonment (with some leaders emerging from prison only in 1945), torture and executions, resistance movements regrouped, reformed and reorganised. In the 1920s, farm and factory disputes and strikes racked up from dozens to hundreds and thousands. Wonsan and Seoul went on general strike in 1929 and 1930 respectively, and in 1930 54,000 Korean high-school students were involved in disturbances across Korea.

Resistance groups were already operating from Manchuria, and following Japan's annexing of the area in 1931, Chinese and Korean guerrillas co-operated in carrying out merciless attacks on Japanese troops. By the mid-'30s, three anti-Japanese armies were operating in the Manchurian area, called the North Eastern Anti-Japanese United Army (NEAJUA) that had Chinese and Soviet support. Many partisans fled into the Soviet Union and there they were armed, trained and filled with political thought. Japanese forces were harried, pinned down and cut up in the region's cold, harsh terrain, and it was from this frozen hell that a future leader, Kim Il Sung, would be forged. Although later DPRK historians would shroud his early years in myth, what's not in doubt is that this charismatic young leader (born in 1912) wreaked enough havoc to warrant the Japanese assigning a crack unit to track him down.

Japan's imperial plans led to full-scale war with China in 1937 and the US in 1941. Imperial overstretch required Koreans to take the higher jobs they'd always been denied, and enter the Japanese army. All this achieved was to create a stock of Koreans that would later be branded collaborators and compound post-war misery.

By late 1945, Japan was on the brink of defeat. As he had promised the Americans months earlier, Soviet Premier Josef Stalin prepared to launch war against the collapsing Japanese forces in east Asia. To hasten Japan's surrender and draw an awesome close to the east Asian war, US President Truman dropped two atom bombs on Japan, days before the Soviets were due to attack. The Soviets carried on, routing and taking prisoner Japanese forces in the east and landing their own forces in northern Korea.

The US proposed a joint occupation to 'share the burden' of rebuilding the country, dividing the country into North and South by the latitude line of 38° across Korea's midriff. The Soviets agreed, and in early September US forces arrived at Incheon to take their zone of control.

The Soviets wanted a friendly communist nation on their borders, and the Americans wanted anything but another communist nation slap next to their new Asian base, Japan. With the two worlds of communism and capitalism about to collide on a global scale in the Cold War, the Americans and Soviets set about looking for suitable leaders in their halves of the country. Neither side paid much attention to the wishes of the Koreans, and with French and British agreement, the Soviets and US agreed a five-year trusteeship of Korea in which time they would instigate elections for one national government.

Although they disagreed on many things, none of Korea's indigenous political groups took well to the trusteeship, but the trustees considered them too incoherent and politically immature to run the country, as in fact it had been run by the Japanese for the last 35 years. There was already a government-in-waiting in Korea, the Korean People's Republic (KPR), formed by political leader and former political prisoner You Un Hyong and presided over by Syngman Rhee, president of the self-proclaimed Korean government-in-exile. But US forces' commander General Hodge regarded the KPR as crypto-communists, mainly for its popular policy of land reform, and, governing the South with remnants of the Japanese colonials' assistance, set about closing down all 'communist' activities. In the South, left-wing groups, labour unions and advocates of land reform were banned and imprisoned, and communist newspapers closed. Korean Communist Party leader Pak Hon Yong fled north. In the North, the Soviets had reluctantly cobbled together a coalition of communists, nationalists and Christians as well as considering the KPR, but their trusteeship would be pointless without installing a good communist in charge. In that they already had the youthful but toughened officer Colonel Kim Il Sung, freshly arrived in October 1945.

**KIM IL SUNG AND THE KOREAN WORKERS' PARTY** Only 34 years old, Kim had spent most of his life outside Korea, with years in Stalin's Soviet Union, leading his own reconnaissance brigade into Manchuria for the Red Army. Tough, straight-talking and respected by his Soviet supporters, he had a loyal core of fellow guerrilla-fighters. His military background and impressive record of nationalist resistance was key to his ability to organise and get the forming People's Army on side. He was placed to lead the provisional government of the Communist Party set up in 1946. In August 1946, the communists merged with their political opponents, the more social-democrat New People's Party, a group led by Koreans formerly based with the Chinese communists in Yanan during the war years and which appealed to the educated middle class. The merged party was the North Korea Workers' Party, thus a politically broad church with mass appeal. Cadres toured the country, appealing to the peasants to join the Party and break their bonds with their suppressive landlords in the new Korea. A rural groundswell signed up for the Party that swiftly dominated all politics, and they were rewarded with a revolutionary land reform that dispossessed landlords and distributed the land among the peasants, while the Japanese-owned industries were nationalised as a Soviet-style two-year economic plan for industry was put in train. To be sure, soon enough, the Christian and nationalist politicians would be made redundant, if not arrested. Meantime, the Yanan faction were more useful than obstructive to the functioning of government.

In the South, Syngman Rhee, now in Seoul, survived the KPR's demise and agreed to the trusteeship if the Americans helped crack down on any political protest against Rhee, which, being usually from left wingers, the US command did so approvingly. With US provision of financial incentives for Rhee's supporters, and some local military arm-twisting for Rhee's detractors, Rhee became South Korea's dominant political leader. Not dissimilar tactics allowed the Soviets to establish Kim Il Sung as the key political leader and he set up a military-based administration in Pyongyang.

By 1947, either side of the parallel had its own government, with Kim Il Sung's communist, Soviet-backed regime in Pyongyang and Rhee's right-wing, US-supported regime in Seoul. These provisional governments were necessarily authoritarian to quell sporadically violent unrest and factional fighting, and get the economy going again. But Korea's unification was a fading vision. Nationalist efforts to negotiate a unification treaty floundered because the two domestic governments' temporary set-up gave them questionable political and legal power. Their leaders were getting along as badly as their Soviet and American supporters, without whose backing no meaningful deal was possible.

Realising its increasingly heated relationship with the Soviets was obstructing unification, and that the Soviets were too stubborn to agree on anything, the US decided that a unitary government should be decided by the Koreans themselves. In late 1947, the US requested the United Nations to organise a general election for all Korea. The Soviets suspected foul play, justifiably as both powers had helped ban, incarcerate and assassinate (including Yo Un Hyong) the more radical opponents to their favoured leaders. Fearing their man Kim Il Sung wouldn't win, the Soviets refused elections for their half, but elections in the South were held in May 1948. This election established, under President Syngman Rhee, the Republic of Korea (ROK), recognised as Korea's legitimate government by the Western powers. The Soviets then organised their own northern election in August, delivering Kim Il Sung as president of the new Democratic People's Republic of Korea (DPRK) which was recognised as Korea's legitimate government by the Soviets and their communist allies.

Korea had stable governance, if under two groups and not one. Resistance now to Rhee's government continued but was pushed underground and into the hinterlands. The farms and factories were producing, although the idiocies of a divided economy were immediately manifest, with most of the factories and power in the North and the farms in the South. The North–South border was closed and there were regular, large skirmishes across it by opposing militia. But the situation was stable enough for US forces to withdraw in June 1949, leaving a few military advisers and promises of military aid. The Soviets departed the North, leaving weapons and weapons' factories for the North's 'defence'.

Independent at last, Rhee and Kim immediately began to whip up their halves about the urgent need for unification, and persuading their populace that only military force could achieve this. Barely five years after Japan's hated rule had collapsed, Korea was heading to war with itself. Pre-empting Rhee's plans for unification, Kim Il Sung and Pak Hon Yong visited Stalin in April 1950, assuring him that they had enough supporters in the South to ensure a swift, decisive victory. On 25 June 1950, 70,000 North Korean troops smashed southwards across the 38th parallel. The Korean War had begun.

**KOREAN WAR** In the West it is firmly believed that the DPRK was the aggressor, with the war started by the invasion of northern forces into the south in June 1950. There is also a theory that the Korean War was started by South Korea, and the North simply responded in kind, although if that was the case then the southern offensive into North Korea must be deemed as spectacular a failure as the success of the North's counter-attack.

A low-level war of border incursions and raids by forces of both sides had been going on for some time, years even, before June 1950, but the attack from the North on 22 June was the most decisive. While the success of the DPRK assault suggests a long and hefty build-up, the North was not devoid of provocation, and the unfortunate inevitability of the division of Korea and the political gulf between the two states was always going to be very messy. But both states then, as now, were and are committed to reuniting one country, a country split by outside forces with a map and a pen.

Northern forces hammered southwards with the lightly armed, poorly trained southern forces retreating in such panic they destroyed bridges that their own troops couldn't retreat across. Within a week, the North had taken Seoul, but as swiftly, the US and United Nations had voted to intervene on the South side. Fifteen countries' forces were combined into one UN command under US General Douglas MacArthur. The decisive move came in early September, as the DPRK army compressed the South around Pusan, a US Marine division landed at Incheon and cut the DPRK supply and reinforcement routes. The UN force heartily battered the DPRK army back over the 38th parallel, then pressed on to unite Korea under UN auspices. However, China's newly established communist government grew very wary that, besides their North Korean brothers losing, Korea under the Americans could only serve to harass communist China. China's premier and foreign minister Zhou Enlai threatened direct military intervention if American forces crossed the parallel and didn't leave the liberation to southern troops. Nonetheless, MacArthur was eager to finish the job, and by October's end, UN forces had reached the Yalu, taking Pyongyang by land and Wonsan by sea and pounding every city from the air. The Chinese, as they'd threatened, counter-attacked in late November with hundreds of thousands of troops. The UN Command was unprepared for the attack and the evil winter weather, and within two months they had been pushed 30 miles south of Seoul. There they dug in, and the Chinese suffered their own staggering losses in April and May. Herein the war ground into stalemate as both sides to'd and fro'd around the 38th parallel.

Armistice talks were proposed in June 1951, to which the UN commander General Ridgeway (who replaced the too-hawkish MacArthur) agreed. Two years of negotiations followed while scores died in futile battles every day. Along the way, US President Eisenhower, elected on a promise to end the war, threatened the DPRK with atomic attack.

On 27 July 1953, the US, China and the DPRK signed an armistice at the small village of Panmunjom, south of Kaesong, ending the fighting but not the war: peace has never been officially declared. The cost of the war has been estimated at around three million Korean civilians and 700,000 soldiers, a million Chinese troops, 54,000 American soldiers and 3,200 from the other allied countries. Many of the northern civilians were killed in air-raids, in which a greater tonnage of bombs was dropped on Korea's cities by the US air force than either Nazi Germany or Imperial Japan ever received. And as for a unified Korea...

## THE REIGN OF KIM IL SUNG TO TODAY'S DPRK
**The DPRK domestic set-up** The war hadn't achieved a unified Korea, nor dislodged or destabilised either government. So now we will look at the set-up of the DPRK government and its development.

Notwithstanding minor constitutional changes, the balance of power (at least in theory) rests between three main branches of government: the state, the party (Korean Workers' Party, KWP) and the military. All are made up of various agencies and committees with varying levels of interdependence and autonomy. Each branch of government has its own agencies and supporting bureaucracy, and also ownership and control of different elements of the economy.

From the DPRK's founding, the top state post was that of premier, a post that with a cabinet known as the Administration Council ran the country through numerous ministries. Kim Il Sung held that job until 1972 when the more senior post of president was created. The president and the council are elected by the Supreme People's Assembly, that consists of 674 representatives, voted in by popular election every five years. This body appoints the judiciary, passes laws and calculates the annual budget.

Juche is a Korean word of two syllables, Ju meaning 'master' and Che meaning 'oneself', so literally translated it means 'Master of one's self'. Although the term first became widely used in 1955, most DPRK histories trace its origin back to June 1930 when the young Kim Il Sung outlined a new path for the Korean revolution at a meeting of revolutionaries in Kalun. Kim Il Sung's father Kim Hyong Jik, when president of the Korean National Association, advocated the idea of Chiwon – 'Aim High' – to achieve Korean independence. This idea and the tenets of Marxism were important sources for Juche ideas. Juche (ju-chay) also known as Kimilsungism, is the socio-political philosophy developed by Kim Il Sung and expounded upon by Kim Jong Il that is the governing philosophy of the DPRK, as stipulated in Article 3 of the 1998 DPRK Constitution, towards realising the ultimate socialist state. Juche is celebrated by its followers for its 'scientific' answers to questions of man's destiny and, as the plaques at the base of Pyongyang's Juche Tower show, Juche has (small) followings worldwide. This is a brief outline of the Juche idea and what it means for the country and its people.

Juche states that man is the master of everything, and decides everything. Man is distinguished from the other countless physical and organic entities surrounding him by possessing the three attributes of creativity, consciousness and Chajusong, which means 'independence' in a broad and more profound sense. Chajusong is man's innate will to live, to develop independently, and master his own destiny and world.

Chajusong involves man overcoming and subordinating the will of nature to his own ends. Man adapts the environment to suit him, distinguishing man from other organisms like plants and animals that adapt themselves to their environment.

Animals can mould the environment for themselves, but their endeavours are purely instinctive, whereas man has developed and learnt (eg: building shelters, developing from caves to mud-huts to brick houses to tower-blocks) and is improved by his creativity. Man's consciousness allows him to observe and understand the properties of his environment and manipulate it thus.

Chajusong and creativity are related as recreating the world can only be done in order to master it, and consciousness realises that Chajusong requires creativity to achieve mastery, recognising Chajusong's needs and directing man's energies into moulding his surroundings accordingly. Therefore, all subjugation is to be resisted, and Juche strongly denounces dogmatism and flunkeyism.

There's also man's social and political life, critical because the three attributes are only realisable in social contexts, through linear education and thought development. Man can only progress beyond his instincts through education, discussion and practice to realise his Chajusong, consciousness and creativity.

There's no plan to the universe. The existent physical, spontaneous relationships between physical entities are due to their particular properties that have fallen into being. Man is the only pro-active transformer of the world. In the Juche world, nothing has value beyond its potential use or harm to man. In capitalism, value and worth are given monetary form, and greed prevents serious scientific advancements from benefiting society (consumer durables do not endure but are designed to break). This value system is also subjective and therefore unscientific and irrational and no way to run a society. Juche insists it must be in the interests of the individual to be engaged, but engagement comes through exciting and channelling his energies towards societal ends. Machines and materials can never be valued over man, for they are useless without men and exist only to serve him and society.

Marxism espouses that socio-historical progress comes from developments in the production of material wealth. Transformations in social history have come about through changes in the productive forces, production relations and production of material wealth.

Juche argues that history is the process of the masses enhancing their position and role to realise Chajusong. The masses struggle for Chajusong; when society's structure denies or constrains Chajusong, then society is changed. In international diplomacy, Juche demands each nation stand its own ground and defend its collective Chajusong. The DPRK put this into practice by maintaining a steadfast independence and neutrality during the difficult years of the Sino–Soviet split. The DPRK refused to join COMECON (the Soviet bloc economic union). In the mid-1970s the DPRK became a member of the Non-Aligned Movement and established good relations with many Third World countries. In recent years the DPRK has stood up to pressure from the US. Their life and soul is independence, and they must act as sovereign nations, pursuing paths to further their independence without buckling to outside interference or pressures. This means also that a nation's true Chajusong can only be achieved through economic self-sufficiency, for any reliance on others shifts power into their hands. Similarly, to prevent the wrong class from controlling and abusing the power of the state, the masses must seize control of the state and its economic means of production. Society's structure is underpinned by its forms of economic production, so seizing them is the first means to change society into more advanced states as the masses need. History is a series of struggles, from primitive society through feudalism to industrialisation, involving the struggle to subdue nature, wherein the creative processes are fostered, practised and developed.

To realise Chajusong the masses must be brought up to be the masters of society, and be free of all exploitation and oppression. Old ideas die hard while imperialists continue to infiltrate and spread reactionary ideas, so even the liberated need remoulding. Ideological remoulding eliminates old ideas incompatible with man's Chajusong and equips him with the progressive ideas needed for independence and creativity, but it's hard work. People need to be remoulded like nature.

In 1975 the line of the Three Revolutions was put forward – the ideological revolution, technical revolution and cultural revolution. Basically the ideological revolution was to be complemented by the technical revolution to free people from the shackles of outdated technology and liberate people from back-breaking work. The cultural revolution would bring everyone up to the standard of an intellectual. Progressive ideas mean a high level of scientific and technical knowledge, with a strong physique. Thought determines men's worth and quality. Knowledge doesn't mean respectability, because much knowledge and bad ideology is disastrous. Only sound ideology, via good ideological remoulding, can direct knowledge to society's benefit.

Juche is built around the interests of the masses, so the masses must learn Juche and accept the organisation required to imbue them with the philosophy of revolutionary struggle, i.e. the struggle to defend their Chajusong, their life and soul. For revolutionary tasks to succeed, political work must educate and rouse people into action, and the fostering of their zeal must be prioritised over all other work. People cannot simply be ordered to a particular goal; they must have their hearts set to it, wherein no challenge is too great. The political persuasion and education of people must be tailored to their backgrounds, trades, etc. One persuader per ten workers is a good ratio for intilling revolutionary fervour.

Above all, harnessing this zeal requires good leadership from the party and its leader. The leader is the brain to the body of the masses and is the supreme representative and embodiment of their interests; his acts represent their will. He leads them to victory and so devotion to the leader is the highest expression of revolutionary zeal.

*With many thanks to Dermot Boyd-Hudson for his help here. The above is sourced from* The Immortal Juche Idea *by Kim Chang Ha, Pyongyang Foreign Languages Publishing House, Pyongyang Korea, 1984. For further information visit Juche Idea Study Group of England (www.language-museum.com/jisge/), or Study of the Juche Idea (www.cnet-ta.ne.jp/juche/defaulte.htm).*

The KWP is not the only political party. There's also the Tonghak-derived Chondoist Chongu Party and the Korean Social Democratic Party, concerned with peace, reunification and the imposition of a social democracy for one Korea. In practice, the assembly is dominated by KWP representatives and the assembly ratifies policies already decided by the KWP leadership. The top KWP leadership post is the General Secretary, who works with a small advisory group known as the Politburo, and both consult with the Central Committee, a several-hundred-member group that discusses state and ideological policy. The General Secretary, Politburo and Central Committee run the party between party congresses that until the '80s used to happen (very) approximately every four years. Congress involves a few hundred party officials from across the country debating policies put to it by the leadership. Congress elects the Central Committee and Politburo. A Central People's Committee was created in 1972 that would supersede the Politburo, but isn't considered much more than symbolic.

The final branch of power is the military, the Korean People's Army (KPA), whose top posts are Supreme Commander and the Chairman of the National Defence Commission, ultimately commanding millions in service and industry.

As said above, each branch has its own sector of the economy under its governance. What these sectors produce, the people they employ in what conditions, income generated and to what end the goods and income are put, all have a bearing on the relative balance of power of the three power branches. Nor is any one branch totally independent of the other. If the KWP dominate the agencies of the state, then the KWP is de facto the state, then the General Secretary of the KWP wields great power. The army, however, has a firm monopoly on employing the nation's fit young men who themselves have a firm interest in joining up and working in the army's own economy sectors and networks. Commanding the army is critical, and when the Korean People's Army (KPA) was founded in early 1948, its leader Choe Yng-gn and its tens of thousands of troops were the hardy stock of guerrilla-fighters in Manchuria; Kim Il Sung's kind of people, and he was their kind of leader.

The different branches of government indeed have their own newspapers. While the subject matter may obviously differ, the unquestioning support and veneration of the Kims does not. Dissenters are noted and their opinions discounted; if they persist, they're publicly named, denounced and demoted (they used to disappear). This is largely the result of the extremely personalised rule of the country that Kim Il Sung inculcated from the immediate post-Korean War period, for the top posts mentioned would soon all be staffed by one man: Kim Il Sung.

Elections do happen. Michael Harrold, in *Comrades and Strangers* (see page 225), describes the visit he made for the election of the People's Assembly, explaining that he could see that the official turnout figures of 100%, of which practically all were voting for the Korean Workers' Party, were not inconceivable considering how much 'fun' voting is. Taken by his friends, wearing their 'Sunday best', he says:

> At the polling station – for the Ansan Guest House it was a nearby secondary school – there were crowds gathered and music being played. The people were organised into large circles, dancing.
>
> Taking the lead were, as usual on such jolly occasions, the old women, and they were pirouetting madly yet gracefully, coloured scarves held aloft, to the sound of some pretty uninspiring music being scratched out by a gramophone. I knew it was going to happen and so I tried as best I could to fade into the background. But it is hard for the proverbial sore thumb to become invisible, and it was with a shout of glee that one old lady spotted the foreigner in their midst. 'Have you come to vote?' she cried, to laughter from those around her. 'Vote for the glorious Workers' Party!' shouted another.

**Kim takes charge** Before the Korean War was over, Kim Il Sung took action to consolidate his position as leader. Across every echelon of the DPRK government were Koreans with a variety of backgrounds in terms of class, education, and their roots in the country with lifelong ties of friends and family. Aside from these loyalties, their individual political opinions, and the factions thus created, were influenced by where they had served their political apprenticeships during the anti-Japanese war, in the Soviet Union, China, in Korean guerrilla activities or outside Asia altogether. Kim was not one to wait for any disagreements with his policies to snowball into opposition and challenge to his leadership. Purges of the KWP began in 1952 when he indicated that some cadres were infected with sloth and other vices. He upped the ante in his expurgation of potential opponents and, by the end of 1955, a dozen senior figures had been imprisoned or executed on charges of spying for the US, including the former Korean Communist Party leader, Pak Hon Yong.

Thus emboldened, Kim set out his own vision for Korea, to set up the country's political economy along the same lines as Stalin had done in the Soviet Union from the 1930s and '40s where Kim Il Sung had been trained and based for years. Kim Il Sung committed the DPRK's economic growth to heavy industry, a very centralised form of governmental control and unquestioned, highly personalised leadership, which has drawn many parallels with Stalinism. But simply transposing the 1930s' Soviet model onto Korea wouldn't take into account Korea's unique circumstances and history, certainly not for Kim. His Juche philosophy, Marxism infused with Korean nationalism, was soon to become the governing philosophy of the DPRK.

**Kim consolidates** However, the Soviet Union's Premier Nikita Khruschev denounced all things Stalin in 1956, and a few Soviet-Koreans in the KWP criticised the leadership for the direction in which it was taking the country. Beating his detractors with the stick of nationalism, by late 1956 most of the Soviet-Koreans and the Yanan Koreans from the former New People's Party had been purged from the KWP for their 'foreign influences'. Up through the ranks of the party and the state bodies, Kim promoted his anti-Japanese guerrillas, rough, tough, hardy folk, of common stock and educated as such, promoted more for their ties to Kim than for their technical or political talents. Meanwhile, Party membership was growing into millions across the country, taking in a groundswell of farmers and peasants, the people whose origins paralleled those of Kim's senior appointees in the Party and agencies of government. By the end of 1958, through purges and promotions, Kim's grip on the KWP was iron-tight. Over the next decade he consolidated his personalised rule through fewer Party congresses, more purges and a developing personality cult with a heavy military flavour (see box, *Cult of the Kims*, pages 28–9).

**Foreign policy** It's a misnomer to write of the two Korean regimes' relations to each other as 'foreign relations'. The DPRK and ROK have always been the two halves of the Korean whole, yet undeniably their want and efforts for reunification have dominated their political environments. However, as both regimes and their backers recognised only themselves as Korea's legitimate government, reunification only ever looked possible through one regime removing the other, and, as no formal peace was ever declared, the peninsula has spent the years since 1953 on a war-footing. Tensions between the three sides (for the US has long had a permanent, well-armed, military force in the ROK) oscillate to this day, and the last half-century of relations has been a cycle of negotiations and brinksmanship interspersed by bizarre feats of violence.

Everywhere, everywhere, everywhere in the DPRK there are images of the 'Great Leader' Kim Il Sung and his son the 'Dear Leader' Kim Jong Il. The leaders' portraits hang side by side high on the walls of the largest public halls to the commonest private rooms, and are cleaned with dustcloths assigned only to that task. Their faces peer out from the paintings and mosaics emblazoning buildings, walls, junctions and the badges on people's lapels. Bronze statues of the Great and Dear Leaders front buildings, top hills, dominate town squares across the country, and the leaders' philosophical treatises and teachings, carved in stone, flank public squares and highways or are enscribed onto Korea's holiest mountains and boulders.

During his leadership, Kim Il Sung managed to visit nearly every city, town, village and farm, factory, military base, construction site, port, nursery and hospital, dispensing 'on-the-spot guidance', every occasion being marked on a map in Pyongyang's Korean Revolution Museum. His every word was noted and filmed by accompanying officials and journalists, to be looped in print and film. His birthplace at Mangyongdae is a shrine, visited daily by throngs of pilgrims. All that he touched or commented on has become hallowed ground: the seat he took on the metro; a tree he remarked upon in Wonsan; rooms he visited in rural schools have plaques detailing the time, day, comment, and the same is happening for Kim Jong Il.

Buildings are named by the date that the leaders visited them, or have meaning built into their grouting. The number of stone slabs on Pyongyang's Juche Tower, built for Kim Il Sung's 70th birthday, equals the days that he had been alive. The lowly cabin where Kim Jong Il was reportedly born in 1942 is exactly 216m from a mountain behind it, a distance that miraculously mirrors Kim Jong Il's birthdate of 2/16, a day marked by a double rainbow and a bright star in the sky, and the news spread fast (born in a lowly building, midwinter, bright star, the news spread far and wide … are all Messiahs born this way?).

DPRK history is not completely soaked in such colourful myths (although the mythologising of Kim's forebears has seen his great-grandfather accredited with the sinking of the *General Sherman*), but every subject taught from nursery to university is infused with the wisdom of the Kims and Juche. Departments at Kim Il Sung university are devoted to studying their writings that cover everything from economics to art to

For the DPRK, the creator and perpetuator of Korea's division has always been the United States and its puppet ROK government. For the United States and ROK, peaceful reunification has been impossible with an uncompromising communist regime. To the West, the DPRK has been a warmongering pariah as a Soviet puppet or, worse, on its own initiative. If the DPRK regime was determined to be free of all outside pressures or coercion, as Juche aspired, then the country would be assisted into isolationism by throttling US economic sanctions. The continuity of the situation partly stems from the vehemence of Washington's anti-communist policy, and on the DPRK side from the longevity of the Kim dynasty. The issues over which the DPRK and ROK have disagreed have remained the same, with some fluctuations in relations through the changing regimes in the south (the ROK has been the democracy it is today since 1989).

The DPRK and ROK made stuttering attempts at reconciliation almost immediately after the armistice. At the 1954 Geneva Conference, Kim Il Sung proposed an all-Korean commission to discuss reunification without any foreign interference or forces on the peninsula. A confederation of the two Koreas would be empowered to oversee their own foreign and defence policies, but that died a death. Tentative moves for rapprochement were made by the DPRK in 1960 following the removal of Rhee from office, but Seoul's new military regime would have none of it.

opera. Films and plays exist to propagate the greatness of DPRK socialism and its ultimate victory over imperialism, and the Kims' role in this.

Kim Il Sung has affected time itself. His birthday is a national holiday and the DPRK's years are counted since Kim Il Sung's year of birth. And he's still in charge. In 1998, four years after his death, Kim Il Sung was made 'Eternal President' of the DPRK by the Supreme People's Assembly.

As Kim Il Sung's rule became sharply more personalised and authoritarian from the 1950s, so his deification commenced, and his leadership was based on an expanding personality cult derived from Stalinism, with himself commanding a mass party and centralised command economy. He was feted as a military hero, a philosopher, a father of the nation figure, a genius who intervened in the most personal way with on-the-spot guidance, whose comments were canonised and whose critics disappeared. Many if not most people would have seen him in the flesh at some time in their lives, as he spent more time touring the country than in the capital in the 50 tumultuous, traumatic and spectacular years in which he dominated the country's public life. From the late 1960s, the monumentalism of his character was being matched in massive architectural works, and from thereon, the DPRK's history was his story.

From then on his son Kim Jong Il was promoted in government and print as the only man with the cojones to succeed his father. In a drawn-out succession, Kim Jong Il took over the significant post of General Secretary in July 1997, after three years of official mourning for Kim Il Sung had elapsed. In 1998, Kim Jong Il became Chairman of the National Defence Commission, de facto president – but the latter title went to Kim Il Sung, herein the 'Eternal President'.

Transferring power from father to son reflects Korea's history of dynastical rule, and the country's authoritarianism has parallels with Korea's preceding Confucian-based regimes, based on deference without question from subordinates to superiors. That Kim Il Sung is still venerated and worshipped as the country's 'Eternal President' is a modern extension of ancient ancestral worship, something that continues at all societal levels in today's ROK, and as alluded to above, the cult has distinct Christian tinges (why else would Billy Graham and Kim Il Sung get along so famously?).

Kim was not disconsolate by this rebuff, however. Socialism was working. By 1960, the DPRK GNP was US$140 per capita, hammering the US$100 of the ROK, an impressive recovery that was partly explicable by Soviet and Chinese aid. The DPRK jostled between the two powers for aid, playing one off against the other and thereby being the pawn of neither, but Khruschev's favouring of coexistence with the capitalist West was unacceptable to Kim who considered coexistence tantamount to defeat. Deteriorating Sino–Soviet relations in the 1960s led the DPRK to back China at the cost of its Soviet aid but Kim was worried that the two would fall out to the detriment of their shared beliefs. He was scathing about China's evident failures to publicly lambaste America's engagement in Vietnam. However, China's Communist Party was lurching into extremes, soon to culminate in the Cultural Revolution, and returned fire that Kim was too pro-Soviet. Sino–DPRK relations soured, just as a spate of violent incidents marked US, ROK and DPRK relations in the late 1960s. In January 1968, a team of DPRK commandos were caught and killed on a raid on the ROK president's house. Two days later, an American spy-ship, the USS *Pueblo*, was captured by the DPRK navy and the crew held captive for a year. All 31 crew-members of an American EC-121 spy-plane were killed when it was shot down by a DPRK MiG fighter in April 1969, and in August a US helicopter was downed as it strayed across the DMZ into the DPRK.

In the early 1970s, thawing Sino–US relations and reduced US forces in the ROK goaded more inter-Korean talks. High-level talks alternated between the two capitals and a crucial joint communiqué was issued in July 1972, which was a milestone for ROK–DPRK relations (another milestone that year was the creation of the post of president of the DPRK, which Prime Minister Kim Il Sung was elevated into). Work towards reunifying the country would be without foreign interference and without force, and with reduced slanging matches (the media attacks on one another had descended from acerbic through vitriol to scraping for insults). A Pyongyang–Seoul hotline was set up, as was a South–North Coordinating Committee (SNCC) for further negotiations and implementing the agreement. But it was a false dawn. The SNCC met only three times. The DPRK stressed that reducing inter-Korean armed confrontation was a prerequisite to all else, demanding in particular that US aid to the ROK must stop. Seoul preferred both Koreas' political systems be recognised, with mutual non-interference and economic co-operation preceding arms reductions.

Pyongyang proposed replacing the armistice with a peace agreement. The ROK side was worried by a reduced US presence and the communist victory in Vietnam. A call from the DPRK for South Koreans to overthrow President Park's government wasn't conducive to successful negotiations. Tensions escalated along the DMZ and the Pyongyang–Seoul hotline was cut. At the beginning of the decade, the Korean People's Army had some 400,000 frontline troops; by the end, this figure had topped a million. Evidently the two sides weren't getting along so well and arming themselves to the teeth was one way to deal with relations.

**Casting further** Jostling for favour between China and the Soviets, and apparent unending aggravation with the ROK and US, the net for friends and funds was cast further in the early 1970s. From 1972 to 1974, the DPRK government procured large loans of foreign capital, machinery and funds from countries like Sweden, France and Japan, machinery and funds to create new export industries that would repay the lenders. To further its nuclear power programme, it joined the International Atomic Energy Association (IAEA) in 1974, and the DPRK was accepted into the Non-Aligned Movement (NAM) in 1975. Kim presupposed that this neutral group of developing nations, not really involved in the machinations of the Cold War, would be a good place to promote his anti-imperialism and be a supporting crowd for the DPRK, especially in United Nations negotiations. While Kim was to be held in high regard by the NAM, it wasn't quite the coherent and cohesive freelance political force he had envisaged. Nor were the capital loans from elsewhere being paid off by its exports, and the Ministry of Finance defaulted on the country's foreign debts, which would cost it dearly later (see *Economy*, page 45).

By the end of the '70s, the DPRK leadership was somewhat galled by China's warming relations with America and Japan, but this spurred some further discourse between the two Koreas in 1980, with a plethora of meetings over discursive details between them. Ultimately, the talks went nowhere, however, as General Chun Doo Hwan established military rule in the ROK and was not up for negotiating. In October, Kim Il Sung proposed establishing the Democratic Confederal Republic of Koryo, with both sides equally represented in a national assembly and a confederal committee with charge over national defence, foreign affairs and economic coordination. Coexistence was the key feature; both regimes would continue in lesser forms within the confederacy. Chun rejected the idea, much to the annoyance of Kim, who then allegedly took direct intervention in the ROK political realm by ordering the assassination of Chun's cabinet in Rangoon in October 1983.

DPRK assistance and relief to the flood-stricken South in 1984 led to discussions on humanitarian and economic co-operation. In 1985, performing arts groups and sports teams were exchanged and separated families briefly reunited for the first time. In the Party's higher circles, ideas of minor economic reforms similar to those China was taking were banded about as the economy slowed and the last seven-year plan evidently wasn't delivering. Capitalist enterprise zones were considered and a joint-venture law enacted, but there that train of thought was halted. Kim Il Sung visited the Soviet Union in May 1984 and it appeared that everything was forgiven and forgotten for a new phase of rapprochement and new economic, military and diplomatic links resumed. Immediately, the DPRK's fortunes lifted; yet now the fortunes of the DPRK rested with Soviet success.

Talks with the ROK ground to a halt in late 1985, and were suspended in January 1986. As usual, provocative joint US–ROK military exercises, performed annually since 1978, were blamed, but unusually, the DPRK didn't resume dialogue afterwards. The aftermath of the Rangoon bombing had been weathered and the DPRK hadn't changed its bargaining positions.

**The ROK makes friends with the DPRK's friends** However, the international situation was changing. By the late 1980s, the ROK economy was soaring, approaching output levels ten times those of the DPRK. The ROK economy's success and the power this bought attracted both the USSR and China as they dallied towards economic reforms of the capitalist kind, and humanitarian and sports exchanges began between China and the ROK. Indeed, the ROK had been wooing communist nations since 1984, and in 1988 the ROK's newly elected president Roh Tae Woo's outreaches to the North cemented ROK relations with

## THE RANGOON MASSACRE

On 9 October 1983, the ROK's leader President Chun Doo Hwan, while on a state visit to Burma, went to lay a wreath at Rangoon's martyrs memorial. Due to traffic problems, Chun's car was delayed in arriving, and just as he did so a bomb exploded at the memorial, killing 21 people and wounding 46. As well as four Burmese dignitaries, 17 ROK government officials, advisers and journalists were killed, including the ROK foreign minister and deputy prime minister.

Burmese police managed to arrest their first suspect two days later, despite the man trying to blow himself up with a hand-grenade. Two more suspects alerted to the police by villagers also tried to commit suicide with grenades, but only one succeeded. The two surviving agents were interrogated into revealing their DPRK origins.

the Soviets and China. The world was presented with the ROK's new glories at the glittering 1988 Seoul Olympics, attended for the first time in 12 years by virtually all communist and capitalist invitees, with which the ROK was star ascendant. The DPRK's offer to co-host the games having long gone by the wayside, they accepted ROK financial aid in return for a promise not to disrupt the games.

The DPRK leadership seethed as its rich brother befriended all its old allies. So, unseen, DPRK diplomats in Beijing made contact with their American counterparts just after the Olympics finished, a prescient move as a year later, the DPRK's greatest allies in eastern Europe evaporated with the Soviet bloc. Soviet trade declined in 1989, and in late 1990, the Soviets announced no more aid, no more barter, just hard currency. The DPRK's world of friends was gone almost overnight, and things looked bleak.

**Japan** One route out could be Japanese investment, but that would need better relations. For many Koreans, North and South, Japan is still the great unforgiven for its colonial rule of Korea. Koreans are still aggrieved that it was the victim, Korea, that was divided and not the aggressor, Japan; something that many Japanese also consider an injustice. Worse, Japan's economic revival stemmed from massive US financial and capital investment poured into the country to make it an operational base for fighting the Korean War. Kim Il Sung was brought up mind and soul in fighting the Japanese. Anti-Japanese resistance was infused into Juche and every history book in the country.

The Japanese government recognised only Seoul as Korea's legitimate governing body, so DPRK–Japan relations were largely through informal channels, including trade links via the association of Koreans in Japan, Chochongnyon, that gained several hundred million dollars of investment over the decades. Japan was to be by the 1980s a major trading partner with the DPRK. Officially, DPRK–Japanese relations were generally poor at best, exacerbated by a spate of kidnappings by DPRK special forces of Japanese citizens in the 1970s and '80s and defaults on large loans. In 1990, a Japanese delegation in Pyongyang, trying to have a fishing-boat crew released from spying charges, were presented with the suggestion by DPRK foreign officials of normalising relations. Haggling would continue for the next decade, but it was a start.

Still, destitution loomed. China's economic reforms were glanced at and a free trade zone was set up in December 1991, but substantial economic reforms were an anathema to Kim and everything five decades of socialism had cost. The late 1980s to '90s were not marked by pro-capitalist radicals arriving in the DPRK government. Indeed, the Politburo and Council were staffed more by ageing anti-Japanese guerrillas: Kim buttressed his beliefs by surrounding himself with his oldest cronies. And it was in the late 1980s that Kim's regime showed its old mettle, over the nuclear issue.

**Nukes in Korea** By the late 1980s, the international community (mainly the ROK, US and Japan) became concerned that the DPRK was producing weapons-grade uranium and would soon have the nuclear bomb. The DPRK Foreign Ministry was vague on the issue but cited the many threats made to them with US tactical nuclear weapons on the peninsula. Inspections of the DPRK's nuclear facilities by the IAEA were repeatedly refused. Tensions rose and some US senators advocated bombing DPRK facilities at Yongbyon, north of Pyongyang.

In fact, the DPRK had hankered to join the exclusive club of atomic powers practically since the country's founding, and as said, in 1974 the country joined the IAEA, the international agency that gives out nuclear know-how – for strictly peaceful means, mind. For years it seemed that the DPRK's intentions were peaceful enough, which were borne out in 1985 when the DPRK signed the Non-Proliferation Treaty of Nuclear Weapons. Only by 1990 was it obvious that DPRK's nuclear electricity reactors weren't really big enough for serious electricity production but could deliver lots of plutonium and enriched uranium: bomb material. However, Pyongyang did agree to talks at the prime-ministerial level with the ROK, and following rounds of bi-capital talks, in September 1991 the five permanent members of the UN Security Council approved both Koreas' membership of the UN. The following month, US President Bush announced the withdrawal of US tactical nuclear weapons from the peninsula, heralding a breakthrough in inter-Korean relations. In December, both Koreas signed the Agreement on Reconciliation, Non-aggression, Exchanges and Cooperation between the South and the North. It was a landmark agreement. The DPRK officially recognised the ROK's existence for the first time, and vice versa, and they agreed to negotiate a formal end to the Korean War.

Joint sub-committees were set up to develop economic ties and communications, cultural exchanges, united sports teams representing both Koreas, and familial reunifications, on top of measures to deflate military tensions. They also agreed the joint Declaration on the Denuclearization of the Korean Peninsula that would set up an effective bilateral nuclear inspection regime.

Not that all this brought peace. In 1992 IAEA inspectors noted discrepancies between amounts of plutonium produced and how much they found, and complained of restricted access to plants. Tensions roller-coasted with DPRK stick-shaking and America's Congress called for increased sanctions, if not bombing. With the economy stalling through diminishing harvests and no energy supplies, the DPRK threatened to cancel its treaties unless dialogue and aid began. US President Clinton ordered sanctions in mid-1994 and the DPRK withdrew from the IAEA. In desperate diplomacy, former US President Jimmy Carter visited Kim Il Sung in July 1994 and brought some diffusion of tensions with a possible 'aid for atoms' agreement. The octogenarian Kim Il Sung, back to the wall, was still demanding no surrender, not without a good price anyway. In October, the DPRK and the US signed the Agreed Framework, to wit the DPRK would freeze (and partly dismantle) its nuclear programme, stay in the NPT and allow full inspections. The US would provide 500,000 tonnes of fuel oil annually (replacing the lost imports from Russia) and lead a consortium to build two light-water reactors by 2003 (nuclear reactors but less potent) through the Korean Peninsula Energy Development Organisation (KEDO). The DPRK got some guarantee of energy supplies and a nuclear-free peninsula finally looked possible.

**Kim Il Sung departs** On 8 July 1994, Kim Il Sung died suddenly of a heart attack. He was 82. His sudden passing was profoundly traumatic for the DPRK people. He had led them out of the bitter ruins of the Korean War, and placed himself at the helm of the country's reconstruction and development into a providing, fiercely sovereign state.

**The succession** From the early 1970s, the man feted and groomed as the DPRK's next leader, the rightful heir of Kim Il Sung's power and authority, was none other than Kim Jong Il, Kim Il Sung's first son. From 1980, Kim Jong Il was given numerous successively higher positions in the Party, and that year it was announced that he would indeed succeed his father, and his own thoughts on Juche were published shortly after. Little was known about the man, however. He was rarely seen in public in the way that Kim Il Sung toured the lands, and was rumoured to be a recluse, who spent too much time watching the Western films in his incredible collection, films that if anyone else had been caught with them

*Dr James Hoare, Chargé d'Affaires of the British Embassy to Pyongyang 2001–02*

The division of Korea in 1945 had little to do with any historic or cultural differences on the peninsula. For about 1,000 years, Korea had been a unified political entity, with a remarkable homogeneous population. There were linguistic and other differences among those people, but the 38th parallel, the line chosen in 1945, bore little relation to them. Rather it was selected by the United States since it seemed the very least that the Soviet Union would accept. Just as important, in those opening days of the Cold War, it gave control of Seoul, the country's capital since 1392, to the Americans. But the Korean people never accepted the division.

However, the failure of either side to win an outright victory in the 1950–53 Korean War meant that the division has been perpetuated to this day. The war ended the 38th parallel's formal role. The line of actual military control, which became the Military Demarcation Line with the signing of the Armistice on 27 July 1953, though it ran close to the 38th parallel, did not follow it exactly. Instead, the South Koreans held territory above the parallel to the east of the truce village of Panmunjom that had been in the North before the war. The North, for its part, held Kaesong, capital of the country in the last but one dynasty, and the Ongjin peninsula, both south of the parallel and both in South Korea before June 1950.

After the signing of the Armistice, while both Koreas claimed to work for the reunification of the peninsula, each set about the creation of a separate state. They did not deny the essential historic unity of the peninsula, but each side drew on cultural and historical material that could be used to stress its legitimacy, and in the process downplayed the claims of the other side.

In the South, this meant stressing the role of Seoul, the capital of a united Korea from 1392. The speech of Seoul was presented as the 'national language'. At the same time, South Korean propaganda emphasised the tradition of the Silla kingdom. Silla, one of the traditional 'Three Kingdoms' of Korea, with its capital at Kyongju in the southwest of the peninsula, had unified much of the peninsula under its rule from AD668. Silla's role assumed particular importance after Park Chung Hee came to power in 1961, since he

would have meant a trip to the mines. Favoured actresses and directors of ROK films were apparently kidnapped and brought to him, and much has been written about Kim's preference for film femmes. The difficulty is that whereas DPRK publications about Kim Jong Il venerate him, ROK publications are at the other extreme with the most salacious, scurrilous tales that can't be trusted.

But following Kim Il Sung's death, the West wondered whether Kim Jong Il would indeed take over. Could an entire regime, a system of governance, built around one man in fact and fable actually survive his loss and the handover to a.n.other, even if the successor was his son? Questions arose over who was really in power. The posts of general secretary of the KWP and president of the DPRK remained empty while the country remained officially in mourning for three years.

During this time, the country, through floods, droughts and the breakdown of energy supplies (see *Economy*, page 45) entered into its first great famine. The trickle of defectors crossing into China was turning into a stream of refugees fleeing over the Yalu. In 1995, United Nations relief organisations received unprecedented requests to see the situation. Food and medical aid were forthcoming over the next months and years, from, among others, the US, Japan and ROK, but the politicking going on in the country's leadership was impenetrable at best. An indication of business as normal north of the DMZ came

came from that part of the country. The tradition of concentrating on Silla continued under his successors, since they too came from the southwest.

Although for North Korea, Seoul was to remain officially the capital until 1972, with Pyongyang listed only as the 'temporary capital', much stress was laid on Pyongyang's much longer history compared with that of Seoul. Indeed, Pyongyang was proclaimed to be the site of the capital of Tangun, the legendary ancestor of the Korean people. The speech of Pyongyang was promoted as the 'standard language', in the North. Historically, North Korea looked to another of the 'Three Kingdoms', Koguryo. Koguryo had been the largest of the kingdoms. At their greatest extent, Koguryo's territories stretched north far into what are now China's northeastern provinces, and south to Han River valley around Seoul. The kingdom's warriors also acquired a reputation for fierceness in battle.

North Korea has placed much emphasis on these themes. There has never been any claim that these are the only strands in Korean history but the stress is on the importance of the Pyongyang region and the superiority of Koguryo over Silla. The role of Pyongyang as an older capital than Seoul has been boosted by the claim that this was the capital city on earth of Korea's mythical founder, Tangun. Even more conclusive evidence, in North Korean eyes, for the sacred nature of Pyongyang and its claim to centrality in Korean history, was the alleged confirmation in the early 1990s that a tomb just outside the city was that of Tangun and his family. Refurbishment of the tomb of King Tongmyong, the supposed founder of the Koguryo dynasty, also just outside the city, reinforced the claimed importance of Pyongyang in the (unified) nation's history. No doubt an additional factor was that Kim Il Sung, ruler of North Korea from late 1945 until his death in 1994, came from the small village of Mangyongdae, just outside Pyongyang.

In addition to these factors, the continued North–South division has enhanced a sense of separateness. In vocabulary, customs, politics and general behaviour, North and South have grown apart. They no longer sing the same words to traditional songs, for example, even though the tunes remain the same. Increasingly, it is unlikely that they would even use the same instruments. None of this is irreversible, but the emphasis on separateness means that eventual reunification will be that bit harder.

in December 1996 when a DPRK submarine ran aground off the ROK coast. Twenty-six commandos swam ashore and so began a violent manhunt which led to the deaths of all the commandos and 13 ROK soldiers and civilians.

The most serious indication of internal dissent was the defection to the ROK of the ageing International Affairs Secretary, Hwang Jang Yop, in February 1997. Hwang was a senior Party member and committee chair, an interpreter of Juche philosophy and a man of very high standing with bountiful perks of state, had he wished to indulge. But he was an aesthete and a man of principle who would go on to tell his southern hosts that the regime was collapsing from within and couldn't have long to live. The rest of the world looked on, awaiting implosion.

In October 1997, Kim Jong Il indeed took the post of general secretary of the KWP. Kim has also been confirmed as commander-in-chief of the Korean People's Army, so he is nominally in charge of both halves of the power duopoly of the KWP and KPA that runs the country today.

There was not a noticeable change in policy in Kim's first months. To the poker table of the diplomats' casino, the DPRK brought its sophisticated multi-stage missiles. In August 1998 a Taepondong 1 missile sailed over the northern end of Japan, proving to the world that despite all the rumours, the regime was alive and well enough to build and launch that kind of weaponry.

Seriously unimpressed, the Japanese government promptly withheld US$1bn earmarked for the already delayed reactors. The US Congress would also suspend some oil shipments over DPRK missile sales to America's enemies. As a result of the 'Berlin Talks' between the US and DPRK in late 1999, the Clinton administration lifted some sanctions and offered food aid in exchange for the DPRK freezing its missile programme. Was this a breakthrough?

**Foreign relations** From the late 1990s, the DRPK began to reap the rewards of what was a remarkably successful diplomatic campaign. By the end of 2001, full diplomatic ties or the means to set them had been established with the EU and 13 EU countries (including the UK, France, Italy, Spain, Germany and the Scandinavians), the Philippines (completing the ASEAN nations, except Burma), Canada and Australia.

**Relations with Japan** Meetings and negotiations have followed throughout the decade since the 1990 breakthrough, and full diplomatic ties were looking as likely as a few long-standing issues might allow.

The DPRK is demanding recompense for Japan's colonial crimes, including the issue of Korean 'comfort women' in Japan, while the Japanese demand the return of a dozen Japanese abducted in the 1970s and '80s. Today, Japan is concerned over the DPRK's nuclear and missile programmes.

These days, more pragmatic concerns of the DPRK leadership could mean billions in Japanese investment might suffice as 'recompense'. Chochongnyon does most of the DPRK–Japan trade in technology transfers and goods (used cars) that now amount to around US$600 million a year. Communications (phones, flights, ferries) and cultural links are also operating, and Japan has donated considerable funds and foodstuffs to stave off the DPRK famine. Great headway was made in 2002 in re-establishing diplomatic ties between the two countries, but Japanese fears that aid for the reactors may end up in military hands has led them to shelve funding. The DPRK still demands apologies backed up by hard cash.

**Relations with the US** DPRK–US relations also improved considerably during the late 1990s, and US President Clinton was poised to be the first US president to visit the country (notwithstanding they were still technically at war). US Secretary of State Madeleine Albright visited in October 2000. Much of the progress in DPRK–US relations stemmed from the build-up in trust that had been going on since 1994, but the clincher to warming relations was a pro-negotiation Washington which allowed the ROK President Kim Dae Jung to lessen tensions between the two Koreas with his 'Sunshine Policy'. This precipitated a virtuous cycle of US–DPRK relations, and the US and DPRK media began to use substantially less colourful language when describing the other. The peace wasn't confirmed but the propensity for war to break out was reduced far below any other time. However, until a peace treaty is signed by all sides, US and ROK relations with the DPRK can, and do, change with their administrations.

**Southern sunshine and a new dawn** The greatest diplomatic advances, those that may have precipitated all others, were with the ROK and their President Kim Dae Jung's 'Sunshine Policy' with the country. The former political prisoner and activist policy was a more pragmatic acceptance of the North, encouraging permanent economic and diplomatic assistance and cultural exchange, and the DPRK has reciprocated the approach. In late 1999, the ROK basketball team visited Pyongyang and the DPRK team went to Seoul. In June 2000 was the historic summit in Pyongyang between the two sides' heads of state. It began with a hurrah as, stepping from the plane at Pyongyang airport, Kim Dae Jung was surprised to see Kim Jong Il awaiting him at the foot of the stairs. The warmth and cordiality of this moment set the tone for the summit.

More families were reunited on Liberation Day, August 2000. In September, the ROK and DPRK teams marched together at the Sydney Olympics. The ROK held half of the World Cup football games two years later, and although no ROK-team games were shown on DPRK TV, after the tournament the two sides had their own friendly, with one flag and a traditional folk song replacing their respective anthems. It was a fitting 0-0 draw. On the subject of football, the ROK team's performance in the 2002 World Cup was a magnificent surprise; however, they were not setting a precedent.

Other developments were an ROK promise to finance the rehabilitation of the DPRK's infrastructure. Road and rail links between the two sides are being constructed across the DMZ, which involves the partial de-mining of this section. It's hoped that Kim Dae Jung's successor, President Roh Moo Hyun, can extend the diplomatic roads into the north.

And there are changes afoot within the country. In January 2001, three central DPRK newspapers published a joint editorial proposing to develop the economy in a profitability-oriented manner, basically a public declaration from across the country's power structure that the DPRK was not shuffling but stepping towards market liberalisation. In January 2002, the official 'Arduous March' phase of the country's development (or contraction) was declared over. So would begin the 'Construction of the Powerful State'. Two months later, the titular head of state Kim Yong Nam announced adjustment of economic foundations of the country at the Supreme People's Assembly session.

**Bombs and rockets** However, nothing moves without energy. KEDO (the Korean Peninsula Energy Development Organisation) was dragging along, and as the century turned it was clear the light-water reactors would not be finished by 2003. With the more confrontational George W Bush administration, in early 2001 the US agreed to an indigenous ROK missile programme. In February 2001, the DPRK expressed its frustration that the Agreed Framework wasn't being implemented by the US and that the DPRK might consider the Framework to be defunct. The Bush administration ignored the warning and called the DPRK the 'road-kill of history', placing the country on the infamous 'Axis of Evil' list, which substantially alarmed the DPRK and irritated the ROK. US aid in food and monetary terms declined sharply, although this may have been due to the DPRK's recovering economy.

In April 2002, the White House posted that the DPRK was in full compliance with the Agreed Framework and that funds for the very late reactors would be released, for which a ground-breaking ceremony was held in August. But in contradiction to the White House's release about full compliance, and the commencing of the reactor, in October 2002, in talks between the US and DPRK in Beijing, US special envoy James Kelly reportedly presented evidence to the North Korean foreign ministry officials that the latter's country was engaged in enriching uranium in violation of the Agreed Framework. The North Koreans apparently denied this, and then declared it true, which the US and ROK then disbelieved.

In November President Bush unilaterally suspended oil shipments, the day before presenting the ROK, Japanese and EU delegates sent to discuss the matter with a fait accompli. Winter set in and a third famine loomed for the DPRK as food donations plummeted through overstretch and political malice. Less for electricity, and in wilful defiance of the United States, in December the plutonium-producing

An extremely effective introduction to the modern DPRK and its people would be to watch three films made by the Sheffield, UK-based VeryMuchSo productions, that Nick Bonner co-produced with director Dan Gordon. Whether covering a historic football event, going behind the scenes at the Mass Games or catching up on US defectors to the DPRK – alive and well – the films are truly ground-breaking in terms of access and insight into the ordinary lives of North Koreans (although the films' subjects are rightfully extraordinary people in any scenario). The films have received acclaim and awards both in the Western media and the DPRK itself.

The first was the barnstorming film *The Game of Their Lives*, catching up with the thousand-to-one-against DPRK football team in the 1966 World Cup, which created football history by becoming the first Asian team to make the quarter-finals, which they did with an incredible, historic 1-0 win against the much-fancied Italian team. The North Koreans would go on to lead Portugal 3-0 in the quarter-final before the latter came back to win 5-3. Nothing was heard of them after 1966, and rumours abounded that the players came home in dishonour and were sent to labour camps.

None of it was true, and seven of the original team were still alive when the film was made. It took four years of negotiations, but the film-makers were not only granted unprecedented access into the lives and homes of the players, but in 2002, the team was brought back to Middlesbrough, where the team played, to a heroes' welcome, in what was the biggest cultural exchange with the West. A crowd of 33,000 gave the players a standing ovation at Middlesbrough's new stadium and the DPRK flag was flown over the town hall.

It is the first film to have official access to ordinary North Korean citizens and unfettered, uncensored interviews with them as they talk openly about their memories of 1966, the rebuilding of Korea after the devastating Korean War, and their lives today. *The Game* shows never-before-seen archival footage, filmed by the North Koreans in England in 1966. (Curiously enough, a couple of years later, the unlikely success of the odds-against US football team in the 1950 World Cup was celebrated in a film, entitled *The Game of Their Lives*.)

'Even for an American, it was enough (no lie) to bring tears to your eyes,' reported CNN *Sports Illustrated* and among four awards *The Game* won the Royal Television Society award for Best Sports Documentary. Kim Jong Il has also seen and lauded the film.

On the heels of this success, VeryMuchSo was granted permission from the North Korean authorities to make a second documentary, *A State of Mind*. Filming started in early 2003, following the lives of two young gymnasts, 13-year-old Pak Hyon Sun and 11-year-old Kim Song Yun, and their families, for over eight months in the lead-up to the Mass Games. As Gordon put it, there was no story per se, it was essentially just following the gymnasts and their lives with the hope that something would develop. With subsequent visits, the characters did warm and relax in front of camera, which added to the quality of the film, and bit by bit access to home life, trips to the countryside and a much more intimate portrayal were attained – a remarkable insight into a part of North Korean society never seen in the West. As their Korean minder explained, 'You have to understand, no-one has ever been allowed to see, let alone film, what you are witnessing.'

All this paved the way to making the most recent and possibly most contentious film, the 2004 production *Crossing the Line*, concerning the fate of US soldiers who defected to the DPRK during the 1960s – when the Cold War was at its height and a war on the peninsula was not just possible but probable.

Yet, a total of four US soldiers, sent to the DMZ to keep the peace and protect the 'free world', instead carried out the simplest yet most dangerous act of just stepping across the demarcation line and defecting to the DPRK. The film concentrates mainly on James Dresnok, or 'Comrade Joe', who defected in 1962 and was for a while a coveted star of the North Korean propaganda machine. Dresnok would, along with the three others, become author and signatory to reams of propaganda leaflets dropped on the South detailing the virtuous wonder and wealth of their new found home. They provided the voices behind some of the propaganda tannoyed over the DMZ to the US and ROK soldiers on the other side. In a a further twist, they found film fame with roles in DPRK films vilifying the US, with Dresnok typecast as an evil American and making firm friends with several North Korean film stars who appear in *Crossing the Line* and discussed the importance of film to the DPRK's propaganda machine.

But the defectors were soon forgotten. Not until 1996 did the Pentagon admit that the four were in the DPRK – all four listed as deserters but it would be another six years before the story began to crack open. Then the DPRK confirmed to the Japanese government that its agents had kidnapped 13 Japanese nationals to teach Japanese and customs to North Korean spies. Of the five surviving kidnapped Japanese, one, Hitomi Soga, had married US defector Robert Charles Jenkins. By this point, the film-makers were almost alone in knowing Dresnok was alive as well, speaking Korean as his daily language, the father of three sons from two wives.

The film was the world's first contact with Comrade Joe in almost half a century. Gordon called it 'the biggest risk', combining as it did the governments and armed forces of the US, North Korea, South Korea and Japan, although neither the North Koreans nor the US army ever tried to interfere with either filming or the editorial. The film not only takes in the curious worlds of American servicemen who defected to their country's most committed enemy, and the trial of one for desertion, but also involves the Japanese victims of the DPRK's kidnapping.

Two years of negotiations in getting access to Dresnok and his family succeeded in the crew filming them over the course of a year, and a year fraught with a tumult of events. Within a month of filming commencing in June 2004, Jenkins would leave the DPRK and surrender to the US army in Japan to face court martial. The return of his wife Soga to Tokyo had gone from a short visit into an indefinite stay, leaving Jenkins and their two daughters in Pyongyang. Jenkins' health deteriorated, but he faced arrest and deportation for deserting the US army if he also went to Japan. Jenkins and his wife were reunited in neutral Indonesia – but then he surrendered. At his court martial Jenkins alleged that Dresnok would beat him in interrogations, and the film-makers were in North Korea interviewing Dresnok when he heard of the allegations.

Extraordinary events in an extraordinary land at an incredible time, with real people being caught up, destroyed, saved and betrayed by their own humanity within a whirlwind of an ongoing clash of ideologies, cultures and propaganda. But one facet of Dresnok's story is all the more incredible and encouraging. One of the allegations was that the DPRK deliberately kidnapped foreign women to marry the Americans to have Western-looking children who could be sent to the West as spies – ie: a deliberate spy-breeding programme. Dresnok's two boys are fully integrated into North Korean society, with one attending Pyongyang University of Foreign Studies with ambitions to be a diplomat, and the other serving as a soldier in the Korean People's Army, patrolling the DMZ from the northern side.

*VeryMuchSo Productions, in association with Passion Pictures, the BBC, E Pictures, Koryo Tours, IFG2, Cinequanon and Dongsoong Art Center.*

reactors at Yongbyon were re-activated. If the United States is really to strike at us for our nuclear programmes, we better make a load of nukes to ward them off, Pyongyang reasoned.

**Rising tensions** Kim Il Sung once observed:

> The imperialists ... make aggression and war their means of existence. Aggression and war are constant companions of imperialism ... The situation has become aggravated to the extreme in Korea today and has engendered the danger that war may break again at any moment not because we committed any act of violating the territory of the United States of America or menacing the sovereignty and security but because the US imperialists have come to our country, thousands of miles away from theirs and stepped up policies of aggression against the Korean people.

Throughout 2003, the situation deteriorated. The US brought in two dozen B-52 bombers to Guam, within range of the DPRK.

In January the IAEA urged the DPRK to 'co-operate fully and urgently' with the Agency or risk being in non-compliance with its safeguards agreement. The DPRK booted out its inspectors and withdrew from the Non-Proliferation Treaty the same month. The IAEA referred the matter to the UN Security Council, while the DPRK test-fired missiles and timed one for the inauguration of the new South Korean president, Roh Moo Hyun (what a day to start work!). With some courage in the face of this breakdown, Roh vowed to carry on the good work set in place by his predecessor's Sunshine Policy.

It did not seem to make sense. The White House had already said the DPRK was in compliance with the Agreed Framework and the reactors were about to begin being built – albeit a decade late. All the years of thawing relations between Pyongyang and Washington may have been thrown out the window by Bush's stupid Axis of Evil speech, but at last they seemed ready to deliver on the deal – more than the Clinton administration, which admitted it had agreed the deal with Pyongyang back in 1994 thinking the DPRK would not be around to take delivery years later.

Even if the DPRK had been enriching uranium or moving towards that, that would have been understandable not because it sought a bomb but because light-water reactors still need enriched uranium to operate, and intermittent deliveries of fuel oil over the decade from the US suggested the latter might not deliver reactor fuel as regularly. And enriched uranium was not under the Agreed Framework – that covered plutonium.

But there was no time for questions, the DPRK had its million-man army and was always being aggressive and the US attack on Iraq was about to begin. Pyongyang demanded bilateral talks with Washington and security guarantees – the two are still technically at war – but Washington refused to put the DPRK on an equal footing and opted for talks involving Russia, Japan, the ROK as well as China. The mood in the DPRK seemed set – the US was intransigent and distracted, and air-raid drills in Pyongyang were being taken very seriously. In July Pyongyang claimed that its Yongbyon reactor had produced enough plutonium to start making nukes. The Six-Party Talks resumed and failed to progress. By October some 8,000 nuclear fuel rods, enough to make six bombs, had been reprocessed. Talks started, stopped, stalled, all the way through 2004, with the monotony broken only in September when the ROK helpfully admitted its nuclear scientists had secretly conducted experiments into uranium enrichment in 2000. The roller-coaster ride began to get a bit wild in 2005. Pyongyang announced it did indeed have nukes. Then, later that year, a breakthrough came at the summer of the Six-Party Talks, when the DPRK agreed to abandon its nuclear programme in exchange for economic aid and security guarantees. In September a Joint Statement was announced.

More talks followed, then, in July 2006, the DPRK fired a fist of missiles into the Korean East Sea off Russia. This was condemned by the UN Security Council, which then urged the DPRK to return immediately to the Six-Party Talks to implement the September 2005 Joint Statement, and imposed an embargo on the trade of missile-related materials, but with fertiliser and food aid also cut off – again.

The DPRK was in no mood for embargoes, and went nuclear: 'The field of scientific research in the DPRK successfully conducted an underground nuclear test under secure conditions on October 9, Juche 95 at a stirring time when all the people of the country are making a great leap forward in the building of a great, prosperous, powerful socialist nation,' KCNA announced, with the blast estimated to have taken place near Gilju, Hamgyong Province, making the DPRK the world's ninth nuclear power.

Estimates of the strength of the explosion varied from less than a kiloton up to 15 kilotons, although most intelligence services aimed at the lower end, particularly from the US government which, having done so much to talk up the hypothetical threat, were now downplaying the reality. Indeed, CIA Director Michael Hayden later called the blast a 'failure' and said 'The United States does not recognise North Korea as a nuclear weapons state,' although this was really a face-saving comment as the US was once again sitting down to talks with the DPRK.

Still, it was 'provocative' and the UN Security Council imposed sanctions against the DPRK, demanding that Pyongyang cease its pursuit of 'weapons of mass destruction' (WMD). The strongest response came from China, describing its 'resolute opposition' to the 'brazen' act, the PRC's delicate way of saying 'we are apocalyptically unimpressed'. Possibly the Chinese had had enough. By the end of the month, the DPRK agreed to rejoin talks, which resumed in December. Still, low farce was still on the menu when the following month the US banned cognac, jet-skis and iPods from export to the DPRK to punish its 'elite'.

Progress came in February 2007 when the DPRK said it would shut down and seal, for the purpose of eventual abandonment, the Yongbyon nuclear facility, including the reprocessing facility. The DPRK said it 'will invite back IAEA personnel for monitoring and verification', and in return receive 50,000 tonnes of heavy fuel oil immediately and another 950,000 tonnes after its nuclear facilities were proven disabled. In addition its demand for a light-water reactor would be discussed at an 'appropriate time' – the terms of the 1994 Agreement were all but reprised but with more scope for 'peace' of sorts to be settled between the DPRK and US. Whether and when the US, DPRK and ROK will ever sit down and formally end the war is not known, but at the time of writing, the process was under way for the return of the remains of dead US soldiers from the DPRK – a good sign – and the normalising of relations is at last being discussed on both sides.

For all the sabre rattling on both sides, the chances of a US strike on DPRK, be it its nuclear sites or other targets, have always been extremely remote. Notwithstanding the DPRK's own claims that the nuclear generators were required for electricity and the right to build nuclear weapons to defend itself from the world's best-armed nuclear mega power with which it is still technically at war, an attack on a North Korean reactor nuclear site would at the least risk the possibility of covering the state, ROK, China and Russia's border areas (and possibly Japan) with radioactive fallout.

Through a treaty signed with DPRK in 1961, China is also obligated to defend the state with all the scope for at the very least a lot of very damaging diplomacy to deal with the threat or reality of an attack (China was drawn into the Korean War principally due to the advance and arrival of US forces on its border and subsequent attacks on Chinese territory).

Of course it is not inconceivable that the DPRK would launch a calamitous counter-attack onto the ROK, what with 37,000 US troops there, although the likely result would be destructive on the North. Any ensuing apocalypse would lead to millions of refugees flooding into South Korea, China and Russia while millions more would die within from the catastrophic breakdown of infrastructural flows. The impacts would lead, not ironically, to US forces being ejected from the peninsula – an imploded DPRK would no longer require an external presence.

Anyway, the region has not collapsed into a firestorm. The sky has not fallen on anyone's heads. Yet.

The most common arguments in the Western media are that the aggressive little dictatorship sought all along to build a nuke and use it as a bargaining chip for more aid – which sidesteps the fact that the DPRK was being threatened by a nuclear mega power with which, someway by mutual consent, it was not at peace. It also overlooks the fact that the accusations about the DPRK's nuclear plans came from the same White House regime that cooked up the WMD intel against Iraq. And the allegations about the uranium enrichment that sparked the whole row were based on whisperings in corridors – hearsay (although while the North Koreans are evidently never to be trusted on anything, they are to be believed when they whisper in corridors?). The world was not even privy to Colin Powell giving a PowerPoint presentation at the UN on the subject, or a couple of dossiers downloaded off the internet. But for some reason, because it involved communist Koreans, it just had to be true. However, in 2007 David Albright, president of the Institute for Science and International Security, compared the Bush administration's intelligence on Pyongyang's uranium enrichment programme to its claims on Iraq's WMD programme being made at the same time and wrote that a large enrichment plant 'likely does not exist; perhaps it never did', adding that the 'vast majority' of the DPRK's plutonium was made after December 2002. The Senate Armed Services Committee has also queried the State and Defense departments' intelligence on the DPRK programme.

A very curious comment came from the State Department's senior diplomat for east Asian affairs, Christopher Hill, as he prepared for bilateral talks with the DPRK's Kim Kye Gwan in New York about proceeding with the February Six-Party Talks agreement. Hill said the DPRK would need to 'come clean' on its uranium enrichment programme for normalisation to move ahead. Come clean? What would be the point of that; surely the intel on the US side was good enough?

Either way, from the off, going public with the allegations, regardless of foundation, was only going to force the DPRK to do what it did, ie: dig its heels in. So why stoke the situation?

One theory is that the new regime in the White House sought a confrontation to exaggerate the power of the 'threats' facing the US, its interests and allies, and justify the continued presence, and further build-up of its own armed forces in that theatre, with purchases from Asian allies for its weapons. A long-time international expert on the DPRK, Aidan Foster-Carter, once ventured what he called a conspiracy theory that in the late 1990s the United States' national missile defence system was under threat of cancellation. A new missile threat would ensure the programme be kept alive and anti-ballistic missiles sold – Japan being a good likely customer. Donald Rumsfeld approached the North Korean military and said that with a Republican White House, he could use his position on the board of engineering company ABB to ensure that the DPRK got its light-water reactors –

if the North Koreans fired off just a few missiles in return to scare the Japanese into buying America's ABM system. The missiles were fired and Japan has indeed bought ABM – only there was no way Rumsfeld was ever going to let the DPRK get its reactor.

Another theory has it that North Korea was listed on the Axis of Evil along with Iraq and Iran as all three countries were preparing to dump the US dollar as the first foreign currency of choice and use the euro instead – ie: the Axis of Euro. Both Iran and Iraq, mega oil producing nations, had threatened or are threatening to, replace the US dollar as the currency of choice for trading in oil with the euro, kicking international currency market demand for the dollar through the floor and smashing the United States' ability to buy oil – being a net energy importer, very, very bad news indeed. It would be galling for the DPRK, also a net-energy importer, to profit from reserves of rising-value euros as the US dollar declined, but the real beef would be the lesson for other east Asian economies, China, the ROK, Japan, Taiwan, those with the biggest dollar reserves for their own energy imports and which would dump the greenback for the euro and make the eurotrading DPRK even richer as the region's currency trader of choice.

A sub-story to the furore over the tests was the seizing of DPRK funds in the Macau-based Banco Delta Asia, wherein some US$25 million was alleged to be part of a North Korean money laundering operation involving counterfeit notes and leading to tough financial sanctions being imposed. But an audit report by Ernst & Young on the BDA found that the allegations were unfounded and exaggerated, with no irregularities on 50 accounts. Basically, the bank was smeared to curtail the DPRK's growing sales of gold bullion – output now at six tonnes a year and rising – a billion dollar business beyond the scope of UN sanctions related to the DPRK's weapons' programmes – and all the more irritating to the DPRK's enemies as gold prices go sky-high, a hard-currency earner of great reach and longevity. (Funnily enough, some of the key chemicals required for gold mining and processing, freely available elsewhere in Asia, have been sanctioned for purchase by the DPRK due to their dual use in WMD.) Hacking at the Macau bank further constricted the DPRK's ability to get foreign currency through bullion sales, on top of limited access to international capital markets, and limiting the state's means to buy oil, fertiliser and food surpluses, already restricted by cuts in trade and aid. Similar charges of money laundering and radioactive dealings were thrown at the DPRK Golden Star bank in Vienna, leading to the suspension of operations after two decades of legitimate work – funnily enough, Austria is the source of most of the euro notes circulating in the DPRK.

What the DPRK wants is to be able to engage and trade with the international financial community like anyone else, with foreign investment, raising of capital and sale of gold on world exchanges. It does not want to depend on China to back it up in crisis and sell its good and labour there at knockdown prices. Indeed some go so far as to say the DPRK seeks to be an ally with the US in competing with China – a buffer state between the two.

Raising the stakes on the peninsula only sets everyone off and not least allows the DPRK military to reassert itself within the state. With the brakes being put on any reform programmes and efforts to engage with the world beyond from within and without, everything takes a back seat to the needs of the military. Inter-Korean relations have been shaken if not stirred with the DPRK's self-confidence bolstered – the United States has been made to lose face, not a thing to crow about in the long term. The state's military has reasserted itself, and regional belief in the power of the US has faltered – while the message to the world is 'the way to defy the United States is to get a nuke as soon as possible'. Right wingers in Japan have been able to reassert themselves and change the country's constitution to allow its military to intercede abroad, for the first time since 1945. The DPRK fought through an appalling war and built itself out of the ashes. For a while it was beating its southern brother economically. It has both enjoyed prosperity and survived the extremes of difficulties over more than 60 years in the face of massive military power, threats, blanket economic sanctions, energy starvation and mass famine. It is not a suicidalist state and reports of its imminent death have always proven exaggerated. Strategies based upon that belief are doomed not only to fail, but also to hurt the weak and the poor first, foremost and worst, as the reapplication of sanctions and the onset of famine without relief laps into the state. And that is the real point. Always the DPRK is talked of as that odd little starving land of bombs, rockets, the man with a bouffant terrifying the world, its elite, and so on, and its people are brainwashed automatons. Well, they're not, and at time of writing, it seems to be easier than before to go see for yourself to find out.

In June 2007, the row over ABM was resolved. The following month, the DPRK shut down and sealed the Yongbyon reactor in the first phase of a deal, and then in September 2007 came what was possibly to be the biggest breakthroughs of all: the DPRK's foreign minister said the state had shown a "clear willingness" to dismantle all nuclear facilities by the end of 2007; and a meeting between the US and DPRK envoys in Geneva led the DPRK's foreign ministry to announce the state was being taken off the US' list of terror-supporting states, a great step towards improving the DPRK's standing in the world and enabling many of the sanctions against the state to be lifted, particularly those relating to companies fearing legal prosecution for 'trading with the enemy'.

Japan's relations with the DPRK are also ongoing in a choppy process of normalisation, with one step back for every two forward. The DPRK remains adamant, like several other east Asian nations, that Japan both apologise and compensate it for the colonial years, and give Korean residents in Japan the same rights as Japanese nationals. Japan demanded the DPRK confirm the kidnapping of 13 Japanese nationals over the decades, which Pyongyang ultimately did in 2002. Japan admitted it had 'caused tremendous damage and suffering' to Korea under colonial rule and sought to help normalise relations with grants and low-interest loans. Then for the sake of taking a step back, in 2007, the Chongryon's offices in Tokyo were raided.

**Inter-Korean relations** While the nuclear crisis raged, Korea got on with healing itself. In mid-2004 the top chiefs of staff and generals of the respective Koreas' armed forces met in what was called a 'breakthrough of monumental proportions', setting up a hotline, shared radio frequencies and working to prevent spats like the ones over blue crabs (see box, page 150) – and instead clamp down on illegal Chinese fishing forays. Propaganda broadcasts by loudspeaker and other means across the DMZ, some of which had been given by United States defectors to the DPRK, were also stopped. Investment into Kumgangsan and Kaesong are continuing. Tourist sales to Kumgangsan were down a third year-on-year in 2006 due to the rocket and bomb tests, but are now picking up again. Relations between the two Koreas will depend in part on the outcome of presidential elections in the ROK and the subsequent policies. Still, inter-Korean sporting events have been ongoing with a joint team for the 2008 Olympics looking likely to go ahead. In addition the harrowing reunions of divided families, happening with increasing frequency in recent years as those most affected start to pass away, have continued.

**Websites** For more on the nuclear issue, try the Federation of American Scientists, www.fas.org. A very good site for current affairs and issues about the DPRK is www.nautilus.org. You can track daily updates at www.nytimes.com, as found at www.kcna.co.jp and www.bbc.co.uk/monitoring. Alternatively, try www.north-korea.narod.ru/pyongyang_watch.htm, or www.worldperspectives.org/dprk/, which is a general interest site. A whole host of sites focusing on the DPRK perspective can be found at www.kimsoft.com and also at www.koreascope.org/eng/main/index.jsp. See the *Media and communications* section, pages 83, for more DPRK sites.

## ECONOMY

The DPRK economy has historically been a command economy. Since the DPRK's inception, the economy has been built along a similar system of centralised control as the Soviet Union's economy in the 1930s. In both cases, the ultimate socialist state was to be achieved through mass industrialisation based on huge increases in agricultural output. Thus achieved, the state provides cradle-to-grave jobs, housing, food, medical care, education, goods and clothing.

In command economies, output is not dictated by the laws of price, supply and demand, but according to targets set by the government. Successive multi-year plans (in the DPRK starting with a One-Year Plan in 1946 and getting longer ever since) demand certain economic sectors to produce quantitive targets (usually increasing) by a certain date. For example, the DPRK's 1978 Seven-Year Plan demanded that coal output in 1984 would rise from 80 million tonnes to 120 million and fertiliser from five to seven million tonnes. The plans include the inputs and incentives needed to increase production.

There is very little private ownership, the state 'owns' and runs industries, banks, transportation, financial institutions, etc as monopolistic enterprises. Workers are assigned to task-oriented work units that compete to (over-) achieve the targets, with rewards or cuts depending on their collective results. Mobilisation and propaganda campaigns exhort the workers onwards and upwards, and the workers can be rewarded from the total of their productivity increases.

Centralised governmental control and direction of each economic sector comes through ministries, committees and agencies at the national level down through committees and agencies at the provincial, county and city levels. The lower levels provide the statistics and information on developments, bottlenecks and issues their superiors need to plan, decide and overcome problems. Party control, as a distinct influence from solely state directives, comes through Party cadre occupying key managerial and committee posts in these sectors.

Planning has become more complicated as the DPRK economy has developed from being predominantly agricultural to an advanced industrial economy, with increasingly complex sectoral interactions and input needs. Ministries and agencies have varied and developed over time in response to planned (and unplanned) situations, the most dramatic being the collapse of the Soviet Union in the early 1990s, but we shall come to this after the following history.

The division of Korea in 1945 cut off the North from the greater agricultural resources of the South, and the South from the concentrations of heavy industry in the North. The infrastructure of industry, road and rail installed by the Japanese colonialists was all very well except that the Korean economy had been run by Japanese, not Koreans, as the Japanese kept Koreans excluded from the higher echelons of education and government of their own country. The majority of the North's population were agricultural and were educated only to that level.

Between 1945 and 1950, the Party prioritised the 'Revolutionising' of the country's agriculture to produce abundance, not famine, and allow its workers to migrate to the cities' industries. A minority of landlords owned most of the land, with the overwhelming majority of peasants living as tenant farmers paying rent in kind (from

50% of crops upwards). Reform came as communist agitators had promised: all land, livestock and buildings held by Japanese, traitors, absentee landlords, religious organisations and Koreans with over five chongbo (2.45 acres) were confiscated and re-distributed among the peasants; theirs but not to sell, rent or mortgage.

Landlords were harassed by police and party cadres, shunned by the peasants and investigated for anti-communist activities. Large and absentee holdings were confiscated first in a seemingly random fashion to avoid inciting any organised backlash by the landlords; lesser landlords either hoped to be spared, or collaborated. At best they received smaller plots, or were run from the province, southwards; otherwise it was hard labour.

The peasants were encouraged into the Party, more land was appropriated, cultivated and funds released for fertilisation and irrigation. Farmers paid tax in kind and sold the rest, although 'patriotic rice' was occasionally appropriated for patriotic ventures, like large building projects.

The Korean War of 1950–53 destroyed the North's cities, their industries and the people that worked in them. War also wrecked the country's agriculture; mass call-up for the army and factories left crops unattended, while raging battles destroyed those that grew. The smoking husk of post-war Korea meant that nothing short of complete reconstruction was necessary. Rapid industrialisation was sought and needed a strong agricultural base, so the first priority was to increase agricultural output.

During and after the war, and into the late '50s, the farms were collectivised into co-operatives, ie: individual farms were combined into larger social, work and administrative units called ri, eliminating the final vestige of capitalist ownership in the countryside. Collectivisation was a practical necessity as the land and labour were pooled to make up for the missing men, but it was also a move of emancipation for women, who both achieved collectivisation and ran the farms, as is still the case today. By late 1958, all farms were collectivised into 3,800 co-operatives of around 300 households each, introducing new planting techniques, chemical fertilisers, industrialised and mechanised agriculture, and electrification through generators and hydro-power.

Farming joined the other economic sectors of industry, trade, culture, etc, that were all under state control by the end of the 1950s, and the productivity increases allowed for increased rural–urban migration to the city factories, based on cheap food at fixed prices for the urbanised workers. Government investment (there being no private) from the 1954–56 Three-Year Plan poured into agriculture, housing and education, but half of government investment was in heavy industry, in mining, coal, steel, copper, chemicals, and manufacturing of machine tools.

These developments were built upon in the 1958 'Chollima Undong' (Flying Horse) movement, the first great mass-mobilisation campaign (and it's never really stopped) where increased output was to be attained through the implementation of the Chongsanri Method and the Taean Work System. In the Chongsanri Method, Party officials were given much greater input in the production process in the farms and factories. Party cadres were placed as hands-on managers empowered to solve any of the problems and use the ideas that workers confronted them with, in a micro-version of Kim Il Sung's own highly interventionist style. Output was also to be increased by whatever means worked, usually increased shares in the output or other material rewards to the group. Group rewards besides, the workers were exhorted to produce ever more with ever less means and time, and were bombarded with slogans like: 'Let us produce more with existing labour and facilities'. This kind of management developed into the Taean system, with more committees between the numerous work levels in a factory from shop floor to CEO, that remains largely in use today. So the Party's economic and political control infiltrated every level of production, and industrial and agricultural management were of concern to the Party as well as the factory managers.

The fire of the 1950s' economic growth was stoked in the 1960s. At this point the economy of the DPRK was racing ahead in income per capita over that of the ROK, and Kim Il Sung confidently predicted that if the ROK got anywhere under capitalism, it'd collapse soon enough anyway. Nonetheless, the DPRK economy saw high rates of growth in all sectors, and critically for its 'defence' and socialist cause, its economic growth and per capita income outstripped the South's throughout the decade. As Juche proscribed, the DPRK had to propagate revolution by force and defend itself from attack from US and Japanese imperialists. A huge proportion of its manufacturing industries were for arms (defence industries were estimated to be up to 30% of GNP in the late 1960s and 1970s, and as high as 26.7% of GNP in 1995 as a 'military first' principle has taken over). Although Juche advocated the economy develop independently, ie: with minimal trade and capital flows from beyond its borders, the DPRK's Soviet, Chinese and eastern European socialist brethren supplied material aid and trade throughout the mid-1980s.

Nor was the DPRK averse to foreign investment from capitalist countries, only that inflows of capital to diversify the economy's output in the 1970s didn't fit the bureaucratic, insular economy and the DPRK defaulted on its foreign debts, excluding it from Western capital markets. Similarly to the other command economies of the socialist bloc, the DPRK's multi-year plans' over-emphasis on heavy industry and commodity export suffered in the commodity market crashes of the late 1970s, while heavy bureaucratic control stifled technical and productive innovation. Capitalist investment from abroad was encouraged. Joint-ventures were allowed from 1984, tourism was promoted in Kumgangsan and special economic zones were set up in Rajin-Sonbong on the Russian border, around Sinuiju and Kaesong. Foreign interest has fluctuated but steady Chinese and ROK investment has been inflowing since the late 1990s. Aid slowed as the other socialist economies spluttered, while minimal foreign trade meant the DPRK hadn't the foreign currency to buy what it couldn't produce itself. Because a quarter of the country's output and technical investment was monopolised by arms industries producing for domestic use, what the economy couldn't produce was a lot. The idea of diverting resources into a nuclear power-cum-weapons programme and development of intercontinental rockets was to use them to bargain, but would bombs and rockets earn more in bargaining than they could lose in sanctions and diplomatic reproach? Well, at least the rockets can always be sold for hard currency.

The DPRK's trade deficit with the USSR became unaffordable. Barter-trading with the USSR was curtailed by the latter for hard currency in 1991, as the Soviet economy staggered towards free-market economics. China followed suit. Soviet trade fell from 55% of the DPRK's 1990 total to 14% in 1991, worsening as the Soviet economy crashed. Soviet fuel imports, principally oil, collapsed by 85%, throttling the DPRK's transport and industries' ability to operate. The ensuing energy crises, compounded by failing hydro-electric power output, affected industrial output of goods (and food, see *Famine comes to the DPRK*, below) with which to trade and earn foreign currency, as flagship state industries' output fell to 20% of the norm.

Simultaneously, aid and trade with the DPRK's eastern European allies died with their socialism, and the DPRK hadn't any significant manufacturing capacity for quality consumer goods to sell elsewhere. The DPRK's trade with 'imperialist' free-market economies (mainly Japan) existed but the links were minimal, its credit record poor, debts accumulating and US sanctions kept the DPRK from

47

Floods don't just destroy growing and stored crops. Soil, tended and fertilised over years, is washed away with irrigation systems, agricultural landscaping, equipment, farms and people's lives. Silt and debris give the floods more physical clout to damage other areas, blocking, damaging and demolishing channels, roads and structures, and the best land is left under a thick scum of sand and silt, that the petrol-less bulldozers cannot shift.

People escaping direct death and injury have to deal with the loss of land and livelihood, and the immediate problem of lost food stores and sanitary water supplies. Damaged and destroyed communications hinder the ability to deliver aid; conversely, people are unable simply to flee to unaffected areas. The DPRK Ministry of Foreign Affairs announced flood damage to be some US$15 billion in 1995.

Either it rains, or it doesn't. Drought also blights Korea's crops, and in 2001 the worst spring drought in 80 years followed the coldest winter in 50 years. Spring's wheat, barley and potatoes were affected, then the drought prolonged to scuttle autumn's rice and maize. Droughts reduce Korea's hydro-power, causing power cuts: refrigerators for vaccines and pumps for sanitary water turn off. Adding insult to injury, the major food-producing areas in the southwest also suffered severe floods that year. Deforestation in the country is one local explanation, the treeless hills drying the micro-climate while rainwater rages down the hillsides with nothing to soak it up. Plots and clumps of new trees are bedecking the fringes of farms and barren hillsides as the government vigorously afforests the country.

Nevertheless, the country's increasingly unstable climate is also on the sharp end of severe droughts affecting Mongolia and northern China as the Gobi Desert expands east.

markets that the pro-independence spirit of Juche might yet have allowed. The DPRK's industries were worn and decades of insulation meant they were comparatively outdated. In late 1993, it was announced that the Third Seven-Year Plan had failed, a staggering admission in itself. The worsening energy crisis then began to break down the country's agricultural basis that had made the DPRK's industrialisation possible, and the DPRK tipped towards famine.

**FAMINE COMES TO THE DPRK** Korea's agriculture has historically been prone to calamity, as the mountainous peninsula has little fertile land in a country prone to flooding and drought. A terrible drought of 1812–13 reportedly led to a million deaths, and during rice riots in 1833 rioters burnt and trashed many parts of Seoul.

The division of Korea left the South with most of the country's arable land, and with the quality, fertile land at that. Regardless of tremendous output increases achieved since the Korean War, food has been rationed for Koreans for many years, with rations based on occupation, age and region, averaging around 220kg per capita annually as a solid supply. Factors that had proved critical to increasing agricultural output included the mechanisation of farming in output and transportation (tractors and trucks replacing men and oxen) and the vast expansion of land under pumped irrigation. Chemical fertilisers and pesticides were also produced and employed in increasing amounts. The DPRK was more than self-sufficient, or self-reliant, in food output. The DPRK's Juche was grown from the fields.

But by the early 1980s, food shortages were being reported as the economy stagnated, and by the 1990s, the situation became disastrous as rations for farmers were reduced, causing upset, and Chinese and Soviet subsidies ended. The DPRK's contracting economy reduced fertiliser and pesticide output, as well as production of new tractors and pumps and spare parts for those already in use. Broken machines couldn't be fixed, and harvests couldn't be reaped or sown. But the critical issue was energy; oil imports from the Soviet Union died with it, and the DPRK literally ran out of fuel. Two-thirds of the DPRK's electricity comes from hydro-power, in irregular supply due to droughts and flood damage, and so irrigation systems didn't work when needed – aside from the mass destruction caused by drought and floods on the crops and farms (see box). Much of the land was exhausted from overuse or fertiliser saturation. Unfortunately, depleted foreign earnings prevented the import of fertilisers, pesticides, parts and oil; they hadn't the money, and this applied to importing food. Workers, soldiers, women and children went from the factories to the fields to supplant the shortfalls in mechanical power, but output slipped then plumbed below minimum subsistence levels. In 1995 and again in 1997 international aid was requested as rumours ripped through the international community of a calamity in the making. The United Nations Food and Agriculture Organisation and World Food Programme (WFP) found in late 1995 that the 220kg average was closer to 170kg, below that needed for minimum nutritional requirements. In summer 1995 WFP estimates for 1995 showed that Korea needed some 4,740,000 tonnes to meet minimum calorific intake, but was deficient in 1,250,000 tonnes, a quarter of a billion dollars' worth in rice alone.

The human cost has been appalling. Estimates of mortality from starvation from 1995 have reached over three million, or over 10% of the total population. UNICEF states mortality rates in the 1990s for children under five rose from 27 to 48 per 1,000, while over 45% of under-fives are still suffering chronic malnourishment and/or stunted growth. Malnutrition compounds people's susceptibility to flood-borne gastro-intestinal diseases, like diarrhoea.

The WFP amongst other international organisations has worked to rehabilitate the country's agriculture through variations in crop and fertiliser use, but restricted access to information and parts of the country has been frustrating. The deficit in domestic food production has fluctuated by up to 1.8 million tonnes in 2001, but international aid in oil and food has been forthcoming, particularly from China. Nevertheless, aid from the South, Japan and the US has sometimes been delayed by wrangling over Korea's nuclear programme on top of long-standing bad relations, and accusations that aid goes to the army first. Aid-funding targets have also frequently not been met on programmes for food relief, vital drugs, immunisation, nutrition, water and sanitation, and education.

In early 2002, the WFP and UNICEF could access more of the remaining provinces and counties. But the floods and droughts continue, and restructuring projects perennially seek funding as the international organisations continue to work in the country.

**REHABILITATION** As the DPRK's agricultural system is renovated, other initiatives are under way. Kim Jong Il has personally led delegations to Russia and China to observe the process of their development from command to fully fledged free-market economies.

Aid and foreign investment are most forthcoming if diplomatic relations are good, for business follows the flag, and the late 1990s and early 2000s saw hugely accelerated diplomatic initiatives with the European Union, Japan, the United States and the ROK. The US had relaxed a broad range of trade sanctions in 1998 but the Bush administration sought to reimpose them from early 2003, notwithstanding constraints on public bodies like the World Bank from loaning funds that came from listing the DPRK as part of the 'Axis of Evil'. Nevertheless, the ROK has made promises to fund the rehabilitation of the DPRK's infrastructure and foreign investment is being encouraged in all industries – from mining to steel and manufacturing – and in new areas like IT and even animation as DPRK restrictions are being lifted. ROK joint-ventures in the DPRK are now worth US$110m export dollars a year, and the economy's long contraction in the 1990s finished in 2000 when 1.3% GDP growth was recorded, followed in 2001 by 3.1%. The Pyongyang Chamber of Commerce was accredited by the International Chamber of Commerce in Paris in May 2000. Many well-known foreign firms are investing in the country, restoring its infrastructure and capitalising on the country's highly educated but low-wage workforce. The capacity to produce and the will to renovate are still very much in evidence among the Korean people. But the building of success breeding success based on solid, trusting relationships with the world beyond takes time. Free flows of information are critical to this.

In March 2002, the government announced that the rationing and therefore the government provision of some goods would cease, ie: be subject to market forces and pricing, which was becoming increasingly the case in some economic sectors anyway. Markets had always existed in some form and clandestine suppliers of goods from China, Russia and Japan had supplemented more usual goods' flows into the country for years. However, the state still provides all shelter. For accommodation, people used to pay a nominal maintenance fee for an apartment which was theirs for life, and a single-digit percentage of wages on utility bills. Bills and rents have gone up significantly to levels (or wage percentages) more akin to capitalist economies. Most significant was the abolition of rationing for basic foodstuffs: money, not coupons, now gets food. Private initiatives in shops and trade are appearing. The 'foreigners' won' was abolished in favour of hard currency trading while the local won was dramatically revalued (from 2.12 won to the dollar to over 200 won to the dollar), although this was establishing nationwide what had been the case in the Rajin-Sonbong Free Enterprise Zone for years. From factories and power plants to restaurants and stalls, the principles of supply and demand are being set in place, while firms seek their own profits and not state help and workers seek monetary bonuses for their labour.

Energy remains the most fundamental issue that the DPRK must solve. Droughts create a problem as two-thirds of the DPRK's electricity comes from hydro-electric power. In addition, completion of the light-water reactors is dependent on the US, Japan and ROK. Finally, in order to secure steady supplies of oil, the DPRK must be able to both access and pay for these supplies. Stabilising relations with these countries will be critical to the future success of the DPRK reforms.

In early 2004, the first billboard advertisements for goods were put up – for Pak cars and small ROK vehicles assembled in the DPRK (one plant being not far from Kaesong). One might point out that the average DPRK citizen does not have the money to buy such a vehicle, the petrol to run it or the inter-city permits needed to use it in a worthwhile way! There are more than a few private cars on the streets and so there are evidently hopes and plans that DPRK will become as car-using as ROK or anywhere else. However, cars also bring dirt, noise, pollution, traffic deaths, road rage and a great deal of extremely tacky infrastructure. If the DPRK could avoid all that, it would be progress indeed.

With a nuclear stand-off going on, across the DMZ in June 2004 came the first inter-Korean trade by road – a convoy of trucks rolling sand from North to South. Any east Asian tiger economy has got to be IT-savvy and the DPRK is proving no exception. Increasing numbers of DPRK businesses have email addresses. There is a burgeoning IT market in DPRK, for brand-new Chinese-made computers with Microsoft Windows software, cheap second-hand ones and the order at least for compulsory computer classes in schools. A DPRK–ROK joint venture, Morning Panda, is manufacturing computers in Pyongyang.

The DPRK is also growing as a resource for out-sourcing of file management and transcription for Western companies. Numerous IT joint ventures with Chinese and ROK partners in software and hardware developments, symposiums, product fairs and factories are being set up and North Koreans sent abroad to get training and data. Co-operative ventures involving the Pyongyang Informatics Centre, the South's Pohang University of Science and Technology (PUST), the Korea Advanced Institute of Science and Technology, the DPRK's State Software Industry General Bureau, and Kim Il Sung University have all been set up in recent years.

Notwithstanding the 'military first' option, investment and development in hi-tech industries, including nanotechnology and bioengineering but principally in IT, are being given high priority, which makes sense with a state that has a highly skilled technical workforce but without the reliability of a modern, efficient infrastructure to put them to best use. But computers and IT classes can cost the equivalent of months of pay for the average North Korean.

Consumer markets are now established as part of the country's economic system. Second-hand bikes from Japan and China are appearing. The Swiss Agency for Development and Cooperation is working on a project with Korea's Central Bank to introduce micro-credit in the more remote rural areas and for farmers to apply business strategies to their investments. Farmers' markets are becoming markets in the broader sense, with more goods available and money to buy them with.

The Kaesong Industrial Park, often featured in the media, especially in the ROK, is advancing. Foreign companies are scheduled to become involved in 2010 and by 2012 the ROK's Ministry of Unification is hoping to attract about 2,000 manufacturers to Kaesong. Currently, there are 55 South Korean firms operating in the joint economic zone, a fifth of all South–North business, with around 500 ROK firms engaging in intra-Korean trade. Almost half of South Korean firms still expect inter-Korean trade to increase despite recent tensions and that the ROK economy is in a downshift.

Observers have cited a noticeable increase in foreign manufacturing companies moving into Pyongyang since 2006, a presence accelerated by progress in the Six-Party Talks early in 2007. In April 2005 the European Business Association was founded in Pyongyang. Joint-ventures involved in banking, shipping, pharmaceuticals production and consumer goods, and European companies seeking opportunities to combine low-cost and skilled labour, see Pyongyang as attractive for the manufacturing and processing of all types of consumer goods and products best-produced on labour-intensive production lines. DPRK-made pianos are going to Austria, a French television station uses North Korean artists to produce cartoons (a section of the Disney film, *The Lion King*, was produced in Pyongyang).

More investigative trips abroad and plans for foreign investment, particularly South Korean investments, have gone ahead. There have been land reforms, enabling individuals and businesses to take ownership of apartments and lease land from collective farms.

At the same time, however, the energy and food situations have remained unsettled. The won has suffered hyperinflation, as have food prices, and the public distribution system for grains, especially rice, had to be reintroduced on a broad basis. In September 2005 Deputy Foreign Minister Choe Su-hon requested that the UN cease food aid to the state as the country had had a good harvest and enough food, and accused the US of using aid as a political weapon, although up to six million of the country's poorest and most vulnerable were receiving aid in some form. Choe also requested that all NGOs leave by the end of the year, a request that was not fully carried through, and arguably linked much to the monitoring requirements from donors as to where the aid ends up. China and

South Korean food suppliers make no such demands. In early 2007 the WFP noted that the average seven year old is 20lb lighter and eight inches shorter than his seven-year-old peer in South Korea, and mothers searching the hills for acorns and bark to feed their families. The rehabilitation of the DPRK's economy and place in the world cannot come soon enough.

**WEBSITES FOR FURTHER INFORMATION** Prospective investors should consult:

**www.kbc-global.com** Roger Barrett at the Korean Business Consultants
**www.tradepartners.gov.uk/north_korea**
**www.eucck.org** European Union Chamber of Commerce Korea

**www.wfp.org** World Food Program
**www.fao.org** Food and Agriculture Organisation of the United Nations
**www.unicef.org/emerg/DPRK.htm** UNICEF
**www.nkeconwatch.com** North Korea Economy Watch

## PEOPLE

Koreans are an ethnically and culturally homogeneous people, as seen in terms of their racial heritage, facial features, language and history. No wars or feuds are as longstanding and bitter as those between two brothers, which describes Korea's division perfectly. The people of both states want unification, but cannot yet agree as to how this will come about. The most obvious difference is that the ROK exists with a significant Western influence, visibly present in capitalist pop culture, that has flowed in through the development of the ROK economy and the presence of American forces there. In the ROK are also some minorities of other Asian nationalities and expats.

The number of minorities in the DPRK is restricted to Chinese and some Japanese, and a minute expat community, whose presence will never undo the country's decades of hermetic existence.

**MEETING THE PEOPLE** Beyond your guides, you may not meet that many Koreans, and Koreans themselves might seem cold or indifferent if they acknowledge you at all. This is not a country where a whole village will pile out to see a foreigner. Historically, foreigners have often not been of great service to Korea and this point is often put to the people.

### EDUCATION

Children in the DPRK attend state nurseries or crèches so that their parents can work normally, and from age four receive a universal, compulsory 11 years of education, beginning with a year in kindergarten. Hence the DPRK has a very high literacy rate. School uniform is universally blue bottoms, white shirts and a red neckerchief. Pupils may have on their arms small badges with horizontal stripes and little asterisks, the number of both patterns indicating a position of responsibility (asterisks determine job) in the school, class or class group (shown by the stripes).

Education has three strong themes of practical knowledge (maths, sciences) and political knowledge (Juche). The third involves 'social education', which Juche prescribes in detail. Children join the Pioneer Corps and the Socialist Working Youth League where they learn the workings of collective life, and children can engage in many extra-curricular skills and activities at the children's palaces around the country. Older children are drafted in at the right times of year to help with harvests and other labour tasks that introduce them to the workers and their world. Pupils progress to high school, then the forces, college or into specialist work units.

From 17 to 25 years of age, Koreans are eligible for conscription into the Korean People's Army (KPA), Navy or Air Force for at least three years. Unless they fail the physical checks to get into the Army, the young can avoid being drafted or have it deferred by attendance at college or qualifying for some kind of reserved occupation. Servicemen and women are not just for defence but are engaged in construction projects and farming, providing supplements to their own rations, or work in one of the KPA's many sub-industries, and one in five people's work relates to the KPA in some way.

Consider also the strains afflicting this country. No family can have escaped unaffected by Korea's division, the war and the recent famines. The DPRK's reconstruction has taken decades of back-breaking work with scant resources, against reciprocated aggression from other countries and based on insecure flows of trade and aid. As the country's allies were lost in the 1990s, so all the health and nutritional gains evaporated as the economy ground to a halt, a time referred to with some understatement as an 'arduous march'. These people have had a time of it.

So it's not surprising that here more than anywhere, friendships take time to build and a lot of trust. That said, those friends made are friends for life and are notably generous and warm. Most Koreans, like anyone else, like a drink and a dance and a picnic in the woods, because all Koreans are people like anyone else. Those much-espoused notions in Western media that the folks in DPRK are lifeless automatons should be ignored. A walk in the park, particularly on a weekend of national holiday, is a great way to meet the locals. Be sure to wave and smile while passing through the country.

**SOCIAL SET-UP** The old Confucian-based order of royal Korea demanded respect for age, learning, filial piety and authority, the last justifying a society based on hierarchy and class. Providing for the individual was secondary to serving the collective. Confucianism is no longer officially practised in the DPRK (and scarcely in the ROK), and the DPRK order has been overturned by a half-century of communist revolutionary rule, but the underlying influence of Confucianism is discernible. Age is still revered (see who gets served first at a table), and so is education. A great success for the DPRK has been the implementation of universal, compulsory education for all. Education is one route to escaping the poverty of one's origins and theoretically makes the basis for a classless society, as communism suggests.

Familial devotion and filial piety are Confucian social currents that the Party puts great emphasis on. Still, the revolution's social impact has been the erosion of old ties of family and broader networks based on kin in the countryside. These ties took a great shock from Korea's division (affecting one in seven Koreans) and the losses of the Korean War. In the DPRK, small villages were merged into large co-operative farms, family and kin moved to the cities as the country industrialised (60% of the DPRK's population is urban) and travel restrictions were introduced, all further eroding the links. However, the family is officially the most venerated, virtuous social unit (if not the kin network) and the above strains have for many people accentuated the importance of their own families.

In the past, one's position in society was inherited as much as earned, and due respect and reward for one's social position underpinned social stability. Today, whether in the Party, the army or just a normal civilian, like anywhere else, people of different livelihoods in the DPRK earn different amounts of money a month.

However, two distinctions with the West are that it's the state and not the market that decides levels of pay, because the state owns everything, and second, pay is (or has been until very recently) of secondary importance to the other lifestyle elements provided by the state, namely accommodation, food and some clothing. Apartment size and food rationing have been graded by job and affiliations, and location. The distinction between town and country isn't just a matter of city limits and checkpoints; the material supply and support for the cities is notably better than for rural areas, and Pyongyang outstrips all cities.

Aside from the distinction of military and Party members, people are categorised according to their general field (workers, farmers, officials, co-operative units) and then graded by specific job, and paid according to scale. There are three main classes, subdivided into 51 sub-grades, into which you are born and from which you can rise and fall.

Regarding social stratification, your starting point in life, your job and location depend on your Songbun, your gauge or 'karma' of political reliability and commitment to the Great Leaders and the Party. Your Songbon weighs heavily on your career prospects, where you will live (town, country, apartment), who you might marry or befriend.

Songbon isn't determined solely by your achievements, but sources from familial backgrounds as well, for Songbun is recorded by the security services and updated continuously. Your ancestors' victories and crimes provide the social context of your birth and your future.

As Kim Il Sung explained in his tomes on Juche, control of the state and its economy was seized from the controlling class and given over to the masses in a remarkably comprehensive overturning of society. Korea's pre-1950 rulers are now ruled by those who are (descendants) of good 'revolutionary' stock, and Songbon sustains that changeover. If your forebears were anti-Japanese fighters, then you probably rule today. Top Songbun gets good military posts, college, careers, apartments and families, and the privileges start young. Children of the elite attend the Mangyongdae Revolutionary Institute near Kim Il Sung's birthplace.

If you descended from factory workers or peasants, your Songbun has a good grounding. Middling Songbun means hard work (revolutionary fervour as Juche demands) can get a job or military posting proximate to Party cadres who might look kindly on you, and higher education is not impossible. If your forebears were Yangban or some form of middle-class professional, well, the odds are stacked. Kim Il Sung stated that 'after liberation we did not reject the old intellectuals because they came from rich families', and intellectuals as an educated class were essential for Korea's rebuilding. But that didn't mean they, or their descendants, were

## INTO THE PARTY

Joining the Korean Workers' Party (KWP) is a good idea, and it has over three million members today, mostly industrial workers, bureaucrats and intellectuals. Weekly meetings on political thought and 'behavioural' issues are compulsory. The most diligent members, exemplary in their knowledge and understanding of Juche, economics and sociology (so very likely well educated) and selflessness in Party work may become Party cadres. Cadres are posted into every element of life here, and the extra hours of study a week are outweighed by enhanced career prospects and raised social status.

In addition to the KWP, there are other mass organisations for people to join, although it seems most are variations on a theme of collective work in the name of the country and the Leaders.

Of the people in uniforms, their colours are approximately thus:

- khaki-green, thick cloth, boots: Korean People's Army, although the detail's in the hatbands – red for army, blue for intelligence
- khaki-green, lighter cloth and red stars on the beret: Workers and Peasants Red Guard Paramilitaries (or Union)
- dark blue: air force
- blue and white, bell-bottoms: navy
- black: civilian police
- azure blue: traffic police and railway police (so, are you in the road or at the station?)
- light grey; construction brigade

'Shock brigades' have their own uniforms for the tasks to which they are detailed.

Civilian clothing provides clues about people's positions or contacts. Until relatively recently, North Koreans were clad in a pretty uniform set of clothes, issued by the state, with men wearing classically timeless suits in heavy dark cloth and women in drably coloured blouses and skirts. Japanese suits, presumably lighter in cloth and colours, used to denote those with the money and connections to get such things; however, this is beginning to change as foreign imports and consumer spending power is making for greater diversity of clothing fashions and status indications less discernible. Virtually everyone in civilian clothing wears a Kim Il Sung or Kim Jong Il lapel pin. This indicates first that you are indeed a citizen of the DPRK; it's also thought that the size, metal and colouring of the pin indicates a wearer's union affiliations, department and possible seniority. But the quality and style of the pins also vary according to income and age, suggesting the societal hierarchal positionings denoted are more generational than deliberate. Children of the higher classes in Pyongyang are reputedly notable not just for their snazzier, foreign clothes, but also in that they might wear their badges on the tips of lapels in a somewhat louche expression of youthful insouciance – they've also been seen in platform shoes. Schoolchildren are usually clad in the classic blue trousers or skirts, white shirts and red neckerchiefs seen in schools across China and Vietnam – outside school, though, they are increasingly seen wearing fashionable clothes.

Vehicles also say a lot about who is driving them, where they're from, possible connections, etc. Vehicle registration plates indicate their origins and sometimes purpose. The most common plate colour is white, for 'public', vehicles from particular government or local departments. On 'public' plates, first is written the vehicle's home city or province, then the vehicle's department number (eg: 88 is tourism, 30 is Ministry of Foreign Affairs, 50 for taxi) then the vehicle's number in that department fleet. Black plates are army, yellow are privately owned (probably donated from Japan), dark blue is diplomat, white with a red star is VIP. There's also red, thought to be for high-ranking Party officials. You might get the spectacle of a VIP visit; the roads are closed as a fleet of black limousines flash and wail past, all flags waving.

innately trustworthy. Good jobs of choice are attainable through Party membership, not possible for someone with bad Songbon, as is higher education and the military; they go where the farms, factories and mines need them, and the only way up is to demonstrate exemplary 'right-thinking' through your work and life. Juche, as every person learns, emphasises self-sacrifice and hard work; dedication and revolutionary spirit can achieve everything, including good Songbon. As the Koreans put it, the best are considered 'tomatoes', red all the way through; 'apples' for the superficially committed, and 'grapes' are nearly irredeemable.

These indicators have deep roots. The use of familial records and professions in Songbon takes precedence over the aged genealogies and land registers used through much of Korea's history to determine people's social class and their entitlements. Today, uniforms are one obvious distinction between the services and the civilians, but the more subtle distinctions in people's apparel, ie: suits and the lapel pins with different styling and colours, could be said to have origins right back in the Sillan bone-clan system that required visual indications of one's social position. Also, how one person's crimes implicated their whole family existed up until the Japanese took over in the 1900s, but has been revived.

For further information try the websites: www.amnesty.org or www.pyongyangsquare.com. Alternatively visit the Academy of Korea Studies, www.aks.ac.kr/EngHome.

**WOMEN** In olden Korea, women were lesser beings, for as Confucius said, wives are subservient to husbands, as the yin-yang symbolises. Women were not allowed to be seen in the streets, effectively under social arrest in their walled homes during daylight, where they tended to their duties as homemakers and mothers. Women had to be veiled to leave the house. The traditional game of see-sawing (jumping up and down on either end of a see-saw) was devised so women could glimpse village life over the garden wall.

Women in modern Korea are emancipated and educated, and in the DPRK their equal status and social rights are enshrined in the constitution. At work, the gender balance is just about 50:50, while professional women have made their careers in the Democratic Korean Women's League Party and the judiciary, and many co-op farms are still run by women in an overhang from the depleted male reserves around the time of the Korean War. Nevertheless, not even the DPRK's social engineering could eradicate traditional male chauvinism that still half expects little more of women than to smile and file.

## LANGUAGE

The origins of Korean language go back to the earliest invasions of the peninsula by ancient Asian tribes, and Korean is considered to be part of the Altaic family of languages. Modern Korean is derived from the language of the Silla, with some influence from China's mandarin language. Another similarity is with Japanese, in that both languages have different grammar and vocabulary according to the level of politeness with which a person of a particular age, gender and social status addresses another. Many Chinese and Japanese words have been borrowed over the centuries, their meanings and pronunciation changing with time.

Historically, imported Chinese texts for Buddhism and Confucianism meant that Korean scholars had to read Chinese, and so used Chinese characters for writing, as can be seen on ancient (and recreated) sites around Korea. Various attempts were made to create an indigenous script over the centuries, until King Sejong's initiative led to a brilliantly simple phonetic script being developed by the mid-1440s. Called hangul, the new written language had 17 consonants and 11 vowel sounds represented in very simple characters, from which all the syllables could be constructed (since then the number of characters has dropped to 24).

Korea's educated elite damned hangul as an idiot's or commoner's means to communicate. The simplicity of hangul meant it did spread with relative ease among the non-elite. The literati argued that this proved their point, while the dual use of Chinese characters and hangul would be a written indication of education and class. Conversely, the literati's opposition solidified hangul's suitability for Kim Il Sung, as a language for commoners was more revolutionary.

The attempts by Japanese colonialists to expunge the Korean language didn't succeed. From 1948 in the DPRK, all foreign influences, from borrowed words (especially Japanese and English-derived ones) to Chinese characters, were expurgated. All DPRK texts are completely in hangul. The DPRK 'dialect' uses Pyongyang as its standard, and northerners think the Seoul accent is nasal. Northern dialect also differs from the South in the former's complete absence of any modern American or Japanese slang. 'Polite' language has also been reduced in the North, from five noted levels down to three. In the ROK, the original number of polite levels and the use of some Chinese characters in writing continue. For words and phrases, see page 219.

# RELIGION

The most important religions (ie: with long historical basis or regional impact) that have succeeded historically across Korea and that still have a presence today are Shamanism, Buddhism, replaced by Confucianism and, following that, Christianity. None 'thrive' in today's DPRK, and there is much documentation on how that is manifest which cannot be summarised in this book, but from the other perspective, there are deep-seated themes for the state's historic opposition to religions in general and the situation is changing, glacially, incrementally, for the better.

Official DPRK figures estimate there to be just 10,000 Protestants, 10,000 Buddhists and 4,000 Catholics in the state today (although ROK church groups cite higher figures), and some 40,000 practitioners in the government-supported Chondogyo Young Friends Party, an adjunct of the Chondoist Chongu Party, which possibly has most official 'favour' for its revolutionary history in the Tonghak movement. These are very small numbers compared with pre-1945 Korea and the present-day ROK (it is estimated up to a sixth of Pyongyang's 300,000 residents were Christians).

The government exercises extremely close scrutiny and control over religious groups, activities and practitioners, and the constitutional provision for 'freedom of religious belief' is not a right that many in the North exercise.

In Korea particularly, many of the religious sites, staff and followers were ill treated by the Japanese. Many of those pastors and practitioners then headed south in 1945 and those that survived the Korean War and remained in the North ceased their worship for their own good.

In China and the DPRK, Christianity has, with some historical basis, been perceived as the vanguard for less benevolent channels of outside influence and control. Some contend that the vehemence of the opposition to the DPRK, particularly in the US, comes from the loss of the worshippers' base and the proselytising and anti-DPRK stance comes from the same American religious right that most sharply castigated the 'loss of China' to communism in 1949.

Communism is inimically antithetical to religion, and the cold pragmatism of its adherents would argue prayers, cathedrals and priests don't grow rice, stop floods or guard against invasion, particularly in a state like North Korea.

The philosophy of Juche also celebrates the power of man and the state and people to have independence of thought, and is widely manifested in forms to capitalise on the fervour of worshippers, inculcating supernatural phenomena and powers to the lives of its leaders (and there are the curious parallels between the Son of God, the nativity and miraculous powers – see *The Cult of the Kims*, pages 28–9).

**SHAMANISM** The oldest religion in the peninsula that took root particularly in the North, shamanism is devoted to the worship of numerous spirits and gods believed to inhabit the elements and in particular the individual spirits inhabiting animals. The spirit believed to inhabit Mt Paektu is one long-surviving example of shamanism. In the North it came to be supplanted by Buddhism.

**BUDDHISM** Buddhism arrived from India in the 6th century BC. An Indian noble eschewed his wealthy upbringing and through meditation achieved 'enlightenment'. Enlightenment here means to escape the cycle of birth, ageing, sickness and death through the renouncing of worldly desires and living in moderation. The soul enters nirvana, a paradise without want. It was Korea's state religion from the 6th to the 14th century AD, and through government patronage, beseeching the Buddha to protect their Korea, grew into a powerful sub-state over the years. This was partly why the religion was swiftly replaced by Confucianism as the state religion from the late 14th century onwards.

**CONFUCIANISM** Similarly to Buddhism, Confucianism was originally more a code of morals and conduct than a religion but attained quasi-religious elements over the course of its 2,500-year history. Although scarcely practised in the ROK, let alone the DPRK, Confucianism is still evident in Korean thinking, shown through reverance for age, learning and desire for social harmony. Confucius was a Chinese scholar from the 6th century BC, who believed study was the way to the truth and the righteous virtues of benevolence, righteousness, decorum and wisdom. These were the virtues to ensure social harmony and stability. He formulated a detailed behavioural code to govern the relationships of the family, community and state, on the premise that stability would arise from everyone knowing their place in society. He espoused that authority and hierarchy continued from the family to the emperor and that there were five relationships to adhere to: sons showing respect, obedience and filial piety to their fathers; subjects loyalty to their rulers; the young revering the old; wives subservient to their husbands; friendships governed by mutual trust. Confucianism increasingly underpinned the structures of government and administration in Korea.

The 1972 constitution said 'citizens have religious liberty and the freedom to oppose religion'. Twenty years later article 68 of the 1992 constitution dropped the 'anti-religious' clause and allowed for 'the construction of religious buildings and the holding of religious ceremonies,' but a pithy insert summarised the state's view of religion: 'No one may use religion as a pretext for drawing in foreign forces or for harming the State and social order.'

In the 1980s, there was a relaxation of sorts when the state allowed for greater freedom of religion, albeit under the auspices of official bodies like the Korean Buddhists Federation and the Christian Federation. In 1988 Pyongyang's Pongsu and Changchong churches were built, and the DPRK began to use foreign religious organisations as channels for dialogue, 'neutral' diplomacy, humanitarian works and business, at a time when the old Soviet networks were winding down.

In particular these have proved fruitful conduits of dialogue with the ROK, and by extension the US, as the churches mainly founded by American missionaries profligate in the South compared with their absence in the North, and on the question of national reunification through Buddhist groups as well.

Since 2005, delegates to the DPRK have included the Venerable Beop Jang, head of the largest ROK Buddhist group and chair of the ROK's national council on religious leaders, and the Catholic archdiocese of Seoul led by the director of the

Chinese philosopher Zhu Xi in the 12th century expounded upon Confucianism to form Neo-Confucianism, with more religious undertones and involving ancestral worship, and it was this form that replaced Buddhism as the state religion in the 14th century.

**CHRISTIANITY** Christianity was first brought into Korea by freelance missionaries moving on from China, and then seeped in via traders and explorers. Christian teachings of paradise in the afterlife and an early release from poverty appealed to the poor and thousands converted, but their teachings were an anathema to the ruling classes, for Christianity dismissed ancestral worship (and therefore the legitimacy of the state rulers!) and encouraged individualism. Several purges killed thousands of converts in the 1800s, but by the 1880s, Protestant missionaries were pouring into the country, and like teachers and doctors were more tolerated for their poverty relief. Such works continued under Japanese rule. After 1945, many Christians headed south as the northern government converted churches for secular use. The ROK is today home to 25,000 churches, while Pyongyang has one Catholic and two Protestant churches. Kim Il Sung's parents were Christians, and there are micro-detectable influences in Juche philosophy and the cult surrounding the Kims.

**TONGHAK** This confluence of Buddhism, Taoism and Christianity was known as 'Eastern Learning' to the Koreans and was propagated by a squire's son, Ch'oe Chu'n. It preached salvation from destitution and placed all men (and women) on an equal footing with heaven, so envisaging a world without any class constraints or barriers. It appealed greatly to the majority of poor farmers, whilst causing panic in the upper classes, and peasants and disaffected Yangban rallied to the cause in their thousands in the early 1860s and throughout the decades to 1894, when the Tonghak mass-peasant uprising came close to destroying the House of Chosun (the Japanese 'rescued' them). The movement morphed into a less spiritual political philosophy that actually survives in some form in today's DPRK as the Chondoist Chongu Party. The proto-Marxist tenets of Tonghak must have saved the movement from the chop of the KWP.

National Reconciliation Committee. Members of the DPRK Christian Federation also attended an international solidarity meeting in Germany.

Religious aid groups like the Buddhist Join Together Society and the Catholics of the Seoul archdiocese have been running food production centres for almost a decade, and the Lighthouse Foundation is preparing to open the Botong River Sheltered Workshop in 2007. The Catholic charity Caritas is the conduit for Catholic aid into the DPRK.

Buddhism is the religion given the greatest latitude, there being an estimated 300 Buddhist temples with religious activities and resident monks in some. They possibly serve to preserve the historical and aesthetic qualities of 'the Korean nation's cultural heritage' more than anything else, as the spotlessness of the sites suggests the monks are the only practitioners. The ROK government and foreign tourists sponsored the reconstruction of the Shingye Temple, destroyed during the Korean War, with completion expected in 2007 and a South Korean monk in residence. Kaesong's Ryongthong Temple was renovated in 2005, with a growing residency of monks. Others are undergoing rebuilding, restoration and rescue from neglect. Since 2000 there has been a Protestant seminary in Pyongyang, reopened with assistance from foreign missionary groups, and in 2003 the Pyongyang Theological Academy for training pastors and evangelists was completed.

The Unification Church is believed to be constructing an inter-faith religious facility in Pyongyang, and the Korean Presbyterian Church is working with the North Korean Christian League to build a third Protestant church in Pyongyang, along with the existing Pongsu and Chilgok – although foreign attendees to services have talked of more being done in the spirit of appearance than actual genuine worship. Pyongyang's first Russian Orthodox church was consecrated last year, with Russian and Korean staff trained in Vladivostok, which arose from Kim Jong Il's visit to an Orthodox cathedral in Russia in 2002. A memorial service for Pope John Paul II was held at Pyongyang's Changchun Catholic church.

For further information:

**www.state.gov/g/drl/rls/irf/2006** International Religious Freedom Report 2006
**www.hrw.org** Human Rights Watch

**www.nkmissions.com** An umbrella organisation for missions to the DPRK
**www.sd.od.org** Open Doors organisation following the persecution of Christians worldwide

## CULTURE

**CINEMA** 'Like the leading article of the party paper, the cinema should have great appeal and inform the audience of reality. It should play a mobilising role in each stage of the revolutionary struggle,' wrote Kim Il Sung.

Should you get to settle in a cinema seat with a bucket of corn, be aware of the educational value of what you're about to see. Categories for DPRK films include historical and literary classics like *The Flower Girl* or *The Sea of Blood*, with healthy infusions of revolutionary thought; socialist-realism films, promoting the success and development of socialism, like *Girl Chairman of the Cooperative Farm* or *The Flourishing Village*; themes of revolutionary tradition, with the Party and its ideals at the centre; and war films, fighting imperialism in its Japanese or American forms. Overarching themes are the oneness of the Korean nation, the realisation of Juche's teachings being the only way to live, and a strong spirit of selflessness and sacrifice being essential to achieving any collective goals, from reaching output targets to achieving national reunification.

In historical outings, common motifs include injustices and atrocities being piled upon lowly villages and families. Fathers get killed early on, providing the rage and reason for the remaining unlikely heroes to 'find themselves' and engage in amazing acts of self-sacrifice. Mothers not performing their own selfless feats, like storming a Japanese-held fort in *The Sea of Blood*, give their children to the revolutionary tasks (ultimately to Kim Il Sung's guidance, who fills the spiritual void of the deceased fathers and becomes the 'father of the nation'). The *Story of a Nurse* celebrates the bravery and vision of a young nurse who follows the army over 1,000 ri behind enemy lines. Just after her efforts are rewarded with Party membership, her unit is bombed. 'Breathing her last,' says a throaty voice, 'she asks that her Party card and her Party fees be forwarded to the Party Central Committee, and dies a heroic death.'

Everyone must watch out for those of aristocratic heritage, inherently unstable people who might try counter-revolutionary activities. In *The First Party Commissioner* a former anti-Japanese revolutionary fighter is sent to the country to form a Party organisation in an iron smeltery. There, workers of former aristocratic stock conspire to kill him, but he crushes their reactionary subversion and establishes the smeltery's first Party cell.

In *Three Revolutionary Red Flags* and *The 100 Days Battle*, the workers are taught how Juche can make them self-reliant to meet the targets of the country's Chollima speed campaigns, which means films also cover issues of the day. From the 1970s, with Kim Jong Il's promotion as Kim Il Sung's successor, a sub-theme became the son taking over the revolutionary charge, and later revolutionary films touch on the class conflicts of the country's new technocrats.

The future of DPRK cinema is safe with Kim Jong Il. Films are Kim Jong Il's passion; aside from his own reputed private collection of 15,000 films, he's had a hand in many of the DPRK's cinematic products, and secured the success of many silver-screen starlets.

Indeed such is Kim Jong Il's love of cinema that he has written extensively (including a book) on the subject and had he not been destined to run the DPRK, he would have been a film director instead. In fact, in a plot straight out of a creaky thriller, in 1978 South Korean film director Shin Sang Ok and his actress wife found themselves accepting an invitation to Pyongyang that couldn't be refused, and during the following nine years in the North as the guest of Kim Jong Il, Shin would make a dozen films that went down very well.

Imports of films and television shows, as well as music, are officially restricted to those from China and Russia, albeit with the forces of modernity and racier ideas filtering in, for the increasingly large number of North Koreans who own CD, VCD and DVD players.

But that is not the only way to see foreign films. Every two years, since the late 1980s, an international film festival is held in Pyongyang, usually in September, at the Pyongyang International Cinema on Yanggak Island (see page 100). For many years the only films shown were from the Korea International Film Production Agency, together with international films from allied communist and non-aligned movement countries such as Iran, Lebanon, Vietnam, China and the USSR (a lot of which would be compelling stuff and not seen at the 'free' festivals in the West). But the range has increased of late to include films from Japan and hits like *Fahrenheit 9/11*, *Cry*, *The Beloved Country* and *Bend It Like Beckham*.

*The Game of Their Lives* won the Special Award in 2002 and *A State of Mind* was shown at the 2004 event. Small numbers of locals are able to visit with tickets distributed through neighbourhood offices, and high-level political figures from the Supreme People's Assembly and the Cabinet, including the Minister of Culture, also attend. Tour operators can arrange this to be the central fixture of a visit.

**MUSIC** Contemporary 'pop' music has rather formally attired men and women in front of suitably suited bands behind panelled music stands, knocking out crushingly sentimental (and quite sexless) numbers about long-distance relationships of friends and family, hometowns, reunification and landscapes, like 'Doves Fly High', 'My Home, Sweet Home', 'The Peak of Mt Gumsoo' and 'Yearning For My Beloved Mother'. Hits to get down to from the Korean People's Army Choir, which you'll certainly see on television, include 'Soldiers Hear Rice-ears Rustle', 'The Leader Has Come to Our Outpost' and 'Warm Feelings Creep Over the Ridge', with a heavy accent on Russian military music. A pop music industry built on teen hysteria, as has spread to Russia and China, just doesn't exist in the DPRK.

The state actively promotes and supports the teaching and production of dance and music in many forms, as long as the output is healthily infused with politically correct ideals.

Kim Jong Il views opera thus:

The creators of music must complete revolutionary opera songs as in The Song of Kumgang-san Mountains: 'For fifteen long years through snowstorms, He fought for the rebirth of this beautiful country, The towering peaks and crystal-clear streams, Praise Marshal Kim Il Sung's kindness in Song.'

*Tell the Story, Forest, A True Daughter of the Party* and *The Fate of a Self-Defence Corps Man* are all hit operas from the 1970s.

Apart from the mass spectacles of Arirang and the Mass Gymnastics, and the medley presented at the Mangyongdae Schoolchildren's Palace, opera, dance and music recitals can be enjoyed in Pyongyang, mainly at the Mansudae Arts and Moranbang theatres.

North Korean children have more opportunity than in many other countries to have state-funded tuition in musical instruments and many are markedly proficient in playing them.

Korean men enjoy beers very similar to those drunk in England and they like a good singalong around a piano, although karaoke is also becoming as widespread as it is elsewhere, replacing the communal singing.

A selection of top tunes can be heard through Andy Kershaw's excellent BBC Radio 3 documentary on the country, which also shows how Koreans are prepared to spontaneously belt out a number, including Sinatra's 'My Way!', and the brilliance of youthful musical expertise.

Specialist tours focusing on the meeting of musicians at places like the Isan Yun Conservatory are possible.

**PAINTING** For depictions of 'ordinary life', the socialist-realism view of the communist world, committed to canvas mostly from the 1930s to the 1960s, is still being exhibited here and produced, albeit on a reduced scale. The rosy-cheeked, flag-flying workers and farmers are depicted gaily hailing each other amid bumper crops, gleaming tractors and glowing blast-furnaces in the rural and urban idyll of the DPRK, while stoic-faced soldiers, chins up and eyes fixed amid blizzard-blinded battle against big-nosed foreigners, are shown defeating imperialism and advancing socialism. A great many paintings are celebrations of the life and achievements of the Kims, who dominate the pictures by the positioning, size and colouring of their figures. Another favoured medium is coloured woodcut prints.

There's little in common with such official art and the traditional painting styles that depict natural scenes of mountainsides, flora and fauna and ancient Korea. These images are shown from a few, deceptively simple brushstrokes of black ink to the wall-sized paintings and murals found in large public buildings. The first great examples of Korean painting are found in the earliest tombs and mausoleums, of scenes from court and portraits of the gods of the day. The Songhwa Art Studio in the Pyongyang International House of Culture is where current trends in DPRK fine art are found, and the Art Gallery on Kim Il Sung Square has an excellent chronological review of Korean art.

**POTTERY** The earliest Korean pottery found regularly is earthenware with combed surfaces, but the earthenware took plain surfacing during the Bronze Age. During the 2nd and 3rd centuries BC, a greyish-blue glaze grew prevalent, followed by the short-lived lead glaze. From China in the 9th century came the green-blue tinge of celadon. Celadon had been imported for centuries from China, where its production was universal, and the techniques and styles were built upon by the Koreans over the next 500 years of Koryo rule, eventually surpassing the wares of China itself and were even exported to Japan. The most sophisticated designs and decoration of Korean ceramics is considered to have occurred in this period, charged by the demand for pottery resulting from the growth of Buddhism in Korea and its prescribed uses of tea and incense. Cranes, willow trees and peony blossom were common motifs, as were the Buddhist-related lotus flowers, carved onto the surfaces and filled with coloured glaze, carved right through the clay or moulded into sophisticated forms.

Meanwhile, the production of white porcelain was being perfected in China and these techniques were mastered in Korea by the late 14th century. Porcelain, being tougher than celadon, gradually supplanted it in common usage. Left plain white or lightly adorned with cobalt-blue designs, the simplified porcelain designs reflected the more frugal, less ostentatious Confucianism that was replacing Buddhism. Such were the skills of Korea's pottery makers that many were kidnapped to Japan by Hideyoshi's forces in 1592 and 1598. Light brown décor on porcelain's white surfaces had by the 18th century taken its place alongside the blue designs, but the most common form of pottery found across the peninsula is still the huge earthenware pickling jars for *kimchi*.

**LITERATURE** A staggering amount of literature produced is dedicated to the works of Kim Il Sung and Kim Jong Il. Juche, revolution and the need for the struggle of anti-imperialism underpin all modern philosophical and historical works, which strive to prove the superiority of socialism over all other lesser societal creeds.

Similarly to facets of culture, writers in the DPRK are state-supported and state-subordinate. From poetry to popular novels, literature must serve to 'depict man and life and serve the popular masses truly', wrote Kim Jong Il. 'We need a humanistic literature, which gives prominence to the principle of independence, the development of independent individuals, and which creates the image of the truly typical man of the new era, thereby contributing to the transformation of the whole of society in accordance with the concept of Juche', clarifying how man prizes, glorifies and will die for independence.

## NATURE AND CONSERVATION

The DPRK has a few national parks, mainly around mountain sites, as in Mt Chilbo, Mt Paektu, Mt Kuwol, Mt Myohyang and Mt Kumgang, which have varying degrees of religious and historic significance and are sprinkled with temple sites, ruined and restored. In these parks and elsewhere, many cultural sites, particularly old tombs and temples, have been rebuilt following the ravages of war, looting, neglect and falling into official ill-favour. Though the parks and other sites accumulatively cover thousands of square kilometres, the country overall has only around 580km² of protected land, and the national proportion of pristine land is less than 1% of the total area. Pollution from heavy industry has turned some local ecosystems into alien worlds, and respite has come not by decree but through economic contraction that has cut the output of the polluting factories. However, areas of extreme human impact contrast with areas of extremely sparse human inhabitation, as around Mt Paektu and the mountains leading into the DPRK's northeast.

The DPRK altitude, long latitude and climatic range make it home to a wide variety of flora and fauna found from temperate evergreen forests through broad-leafed deciduous forests up to tundra meadows. Amongst those species indigenous to Korea and to the northern area specifically are wildlife found in Japan, China and Russia, while the DPRK is a grand roosting place for migrating birds. Across Korea can be found black and brown bear, tiger, sable and deer, and often seen soaring over the peninsula are Baikal teal, white-naped crane and white-bellied black woodpecker, while maple and azalea dowse the land in colour. Wildlife-oriented trips can be arranged through tour operators.

The DPRK has for some time realised the potential benefits of tourism, mainly in the form of increasingly large tours from cash-rich China and Russia and more direct developments by investments by ROK firms (above all else, from Hyundai-Asan), as well as a growing number of much smaller, but nonetheless significant tours organised with Western companies. The financial and infrastructural benefits have to be weighed against the losses in terms of pristine, or as near as, wildlife cover and the erosions and despoliation brought by inflows of booted feet and the places required to transport and accommodate them. But it also means that areas without much hope for economic rejuvenation and means of income become viable again, and environmental sites possibly at risk for wont of any other value become protected by their intrinsic value. In addition, historical sites of forts and temples receive funding for restoration and protection, and sometimes total reconstruction (if not fabrication). In the early years of this century, the DPRK government opened up the possibilities wrought by having sites recognised and listed for their natural and cultural worth with organisations like UNESCO, and this appears to be a growing field of interest in the country; however, there are doubts as to how many of these sites are genuinely 'old'.

# 2

# Practical Information

## WHEN TO VISIT

The rainy season is very humid, cloudy and sticky, and not brilliant for radiant photography as the rain soups up poorer roads and rail lines and curtails access. The best times to go are April to June and September to October, when it is cool, dry and colourful, from spring's heaving tides of white blossoms to autumn's cascades of gold and red. If there are Mass Games on (usually from late April to June) they are an absolute must-see.

## HIGHLIGHTS

### IN PYONGYANG

**Grand Monument on Mansu Hill** You will appreciate its grand austerity and holiness.

**May Day stadium** The best time to visit is when one of the Mass Games events is on. What a show, what a venue!

**Moran Hill** This park on the Taedong's east bank overlooks the May Day stadium and is dotted with relics and pavilions dating across the past thousand years, as well as giving grand views of the city itself. The hill is a sea of cherry blossom in spring, a blizzard of snow in winter, and a cool haven of shade in Pyongyang's baking summers.

### IN THE COUNTRY

**Myohyangsan** Another firm fixture of any itinerary, the mountains of Myohyang are on one hand a beautiful ridge of gulleys bedecked by waterfalls and steeped in Korea's Buddhist history, but also the location for the Great and Dear Leaders' showrooms displaying their hoards of astonishingly gauche gifts from international dignitaries over the years.

**Mt Paektu** A spectacular geological phenomena in its own right, this volcanic mountain lake is the spiritual birthplace of all Korea and is celebrated as such across the peninsula: high, cold, remote and deafeningly peaceful.

**Lake Sijung** On the road south of Wonsan to Kumgangsan, this tranquil place is where the better-off Koreans, Russians and other old friends go to relax in mudbaths, with petrol-cooked clam parties and fabulously clean beaches beyond the electric fence.

**Inner Kumgang** It is difficult – if not impossible – for visitors to gain access to this inner sanctum of this site, which is one of Korea's most sacred, both historically and ecologically. If a trip can be arranged, you should jump at the chance, particularly to visit the Podok Temple, high up on the hillside.

**Kaesong to Panmunjom** The ancient city of Kaesong is very pretty and it and a couple of outlying ancient tomb sites are doable in a day or two. Kaesong's olde worlde charm contrasts sharply with the brash cash of the Hyundai industrial park that is being built between it and Panmunjom. Panmunjom itself is a remarkable testament to positive north–south relations, and a sharp contrast to the infamous, ironically entitled de-militarised zone just a few km further away.

## TRAVEL IN THE DPRK

For tourists, trips to the DPRK take at least two weeks to arrange, for visa applications to be checked out and for the trip's itineraries to be arranged and agreed by both sides. Tourists visit the DPRK only on guided tours, with private transport arranged by the Koreans. Even a solo traveller will have two guides, a driver and a car to zoom about the country, and a guide is with you virtually all the time. The guides have the permits that all Koreans need to travel from city to city, checked at checkpoints surrounding the cities, and which tourists cannot obtain themselves. Access to many parts of the country is completely prohibited, such that even workers for esteemed NGOs like the World Food Programme can't enter large areas. Foreigners' free movement around the country is as proscribed as that of locals, who need good reason to get permits. Combined with the severe shortages of petrol and a very intermittent electricity supply, this means that there is no practical public transport system in the country.

For tourists, the range of places open to visit is limited to the capital, Pyongyang, and a handful of other cities near to national parks that protect mountains deemed significant for their history or wildlife. Pyongyang can be explored freely without guides – most of its bars and restaurants are open to all; but another issue is currency. Until recently, there were three types of currency: the local currency (won), special won for foreigners, and hard currency. The foreigners' won has been abolished, but that doesn't mean that foreigners can use local won. Hence foreigners are limited to the 'approved' restaurants, shops and exhibitions that accept hard currency.

All these limits mean that foreigners are effectively kept to the best parts of the cities and countryside, the well-tended, well-fed areas, where the needs of the locals are being met, so exposure for the average visitor to deprivation doesn't happen. Against the great diplomatic strides achieved in the last five years, a very deep, historical distrust of foreigners is continually worked up by the state-owned DPRK media, but to that end the locals keep their distance and are ultimately very warm rather than hostile. As long as visitors behave themselves within the parameters laid out, the risks to them are very, very few.

## TOUR OPERATORS

**IN THE DPRK** The Korean International Travel Company runs numerous specialist tours, such as mud treatment, spa treatment, golf, steam locomotives (in Kaesong and a new one in Nampo), mountaineering in Kumgang and around Paektu, tae kwon do (Korean martial arts), Korean language learning, Juche learning, plant tours for medicinal herbs and specialist wildlife expeditions.

**Korean International Travel Company (KITC)** Central District, Pyongyang; ☏ +850 2 381 8901, 381 8574; f +850 2 381 7607. There's one office in the basement of the Yanggakdo Hotel.

*China, Beijing* Yanxiang Hotel, 3rd Flr, Qianghuating A2, Jangtai Rd, Chaoyang District; ☏ +86 10 6437 6224; f +86 10 6436 9089
*China, Dandong* Xian Qian Rd, Yuan Bao District Dandong, China; ☏ +86 (0) 415 281 2542, 2810457; f +86 (0) 415 281 8438

*China, Yanji* ☏/f +86 433 2529689
*Thailand* 867139 Moodansilintheb Patanakan Rd, Soi 46 Soun Luang, Bangkok 10250; ☏ (66 2) 321 5797/653 4083; f (66 2) 322 1109

## UK

**Koryo Tours** ☏ +86 10 6416 7544; f +86 10 6415 2653; e (general info) info@koryogroup.com, (reservations) tours@koryogroup.com; www.koryotours.com. This British-run company, based in Beijing, is the leading tour company to the DPRK, with the longest history & greatest reach into the place, & has also been involved in the production of a string of award-winning films, radio programmes & books about it.

**Explore Worldwide Ltd** 1 Frederick St, Aldershot, Hants GU11 1LQ; ☏ 01252 760200; f 01252 760201; e ops@exploreworldwide.com; www.exploreworldwide.com
**Regent Holidays** 15 John St, Bristol BS1 2HR; ☏ 0117 921 1711; f 0117 925 4866; e regent@regent-holidays.co.uk; www.regent-holidays.co.uk

## ELSEWHERE

**Bestway Tours & Safaris** Suite #206, 8678 Greenall Av, Burnaby, British Columbia V5J 3M6, Canada; ☏ +1 604 264 7378; toll free: +1 800 6630844 (Canada & US residents only); f +1 604 264 7774; www.bestway.com
**Tin Bo Travel Service** 2nd Floor, 725 Somerset St W, Ottawa, Ontario K1R 6P7, Canada; ☏ +1 613 238 7093; f +1 613 238 8179/+1 800 267 6668; e tinbo@on.aibn.com; www.tinboholidays.com

**Viatges Pujol** Corcega 214, 08036 Barcelona, Spain; ☏ +34 93 321 9303; f +34 93 419 0334; www.coreanorte.com
**VNC Travel** Catharijnesingel 70, PO Box 79, 3500 AB Utrecht, Netherlands; ☏ +31 30 231 1500; f +31 30 231 0232; e info@vnc.nl; www.vnc.nl (in Dutch)

**TOUR COSTS** On a tour, the cost is determined by numerous factors - hotels, meals, tickets to shows and where in the country is to be visited, etc.

As tours are usually presented as 'costs per day' or cost per entire trip, a comprehensive breakdown of individual elements are difficult to obtain and of no great use anyway, particularly as tours are long-standing arrangements brokered between the agencies inside and outside the country. As said in the accommodation section, the DPRK side prefers (insists) visitors stay in the higher-band, higher-price hotels (and you'll appreciate the quality), and foreign operator packages can be at least 20% cheaper than what going to KITC direct might get.

Most packages include: hotel accommodation and all meals, guides, transportation in-country and the price of return flights in and out of the DPRK - although a very common entry-exit set-up these days is in by plane and out by train (or vice versa). Some packages also include the cost of the DPRK visa and a night's stay in Beijing with transfers to and from Beijing's airport or rail stations.

Not included: pocket money for gifts and extras beyond meal time, tips for the driver and guides (greatly albeit discreetly appreciated); flights to and from China; a double entry Chinese visa (£72 in 2007); provision for Pyongyang's airport departure tax (€11). The main variables affecting cost per person is the season, the length of the tour, group size, destination in the DPRK. Larger groups reduce the overall costs - the daily cost per person of a group 10+ (group sizes being a usual maximum of 16) can be 40% less than a packet of three to five. Those travelling as a 'single', within groups, incur a supplement of €25-40 a night.

A trip can be arranged with two weeks notice but this is very very rare - four to six weeks are what operators demand at the minimum and really the longer the better.

A 'short break' tour to Pyongyang are often at least three nights, possibly being solely based in Pyongyang to see the Mass Games (in the right years) and possibly oriented around another major public holiday. 'Standard' tours, taking in Pyongyang, Myohyangsan and other sites are posted at around nine to 11 days; fully comprehensive excursions go up to 16 days – this would take in practically everything there is to see and would be very intense. More focused specialist tours, to Mt Paektu say, can be arranged, and there are the options to visit Kumgangsan from the ROK.

## GETTING THERE AND AWAY

✈ **BY AIR** Pyongyang's leaving levy is € 10.

### Air Koryo
**From China** The DPRK's national carrier is Air Koryo, and that airline is (at the time of writing) the sole airline flying in and out of the state, notwithstanding the set up of routes with China Southern. Air Koryo operates regular international flights to Beijing and Shenyang. The airline also flies to Vladivostok, Khabarovsk, Bangkok and Macau, but on a descending level of regularity. The airline's domestic schedule reputedly flies Pyongyang to Chongjin, Hamhung, Kaesong, Kilju, Kanggye, Sinuiju and Wonsan, but times, prices and availability for foreigners are not in the public domain. Specialist charter flights to Chongjin, for visits to Mt Paektu, are arrangeable (see Mt Paektu chapter).

Chinese airports charge RMB90 (€ 8.6/US$11.95) for international flights as a 'construction tax' that used to be separate, but is now included in ticket prices.

Prices, times and schedule numbers for the international routes are for late 2007. Prices were given by the Air Koryo office in Beijing, hence the dollar denomination.

**Flights between Pyongyang (FNJ) and Beijing (PEK)** One-way: economy US$197, business US$273; return: economy US$373, business US$526.

| | |
|---|---|
| Tue & Thu | JS151 leaves Pyongyang 09.00, arrives Beijing 09.40 |
| Thu | JS251Y leaves Pyongyang 10.30, arrives Beijing 11.30 |
| Tue & Sat | JS152 leaves Beijing 11.30, arrives Pyongyang 14.00 |
| Thu | JS252Y leaves Beijing 15.00, arrives Pyongyang 17.50 |

**Flights between Pyongyang and Shenyang** One-way: economy US$112, business US$159; return: economy US$217, business US$314.

| | |
|---|---|
| Wed & Sat | JS155 leaves Pyongyang 11.40, arrives Shenyang 11.35 |
| Wed & Sat | JS156 leaves Shenyang 15.10, arrives Shenyang 17.00 |

**From Russia** There is no departure tax for Russia's airports at present.

**Flights between Pyongyang and Vladivostock** This service has been somewhat infrequent in 2007 due to a fall in the number of passengers. One-way: economy US$179, business US$239; return: economy US$349, business US$479.

| | |
|---|---|
| Thu | JS271 leaves Pyongyang 09.10, arrives Vladivostok 11.40 |
| Thu | JS272 leaves Vladivostok 19.40, arrives Pyongyang 20.20 |

There has been until some undisclosed recent point in the past a flight from Pyongyang to Khabarovsk on Mondays and Fridays. This service has been suspended, due to a dearth of passengers, but had been:

Mon & Fri   JS253 leaves Pyongyang 09.50, arrives Khabarovsk 14.00
Mon & Fri   JS254 leaves Khabarovsk 16.00, arrives Pyongyang 16.10

Were the service to resume soon, prices would approximately be US$350 one-way, US$620 return.

**From Thailand** One of Air Koryo's 160-seat Ilyushins has been known to fly Pyongyang to Bangkok on a charter basis. One-way US$450, return US$700

Thu   JS153 leaves Pyongyang 10.30, arrives Bangkok 14.20
Fri   JS154 leaves Bangkok 12.20, arrives Pyongyang 20.00 (although, times & days can vary)

**From Macau**
Mon & Fri   JS187 leaves Pyongyang 08.35, arrives Macau 11.35
Mon & Fri   JS188 leaves Macau 13.05, arrives Pyongyang 16.45 (times & days can vary)

### Air Koryo offices abroad

**China** Beijing: Swissotel, Hong Kong-Macau Center, Dong Si Shi, Tiao Li Jiao Qiao, Beijing 100027; ✆ +86 (0)10 6501 1557/1559, (airport) ✆ 6459 1253; f +86 (0) 10 6501 2591 Shenyang: Qibaoshan Hotel, No 81, Shiywei Rd, Heping District, Shenyang; ✆ +86 24 2325 1922/1937; f +86 24 2325 1936
**Thailand** Room 942/135.4, 4th Flr, Charn Issara Tower, Rama 4 Rd, Bangrak, Bangkok 10500; ✆ +66 (0)2 234 2805/6, 535 3974, (airport)

✆ 535 5974; f +66 (0)2 267 5009.
**Russia** 101000 Mosfilmovskaya 72, Moscow; ✆ +7 (0)95 143 6307; f +7 095 1476300. 41 Portovaya St, Artyom Primorski Krai, Vladivostok airport, 692800; ✆/f +7 4332 307684
**Macau** Rua da Praia Grade 55, 20 Andar-C, Centro Commercial 'Hoi Vong'; ✆ (town) +853 353 6634/353 6635, (airport) +853 861329/861111 ext 3878; f (town) +853 356631, (airport) +853 861329

Air Koryo flights from Pyongyang to Moscow and Berlin are defunct.

In 2004 the EU put Air Koryo on a list of airlines banned from using European airspace, a somewhat meaningless move as the airline has not flown to Europe for some time, although it still advertises flights to Sofia and Berlin.

**Other airlines** In early 2006 China Southern (*www.cs-air.com, www.cs-air.com/en*) began flying a thrice-weekly route (Mon, Wed & Fri) from Beijing to Pyongyang, until political matters led to the service being suspended in early 2007. As the service may yet resume, the codes and times were:

CZ6021   leaves Beijing 13.05, arrives Pyongyang 15.35
CZ6022   leaves Pyongyang 16.35, arrives Beijing 17.10

This schedule was probably an extension of the twice-weekly Beijing–Pyongyang–Beijing route (Mon & Fri) set up by China Northern in 2003, with China Northern having since become part of the China Southern air group (nice and simple eh?).

Some China Southern offices are located:

**China** Beijing: Lst/F Nanfan Hangkong Dasha, 2 Dongsanhuan Nan Rd; ✆ +86 10 6459 0539. Shenyang: 19 Beijing St; ✆ +86 24 2252 5747,
2326 3436, 2326 3429. Hong Kong: Unit B1, 9/F United Center, 95 Queensway; ✆ +85 2 2866 1331

**Netherlands** Byzantiu Bldg, Stadhouserskade 23-B, 1054ES Amsterdam; ☎ +31 20 412 3120/0302  
**ROK** 8F Jungan Bldg, 57-10 (Seosomun-dong

Chung-gu) Seoul; ☎ +82 2 3455 1600  
**Thailand** 491/35-37 Silom Plaza, Silom Rd, Bangrak, Bangkok; ☎ +662 266 5688/7888

Aeroflot and Air China may have flown to Pyongyang in the past, but don't at the time of writing. Check www.aeroflot.ru and www.airchina.com.cn for changes in this. International flights to and from Rajin-Sonbong were investigated in the 1990s and may yet materialise. Direct flights from Seoul to Pyongyang remain the preserve of high-level diplomacy.

In spring 2004, **China Southern Beifang** airlines commenced flights from Shenyang to Pyongyang with the schedule announced as Shenyang–Pyongyang departing 07.30 Chinese time and Pyongyang–Shenyang departing 10.00 Pyongyang time, on an approximately 45-minute flight, on Mondays and Fridays. China Northern had flown Beijing–Shenyang–Pyongyang but the route was badly run to the extent of not making any profit and was halted. A 2002 plan to run a twice-weekly Beijing–Dalian–Pyongyang route during summer has also expired.

**▸▸▸ BY RAIL** There is a very regular international rail service from Pyongyang to Beijing. The T27 leaves Beijing railway station (just inside the second ring road, south of Jianguomenwai Street) at 17.25 on Mondays, Wednesdays, Thursdays and Saturdays, arriving in Pyongyang the next day. The Pyongyang service T28 to Beijing leaves at 10.10 on the same days, and the Saturday train carries a carriage ultimately bound for Moscow. More and more visitors to the DPRK are taking up the now commonly offered deal of taking the train all the way from Moscow to Pyongyang, catching the 23.53 Trans-Manchurian on Friday from Moscow's Yaroslavski station to reach Pyongyang at 17.30 the following Friday; or do it the other way, leaving Pyongyang at 10.10 on Saturday to reach Moscow at 17.59 the following Friday.

At Dandong and Sinuijiu, the two cities straddling the Yalu River border between China and DPRK, the international carriages (Chinese, Korean and a Russian) get detached from the long local trains and pushed across the bridge, from the arms of one side's customs officers into the clutches of the other. Both groups take two hours to sift through your papers and possibly bags. Snack pedlars trawl the train corridors and platforms on the Chinese side, selling noodles to be cooked from each carriage's scalding hot-water urn. If possible, bring lots of savoury picnic foods with a mind to share them with your Korean co-passengers, who'll likely share theirs with you. This writer's experience of the buffet car was that its hand-written menu had ten small dishes for €5.

Beijing to Pyongyang one-way fares in summer 2007 were quoted as US$110 (RMB835, deluxe sleeper), US$91 (RMB690 soft), US$63 (RMB477 hard) with minor variations depending on train nationality and a possible additional fee for booking. Pyongyang to Beijing were similarly priced. Boarding points en route are Tianjin, Shenyang, Dandong and Sinuijiu and prices vary accordingly. Return tickets aren't available from either end. In China, either buy the tickets from the station or go to the informative, English-speaking BTG 69 Ticketing Co Ltd (*Tourism Tower, 28 Jianguomenwai Beijing 100022, China;* ☎ +86 10 6515 0093/24, 6515 8844/2111; f +86 10 6515 8564/5292). There is also the rail route direct from Pyongyang via Rajin-Sonbong into Russia to Vladivostok, as used by Kim Jong Il himself to visit Russia in 2001 and 2002. However, the route is irregularly plied (US$100 one-way, class unknown), being set by date and not by days, if foreigners can get on at all. But it's worth asking about: every question becomes a suggestion. There is a bigger plan afoot to have all Korea linked again by rail and have the Trans-Siberian and Trans-Manchurian railways ultimately connect all the way through to the bottom of the ROK.

Korea was once of course traversed by its railways, lines which were cut when the country was divided, with track first taken up and then blown up in the war. Soon though Pyongyang and Seoul will be just a few train stops apart, for the first time in over half a century. Sinuiju to Seoul would reconnect the Kyongi line running down the west coast. As Hyundai's industrial park at Kaesong is to be connected to this route, ROK company goods produced at DPRK prices will be sent by train, the best combination in speed and freight volume across Asia and Europe (and from Europe to Africa and Asia to the US if planned tunnel routes come off). The east coast Donghae line would go via the port of Wonsan and Onjong-ri in the Kumgang mountains and steam into the ROK. The plans were agreed in 2000, with the railways to be flanked by roads ultimately reaching four lanes in width – some of which are in use already (see *By road*, below).

The tracks have been in place for some time, but a sticking point was the DPRK seeking to resolve a separate issue of the two Koreas' naval demarcation lines. When that demand was shelved, in May 2007 military officers from both sides agreed for a trial run of one northern train going south along on the east coast line and a southern train coming north on the west coast, a truly historic event that went ahead later that month.

**BY SEA** The only direct connection from the ROK to the DPRK is by the Hyundai corporation ferry that sails from Hyundai Sokcho ferry terminal, taking short tours (three or four days) to the Mt Kumgang area on North Korea's southeast coast. The route is the only way ordinary South Koreans can 'easily' visit the North, and makes for an interesting diversionary tour for foreigners in the ROK. A single ticket costs around US$400. Apply to the Hyundai Asian Corporation (*12th Flr Hyundai Bldg, 140-2, Gye-dong, Jongno-gu, Seoul 110-793, Korea;* ✆ *+82 2 3669 3916/3897;* f *+82 2 3669 3690;* e *asan3669@hanmail.net;* *http://english.tour2korea.com/01culture/Application_Form_1.doc*) or ask through KNTO's (South Korean National Tourist Office) overseas branch offices.

From China, there's the Orient Pearl ferry from Dandong that runs to the South Korean port of Incheon three nights a week.

There is also a passenger ferry link to the DPRK from Niigata in Japan, serving as a vital cultural and economic link for hundreds of thousands of Korean residents in Japan loyal to the North. The North Korea service runs around three times a month from Niigata Port (West Harbour Area) to Wonsan, from where the Mangyongbong 92 goes weekly (one-day journey) to Niigata. A lack of diplomatic ties between the North and Japan (under negotiation) preclude non-Korean-Japanese from using this service, but …

Tourists can sail from the ROK to Mt Paektu, by way of Russia and China. The ROK port of Sokcho has ferry routes plying all the way to Zarubino in Russia, from where tourists then bus to Hunchun, China and on to Paektu. The route is run by Dongchun Ferry Company (✆ *+82 2 720 0271; http://dongchunferry.co.kr*). Visas for China and Russia are required.

**BY ROAD** For a long time, the only servicable road links into the DPRK were into the RASON investment zone in the north-east (and hence next to never accessed by westerners) or the bridge from Dandong into Sinuiju (almost exclusively for use by Chinese and Korean traders and their shipments). This changed on 5 February 2003 when a group of 80 ROK officials crossed the DMZ by bus into DPRK on a 40km stretch of road. Another 500 passed through a few days later and this momentous crossing, the first in decades and made as the stand-off between the DPRK and the US looked to be descending rapidly into something possibly deeply unpleasant, showed to the world what kind of invasion Koreans really wanted. The first road freight came by way of truckloads of northern sand going south.

Hyundai tour buses now cross frequently (✆ +82 2 3669 3000; www.hyundai-asan.com). There are also short tours specifically for non-Koreans (✆ +82 2 3669 4164; e jjmariakim@hdasan.com). To that end, the related website (www.mtkumgang.com) is a smart, jolly site that provides a great deal of information, albeit all in Korean, about road tours to the new complex in Kumgangsan (✆ +82 2 3669 3726/3691). Mt Kumgang (✆ +82 2 739 1090) organises tours from the ROK to Kumgangsan.

In 2001 and 2002 motorcycle rallies were held; the International North–South Korea Motorcycle Touring started in the south, then ferried to Kumgangsan and on to Pyongyang, with some spas and a circus taken in on the tour on the US$1,000 jamboree. The tour was run by the Federation Internationale de Motocyclisme (www.fim.ch) in conjunction with the Korea Motorcycle Federation and the Asian Motorcycle Touring Association, and may yet be reprised.

## RED TAPE

The Korean Friendship Association says passports with validity for six months after the travel dates are sufficient for most nationalities, whereas other sources have insisted upon a year. This is something that requires checking with the tour operators.

Visas, usually single-entry, are given for set arrival and departure dates and are designated for exit/entry for Pyongyang, Sinuiju and Tuman. Visas must be obtained before going, and require letters of invitation, whether the visit is for business or pleasure, and your passport should be valid for a year after the travel dates. Because tourists must go on tours, they will either let their travel operator deal with KITC or do that themselves but applications take at least ten days because of how much needs arranging. Along with the application forms of the respective tour company and two (or more) passport photos, travellers must submit a CV and a letter from their current employer verifying the applicant's details. The CV and letter details have to be updated to the day they are checked: a wrong number or date can scupper the keenest tourist. Journalists need special visas, they are not allowed in on tourist visas, and any caught sneaking in are thrown out at their own expense. More importantly, they endanger everyone associated with them, the other tourists, the external tour firm and particularly the Korean guides. It is tantamount to spying. Sneaking into any country without a visa is a bad idea, and the authorities are not amenable. Don't do it. Most people need visas to visit another country; North Koreans need visas to leave theirs.

If you're staying in the DPRK for more than 24 hours you must register with the Foreign Ministry, something the hotel should do, but they will need your passport for an hour.

South Korean tourists can visit on tourist visas but only to the Mt Kumgang complex on the Hyundai ferry and on other occasional tours that are very limited in comparison with the norm (that said, they can and do go by the thousand to the Chinese side of Mt Paektu and to the Yanbian Autonomous Region in China, also known as the 'Third Korea' – see page 216). US tourists were banned in 1995, although a few were allowed in for the 2002 Arirang Festival and there has been an increasing frequency of allowance for a few American tourists ever since to see this spectacular. As this is a situation in flux, it is necessary to check with tour operators.

By far the biggest numbers of tourists into DPRK are Chinese. You'll likely see many jolly bands of middle-ageing, prosperous Chinamen wandering around and you'll share the audience with them for the set shows and other events or venues to which KITC directs its tourists. For many of these visitors, coming to DPRK is something akin to a nostalgia tour, as it is oft observed that DPRK is very similar in looks, organisation and feel to China 20-odd years ago. But this time gap of perceived difference is closing fast.

Remember that you'll need double-entry visas certainly for China or Russia if you're coming through them, which is likely.

**E EMBASSIES AND CONSULATES** Since 1998, the DPRK has more than doubled its cache of fully established diplomatic relations with other countries, with the number of Western countries growing. Still, many don't have an actual embassy in Pyongyang but cover the DPRK from their Beijing embassies. Pyongyang's embassy district is Munsudong, on the east side.

**Bulgaria** Munsudong District, Daedonggang, Pyongyang; ☎ 02 381 7343

**Cambodia** Munsudong District, Daedonggang, Pyongyang; ☎ 02 381 7283; f 02 381 7625

**China** B Kin Mal Dong, Mao Lang Bong District, Pyongyang; ☎ 02 381 3133/3116; f 02 381 3425. This stands out as the biggest embassy & the most efficient. It is very good for getting visas back to China – it can get you business visas in a day for US$100.

**Czech Republic** Apt 39, Bldg 3 Munsudong District Daedonggang, Pyongyang; ☎ 02 381 7021; f 02 381 7022

**Germany** Munsudong District, Pyongyang; ☎ 02 381 7385; f 02 381 7397

**India** 6 Munsudong District, Daedonggang, Pyongyang; ☎ 02 381 7277/7274/7215; f 02 381 7619

**Mongolia** Munsudong, Pyongyang; ☎ 02 381 7322; f 02 381 7616

**New Zealand** The most convenient locations for New Zealanders to apply for visas are likely to be North Korea's embassy in Jakarta, which is cross-accredited to New Zealand, or its embassy in Beijing.

**People's Republic of Korea** ☎ 02 381 7908; f 02 381 7258; e ambassaden.pyongyang@foreign.ministry.se

**Poland** Munsudong District, Daedonggang, Pyongyang; ☎ 02 381 7325/7328/7331; f 02 381 7634

**Romania** Munhengong District, Pyongyang; ☎ 02 381 7336

**Russia** Choson Minjujuii Inmin, Chuji Soryong Tesagwan, Conghwaguck, Pyongyang; ☎ 02 381 1301; f 02 381 1302

**Sweden** Daehak St, Munsudong District, Daedonggang, Pyongyang; ☎ 02 381 7904; f 02 381 7485. Citizens of the US and EU countries without their own diplomatic presence are represented and given consular assistance by the Swedish embassy.

**Switzerland** 3 Yubo St, Munsudong District, Daedonggang, Pyongyang; ☎ 02 381 7645/7646; f 02 381 7643

**UK** Munsudong District; ☎ 02 381 7980/4 (5 lines), international dialling: ☎ 02 382 7980/2 (3 lines), local dialling: ☎ 02 381 2228; f 02 381 7985, international dialling: ☎ 02 382 7983, local dialling: ☎ 02 381 4482 out of hours; ⊕ 00.00–08.30 Mon–Fri.

## DPRK missions

**Australia** 57 Culgoa Circuit, O'Malley, Canberra, ACT 2606; ☎ +61 (02) 6286 4770; f +61 (02) 6286 4795; ⊕ 09.00–12.00 & 14.00–17.00 Mon–Fri

**Austria** Beckmanngasse 10–12, A-1140 Vienna; ☎ +43 1 894 23 11; f +43 1 894 31 74

**Bulgaria** Mladost-I, Andrei Sakharov 4, 1784 Sophia; ☎ +359 (02) 975 334, +359 (02) 974 6111; f +359 (02) 974 5567

**Canada** 151 Slater St, 6th Flr, Ottawa K1P 5H3; ☎ +1 613 232 1715

**China** Ritan Bei Lu, Jianguomenwai, Beijing, 100600; ☎ +86 (10) 6532 1186, 6532 1154 (protocol); f +86 (10) 6532 4862. The biggest DPRK embassy (& one of Beijing's biggest).

**Czech Republic** Na Zaacutetorce 6/89, 160, 00 Prague 6; ☎ +420 (02) 2432 0783; f +420 (02) 2431 8817; ⊕ 08.00–12.00 & 13.00–17.00

**Denmark** Skelvej 2, Dk-2900 Hellerup, Copenhagen; ☎ +45 39 62 50 70; f +45 39 62 50 70. ⊕ 09.00–16.00 Mon–Fri

**Finland** Kulosaaren puistotie 32, 00570 Helsinki; ☎ +358 9 684 8195; f +35 8 9 684 8995

**France** 47 rue Chaveau, 92200 Neuilly-sur-Seine; ☎ +33 (0)1 47 47 53 85; f +33 (0)1 47 47 61 41

**Germany** The Interest Section of the DPRK at the Embassy of the People's Republic of China is now the DPRK Embassy, Glinkastrasse 7, D-10117, Berlin; ☎ +49 (30) 229 3181/3189; f +49 (30) 229 3191. Contact Mr Ri Sang Yu (former GDR Embassy official).

**Hong Kong** DPRK Consulate Chinachem Century Tower, 20th Floor, 178 Gloucester Rd, Wanchai, Hong Kong; ☎ +852 2803 4447; f +852 2577 3644
**Hungary** Beckmanngasse 10–12, 1140 Vienna; ☎ +43 (01) 894 2313; f +43 (01) 894 3174
**Indonesia** PO Box 5003, JKTM Jakarta 12050; ☎ +62 21 521 0131; f +62 21 526 0066
**Italy** Via Ludovico Di Savoia 23, 00185 Rome; ☎ +39 (06) 7720 9094; f +39 (06) 7720 9111
**Lebanon** Mousaitbeh, PO Box 9636; ☎ +961 (1) 311490, 868722
**Netherlands** 43 Pourtalstrasse, Amsterdam; ☎ +41 3195 16621/15704. There is no reciprocal mission in Pyongyang, only the Dutch embassy in Seoul: Koybo Building 14th Floor, Chongro 1-ga, Chongro-gu, Seoul 110-714; ☎ +82 2 737 9514/6; f +82 2 735132
**Romania** Sos. Nordului nr 6, sector 1, Bucharest; ☎ +40 (21) 232 96; f +40 (21) 232 95; ⊕08.00–17.00 Mon–Fri.
**Russia (and Ukraine)** 72 Mosfilmovskaya St, Moscow; ☎ +7 095 143 62 49, 143 62 31; f +7 095

938 21 95, +7 095 143 6312; ⊕09.00–12.00 & 14.00–18.00
**Singapore** 7500A Beach Rd, #09-320, The Plaza, Singapore 199591; ☎ +65 6440 3498; f +65 6348 2026; ⊕09.00–12.30 & 13.30–17.00 Mon–Fri
**Sweden** Norra Kungsvaegan 39, 181 31 Lindingoe; ☎ 767 3836; f 767 3836
**Switzerland** Pourtalesstrasse 43, 3074 Muri bei Bern; ☎ +41 (0) 31 951 66 21; f +41 (0) 31 951 5704; e dprk.embassy@bluewin.ch
**Thailand** 14 Muban Suanlaemthong 2 (soi 28), Phattanakan Rd, Suan Luang, Bangkok 10250; ☎ +66 319 2686 7
**UK** 73 Gunnersbury Av, London W5 4LP; ☎ +44 020 8992 4965; f +44 020 8992 2053
**US** The DPRK Mission in the US is really the Permanent Mission to the United Nations, 820 Second Av, 13th Flr, New York, NY 10017; ☎ +1 212 972 3105/3106; f +1 212 972 3154. DPRK officials are restricted to within a 25-mile perimeter of the building.

✚ HEALTH *with Dr Felicity Nicholson*

**VACCINATIONS** There is no absolute requirement for vaccinations, but the following are strongly recommended. Be up to date with diphtheria/tetanus (ten-yearly), polio (ten-yearly), hepatitis A and typhoid.

**Hepatitis A** vaccine (Havrix Monodose or Avaxim) comprises two injections given about a year apart. The course costs about £100, but may be available on the NHS; it protects for 25 years and can be administered even close to the time of departure. The newer injectable typhoid vaccines (eg: Typhim Vi) last for three years and are about 85% effective. Oral capsules (Vivotif) are currently available in the US (and soon in the UK); if four capsules are taken over seven days it will last for five years. They should be encouraged unless the traveller is leaving within a few days for a trip of a week or less, when the vaccine would not be effective in time. For trips of four weeks or more to rural areas between April and October, **Japanese encephalitis** vaccine is advised unless there are contra indications. The course comprises three doses of vaccine taken over a four-week period. The last dose cannot be given less than ten days before flying out of the UK on a long-haul flight. If time is short then two doses given no less than a week apart will suffice, but the same time restriction applies for flying.

For trips of six weeks or more, **hepatitis B** vaccine should also be considered. If Engerix B vaccine is used, the course comprises three doses given at zero, seven and 21–28 days. This rapid course is licensed only for those 18 or over, and some GP surgeries do not have this vaccine in which case the minimum time to give all three doses is two months. It should also be taken if you are working in a hospital or with children, irrespective of the duration of your trip. Ideally, then, you should go to a doctor or travel clinic at least four weeks before your trip.

Vaccinations for **rabies** are advised for travellers visiting more remote areas, especially if you are more than 24 hours from medical help and definitely if you will be working with animals (see *Rabies*, page 78).

**Tuberculosis** (TB) is spread through close respiratory contact and occasionally through infected milk or milk products. It is very common in North Korea with an incidence of more than 100 cases per 100,000 population. BCG should be considered if you have not had this before and are likely to be mixing with the local population for stays of three months or more. Experts differ over whether a BCG vaccination against tuberculosis (TB) is useful in adults: discuss this with your travel clinic.

There are no reciprocal health care agreements with Britain, so ensure that you have comprehensive medical insurance and that you carry adequate supplies of any prescribed medication that you usually take.

**TRAVEL CLINICS AND HEALTH INFORMATION** A full list of current travel clinic websites worldwide is available on www.istm.org/. For other journey preparation information, consult ftp://ftp.shoreland.com/pub/shorecg.rtf or www.tripprep.com. Information about various medications may be found on www.emedicine.com/wild/topiclist.htm.

*Your Child Abroad: A Travel Health Guide* is a useful resource for those travelling with children and *Bugs Bites & Bowels: The Cadogan Guide to Travel Health* contains information and treatment guidelines for adults.

## UK

**Berkeley Travel Clinic** 32 Berkeley St, London W1J 8EL (near Green Park tube station); ↘ 020 7629 6233
**Cambridge Travel Clinic** 48a Mill Rd, Cambridge CB1 2AS; ↘ 01223 367362; e enquiries@travelcliniccambridge.co.uk; www.travelcliniccambridge.co.uk. ⊕ 12.00–19.00 Tue–Fri, 10.00–16.00 Sat.
**Edinburgh Travel Clinic** Regional Infectious Diseases Unit, Ward 41 OPD, Western General Hospital, Crewe Rd South, Edinburgh EH4 2UX; ↘ 0131 537 2822; www.link.med.ed.ac.uk/ridu. Travel helpline (↘ 0906 589 0380) ⊕ 09.00–12.00 weekdays. Provides inoculations & antimalarial prophylaxis, & advises on travel-related health risks.
**Fleet Street Travel Clinic** 29 Fleet St, London EC4Y 1AA; ↘ 020 7353 5678; www.fleetstreetclinic.com. Vaccinations, travel products & latest advice.
**Hospital for Tropical Diseases Travel Clinic** Mortimer Market Bldg, Capper St (off Tottenham Ct Rd), London WC1E 6AU; ↘ 020 7388 9600; www.thehtd.org. Offers consultations & advice, & is able to provide all necessary drugs & vaccines for travellers. Runs a healthline (↘ 0906 133 7733) for country-specific information & health hazards. Also stocks nets, water purification equipment & personal protection measures.
**Interhealth Worldwide** Partnership Hse, 157 Waterloo Rd, London SE1 8US; ↘ 020 7902 9000; www.interhealth.org.uk. Competitively priced, one-stop travel health service. All profits go to their affiliated company, InterHealth, which provides health care for overseas workers on Christian projects.
**Liverpool School of Medicine** Pembroke Pl, Liverpool L3 5QA; ↘ 051 708 9393; f 0151 705 3370; www.liv.ac.uk/lstm
**MASTA** (Medical Advisory Service for Travellers Abroad) Moorfield Rd, Yeadon LS19 7BN; ↘ 0870

606 2782; www.masta-travel-health.com. Provides travel health advice, anti-malarials & vaccinations. There are over 25 MASTA pre-travel clinics in Britain; call or check online for the nearest. Clinics also sell mosquito nets, medical kits, insect protection & travel hygiene products.
**NHS travel website** www.fitfortravel.scot.nhs.uk. Provides country-by-country advice on immunisation & malaria, plus details of recent developments, & a list of relevant health organisations.
**Nomad Travel Store/Clinic** 3–4 Wellington Terr, Turnpike La, London N8 0PX; ↘ 020 8889 7014; travel-health line (office hrs only) ↘ 0906 863 3414; e sales@nomadtravel.co.uk; www.nomadtravel.co.uk. Also at 40 Bernard St, London WC1N 1LJ; ↘ 020 7833 4114; 52 Grosvenor Gdns, London SW1W 0AG; ↘ 020 7823 5823; & 43 Queens Rd, Bristol BS8 1QH; ↘ 0117 922 6567. For health advice, equipment such as mosquito nets & other anti-bug devices, & an excellent range of adventure travel gear.
**Trailfinders Travel Clinic** 194 Kensington High St, London W8 7RG; ↘ 020 7938 3999; www.trailfinders.com/clinic.htm
**Travelpharm** The travelpharm website, www.travelpharm.com, offers up-to-date guidance on travel-related health & has a range of medications available through their online mini-pharmacy.

## IRISH REPUBLIC
**Tropical Medical Bureau** Grafton Street Medical Centre, Grafton Bldgs, 34 Grafton St, Dublin 2; ↘ 1 671 9200; www.tmb.ie. A useful website specific to tropical destinations. Also check website for other bureaux locations throughout Ireland.

## USA

**Centers for Disease Control** 1600 Clifton Rd, Atlanta, GA 30333; ☎ 800 311 3435; travellers' health hotline ☎ 888 232 3299; www.cdc.gov/travel. The central source of travel information in the USA. The invaluable *Health Information for International Travel*, published annually, is available from the Division of Quarantine at this address.

**Connaught Laboratories** PO Box 187, Swiftwater, PA 18370; ☎ 800 822 2463. They will send a free list of specialist tropical-medicine physicians in your state.

**IAMAT** (International Association for Medical Assistance to Travelers) 1623 Military Rd, 279, Niagara Falls, NY 14304-1745; ☎ 716 754 4883; e info@iamat.org; www.iamat.org. A non-profit organisation that provides lists of English-speaking doctors abroad.

**International Medicine Center** 920 Frostwood Dr, Suite 670, Houston, TX 77024; ☎ 713 550 2000; www.traveldoc.com

## CANADA

**IAMAT** Suite 1, 1287 St Clair Av W, Toronto, Ontario M6E 1B8; ☎ 416 652 0137; www.iamat.org

**TMVC** Suite 314, 1030 W Georgia St, Vancouver BC V6E 2Y3; ☎ 1 888 288 8682; www.tmvc.com. Private clinic with several outlets in Canada.

## AUSTRALASIA

**IAMAT** PO Box 5049, Christchurch 5, New Zealand; www.iamat.org

**TMVC** ☎ 1300 65 88 44; www.tmvc.com.au. Clinics in Australia, New Zealand & Singapore, including:

*Auckland* Canterbury Arcade, 170 Queen St, Auckland; ☎ 9 373 3531

*Brisbane* 6th Floor, 247 Adelaide St, Brisbane QLD 4000; ☎ 7 3221 9066

*Melbourne* 393 Little Bourke St, 2nd floor, Melbourne, VIC 3000; ☎ 3 9602 5788

*Sydney* Dymocks Bldg, 7th Floor, 428 George St, Sydney, NSW 2000; ☎ 2 9221 7133

## LONG-HAUL FLIGHTS, CLOTS AND DVT

*Dr Jane Wilson-Howarth*

Long-haul air travel increases the risk of deep vein thrombosis (DVT). Although recent research has suggested that many of us develop clots when immobilised, most resolve without us ever having been aware of them. In certain susceptible individuals, though, clots form on clots and when large ones break away and lodge in the lungs this is dangerous. Fortunately this happens in a tiny minority of passengers.

Studies have shown that flights of over five-and-a-half-hours are significant, and that people who take lots of shorter flights over a short space of time can also form clots. People at highest risk are:

- Those who have had a clot before – unless they are now taking warfarin
- People over 80 years of age
- Anyone who has recently undergone a major operation or surgery for varicose veins
- Someone who has had a hip or knee replacement in the last three months
- Cancer sufferers
- Those who have ever had a stroke
- People with heart disease
- Those with a close blood relative who has had a clot

Those with a slightly increased risk are:

- People over 40
- Women who are pregnant or have had a baby in the last couple of weeks
- People taking female hormones, the combined contraceptive pill or other oestrogen therapy
- Heavy smokers
- Those who have very severe varicose veins

## SOUTH AFRICA
**SAA-Netcare Travel Clinics** P Bag X34, Benmore 2010;
www.travelclinic.co.za. Clinics throughout South Africa.

## SWITZERLAND
**IAMAT** 57 Chemin des Voirets, 1212 Grand Lancy,
Geneva; www.iamat.org

## PERSONAL FIRST-AID KIT
A minimal kit contains:

- A good drying antiseptic, eg: iodine or potassium permanganate (don't take antiseptic cream)
- A few small dressings (Band-Aids)
- Suncream
- Insect repellent; anti-malarial tablets; impregnated bed-net or permethrin spray
- Aspirin or paracetamol
- Antifungal cream (eg: Canesten)
- Ciprofloxacin or norfloxacin, for severe diarrhoea
- Tinidazole for giardia or amoebic dysentery (see below for regime)
- Antibiotic eye drops, for sore, 'gritty', stuck-together eyes (conjunctivitis)
- A pair of fine-pointed tweezers (to remove caterpillar hairs, thorns, splinters, coral, etc)
- Alcohol-based hand rub or bar of soap in plastic box
- Condoms or femidoms

- The very obese
- People who are very tall (over 6ft/1.8m) or short (under 5ft/1.5m)

A deep vein thrombosis is a blood clot that forms in the deep leg veins. This is very different from irritating but harmless superficial phlebitis. DVT causes swelling and redness of one leg, usually with heat and pain in one calf and sometimes the thigh. A DVT is only dangerous if a clot breaks away and travels to the lungs (pulmonary embolus). Symptoms of a pulmonary embolus (PE) include chest pain that is worse on breathing in deeply, shortness of breath, and sometimes coughing up small amounts of blood. The symptoms commonly start three to ten days after a long flight. Anyone who thinks that they might have a DVT needs to see a doctor immediately who will arrange a scan. Warfarin tablets (to thin the blood) are then taken for at least six months.

**PREVENTION OF DVT** Several conditions make the problem more likely. Immobility is the key, and factors like reduced oxygen in cabin air and dehydration may also contribute. To reduce the risk of thrombosis on a long journey:

- Exercise before and after the flight
- Keep mobile before and during the flight; move around every couple of hours
- Drink plenty of water or juices during the flight
- Avoid taking sleeping pills and excessive tea, coffee and alcohol
- Perform exercises that mimic walking and tense the calf muscles
- Consider wearing flight socks or support stockings (see *www.legshealth.com*)
- Ideally take a meal each week of oily fish (mackerel, trout, salmon, sardines, etc) ahead of your departure. This reduces the blood's ability to clot and thus DVT risk. It may even be worth just taking a meal of oily fish 24 hours before departure if this is more practical.

If you think you are at increased risk of a clot, ask your doctor if it is safe to travel.

Practical Information **HEALTH**

2

**IN NORTH KOREA** Medical facilities in North Korea as a whole are basic, particularly in the rural areas. Hospitals and clinics in the latter are usually able to offer only the very minimum medical care. Clinical hygiene is poor, anaesthetics are frequently unavailable, and the electricity supply to the hospitals (even in the capital) can be intermittent. You should try to avoid serious surgery if you can. Take with you any medication you think you are likely to require because supplies are limited and very difficult to buy. Tourist sites may offer medical facilities.

Use bottled water for drinking and brushing teeth. Avoid dairy products, which are likely to have been made with unpasteurised milk, and boil milk (or use powdered or tinned milk, using pure water in the reconstitution process). Ensure meat and fish are well cooked, and served hot. Be wary of pork, salad and mayonnaise, and always cook vegetables and peel fruit. If in doubt:

PEEL IT, BOIL IT, COOK IT OR FORGET IT.

**Malaria** There are pockets of malaria in the form of Plasmodium vivax in the northern territory. At the time of writing, no prophylaxis is advised (in the form of tablets) but you should always use insect repellents from dusk until dawn (the mosquitoes that carry the disease emerge at this time). It is also wise to wear clothing to cover arms and legs and to make your sleeping accommodation as mosquito proof as possible.

**Dengue fever** This mosquito-borne disease may mimic malaria; there is no prophylactic medication available to deal with it. The mosquitoes that carry this virus bite during the daytime, so it is worth applying repellent if you see any mosquitoes around. Symptoms include strong headaches, rashes, excruciating joint and muscle pains, and high fever. Dengue fever lasts only for a week or so and is not usually fatal. Complete rest and paracetamol are the usual treatment; plenty of fluids also help. Some patients are given an intravenous drip to prevent dehydration. It is especially important to protect yourself if you have had dengue fever before, since a second infection with a different strain can result in the potentially fatal dengue haemorrhagic fever.

**Rabies** Rabies is carried by all mammals (beware the village dogs and small monkeys that are used to being fed in the parks) and is passed on to man through a bite, scratch or a lick of an open wound. You must always assume any animal is rabid, and seek medical help as soon as possible. Meanwhile scrub the wound with soap under a running tap or while pouring water from a jug. Find a reasonably clear-looking source of water (but at this stage the quality of the water is not important), then pour on a strong iodine or alcohol solution of gin, whisky or rum. This helps stop the rabies virus entering the body and will guard against wound infections, including tetanus.

Pre-exposure vaccinations for rabies is ideally advised for everyone, but is particularly important if you intend to have contact with animals and/or are likely to be more than 24 hours away from medical help. Ideally three doses should be taken over a minimum of 21 days, though even taking one or two doses of vaccine is better than none at all. Contrary to popular belief these vaccinations are relatively painless.

If you are bitten, scratched or licked over an open wound by a sick animal, then post-exposure prophylaxis should be given as soon as possible, though it is never too late to seek help, as the incubation period for rabies can be very long. Those who have not been immunised will need a full course of injections. The vast majority of travel health advisers including WHO recommend rabies immunoglobulin (RIG), but this product is expensive (around US$800) and may

## TREATING TRAVELLERS' DIARRHOEA

*Dr Jane Wilson-Howarth*

It is dehydration that makes you feel awful during a bout of diarrhoea and the most important part of treatment is drinking lots of clear fluids. Sachets of oral rehydration salts give the perfect biochemical mix to replace all that is pouring out of your bottom but other recipes taste nicer. Any dilute mixture of sugar and salt in water will do you good: try Coke or orange squash with a three-finger pinch of salt added to each glass (if you are salt-depleted you won't taste the salt). Otherwise make a solution of a four-finger scoop of sugar with a three-finger pinch of salt in a 500 ml glass. Or add eight level teaspoons of sugar (18g) and one level teaspoon of salt (3g) to one litre (five cups) of safe water. A squeeze of lemon or orange juice improves the taste and adds potassium, which is also lost in diarrhoea. Drink two large glasses after every bowel action, and more if you are thirsty. These solutions are still absorbed well if you are vomiting, but you will need to take sips at a time. If you are not eating you need to drink three litres a day plus whatever is pouring into the toilet. If you feel like eating, take a bland, high carbohydrate diet. Heavy greasy foods will probably give you cramps.

If the diarrhoea is bad, or you are passing blood or slime, or you have a fever, you will probably need antibiotics in addition to fluid replacement. A dose of norfloxacin or ciprofloxacin repeated twice a day until better may be appropriate (if you are planning to take an antibiotic with you, note that both norfloxacin and ciprofloxacin are available only on prescription in the UK). If the diarrhoea is greasy and bulky and is accompanied by sulphurous (eggy) burps, one likely cause is giardia. This is best treated with tinidazole (four x 500mg in one dose, repeated seven days later if symptoms persist).

be hard to come by – another reason why pre-exposure vaccination should be encouraged.

Tell the doctor if you have had pre-exposure vaccine, as this should change the treatment you receive. And remember that, if you do contract rabies, mortality is 100% and death from rabies is probably one of the worst ways to go.

**HIV/AIDS** Whilst North Korea still publicly declares itself as HIV-free, there are risks of this infection and other sexually transmitted disease, whether you sleep with fellow travellers or locals. The majority of HIV infections in British heterosexuals are acquired abroad. If you must indulge, use condoms or femidoms, which help reduce the risk of transmission. If you notice any genital ulcers or discharge, get treatment promptly since other infections increase the risk of acquiring HIV. If you do have unprotected sex, visit a clinic as soon as possible; this should be within 24 hours, though may be considered up to two weeks, for post-exposure prophylaxis.

## SAFETY

Petty theft has happened from hotels and other accommodation, so be sure to keep your valuables and passport in safe keeping at all times. Incidents of other crimes against foreigners are very infrequently heard of. Take out full insurance coverage for health, belongings and flights, and cash to cover the trip because the ability to get hold of emergency funds is negligible. Bring all medication that you need and don't expect to get hold of any with any ease in the country. Some form of ID is needed at all times. Visit www.fco.gov.uk for up-to-date advice.

# WHAT TO TAKE

- insect repellent
- a small first-aid kit, with headache pills, contact lens solutions and enough of your own medication (do not rely on getting it in the DPRK; see *Health*, page 74)
- a powerful torch (and batteries) for the lack of street-lighting and evening power-cuts, preferably one that doubles as a lamp for night reading to supplement the low-watt lighting (when it's on)
- quality cigarettes (not American brands) and chocolate are appreciated as gifts for the guides
- instant coffee and any snacks you can't live without
- good reading matter, including this book (!) and any worthy tomes you can donate to the Diplomatic Club to please the fledgling expat community (for whom tonic water is worth its weight in gold!)

## $ MONEY

It used to be that foreign visitors (principally tourists) were barely allowed to see, let alone use, the local currency of *won*. Instead they exchanged US dollars for 'foreigners' won (at a fixed rate of 2.12 won/US dollar), often presented as the kosher currency but its simple designs and very low serial numbers were suspicious. This currency was usable only in special shops, bars and hotels; it controlled the level of exchange, what foreigners could buy, where they could go and what they could do (a 'local' 10 chon piece being needed for public phones and transport), nor could it be converted back into hard currency.

DPRK won, of any kind, is impossible to obtain outside the country and it is illegal to take it out of the DPRK. Foreigners' won was phased out in 2002 and now local won comes in 1, 5, 10, 50, 100 and up to 10,000 denominations at the rate of around 200 to the US dollar, but in December 2002 the US dollar was dumped for the euro. Nevertheless, local won is not necessarily available for foreigners, who are largely restricted to shops and restaurants accepting hard currency.

The accepted hard currency is now the euro. Some exchange facilities in Pyongyang will convert US dollars into euros for local usage, but obviously it's better to bring euros first of all. Convertible currencies are euros, Japanese yen (JPY), British pounds sterling (GBP), Hong Kong dollars (HKD), Canadian dollars (CAD), Australian dollars (AUD) and New Zealand dollars (NZD). To a lesser extent, these currencies, and occasionally even the Chinese renminbi (RMB), are also directly usable for transactions; again, however, the euro is much preferred and more likely to succeed. Foreign exchange is available at the Trade Bank or its agents, and at hotels and some restaurants. The Trade Bank opens from 09.00 to 12.00 and from 14.00 to 17.00 except Sundays. It's best to take euros in low denominations – it's an effort to spend money in the country.

The tour company you use will specify the currency in which they need payment.

Major credit cards (mostly Visa, less often MasterCard, and never American Express) are in theory accepted at the highest-class hotels and a very few of the large shops, but don't expect to use them. Travellers' cheques issued in euros are usable in the bank but not in hotels or shops; those issued in US dollars will not be accepted.

## GETTING AROUND

DPRK transportation is limited, because to travel from town to town and province to province everyone needs a permit, locals and foreign visitors alike (you see the checkpoints around the cities). Locals need good reason to get one from the authorities, which also means the demand, and the need, for inter-conurbation transport isn't there. Foreign visitors' hosts arrange permits in accord with the visitors' itineraries. Buses going beyond Pyongyang are for all practical purposes non-existent. Trains (except for the international routes to Beijing and Moscow) are difficult to get (suffering from power cuts and floods) and may require arranging an extra coach for you. Timetables are not readily available and tickets must be bought through agents before the day of departure, so train travel needs planning. For air travel, there is no domestic air service usable by foreigners except charter flights to Mt Paektu. As everywhere, reconfirm international flight tickets some days before travel, although this is likely to be done by the visitors' receiving party. Bicycles are scarce, are not available for hire and nor are cars except taxis. International driving permits are not valid but foreign nationals resident in DPRK can obtain local driving licences after taking a driving test. Locals walk short distances or hitchhike long distances in army trucks. It's unlikely you'll need to hold aloft your magic cigarettes. You and your group will be ferried about right from the airport in an official bus or car, which is clean and comfortable – and traffic jams are unheard of. Beyond the cities, the roads stretch away as straight as runways, empty of cars, road markings, cat's eyes and lights but with beautifully tended verges and central reservations.

 ## ACCOMMODATION

Hotels come in deluxe, first, second and third class, and there are also guesthouses. The local press often report that the top hotels are 'full' with foreign guests and delegates. It's preferred that you stay in the deluxe hotels, and you'll be informed that's not because they need hard currency more but that that's the regulation, or the other hotels are too inferior for honoured guests, maybe their electricity and hot-water supplies are too unreliable (and yet they're all always full). Point being, it is not impossible to go cheaper, but co-ordinating this in a group tour might be tricky – tours are package deals, based on long-standing arrangements, and for the sake of hassle and considering just how good a top-flight DPRK hotel is, quibbling over a few notes ... well most people don't. The prices and ranges listed are essentially a gauge for those non-tourist visitors or specialist tourists.

Single tourists pay an extra supplement for their rooms. There are some hotels no foreigner can stay at, and it has been the case that certain nationalities go to certain hotels, those from richer countries stay at the pricier gaffs. The greater costs of the top-band abodes is reflected thus: secure hot water and power supplies; more restaurants with longer menus; more entertainment, from billiards to massage and sauna; and greater communications facilities. At the top end is the Yanggakdo Hotel (Pyongyang's most modern and deluxe hotel). In August 2007 the prices were as follows: €370/420 for a VIP double room, €170/200 double deluxe, €105 standard double floors 25+, €95 for standard double below floors 24. Take off €20 per grade for a single.

### HOTEL PRICE BANDS

The following hotel band prices for double standards are approximate:

| | | |
|---|---|---|
| **DELUXE** | $$$$ | €100+ for a standard double |
| **1ST CLASS** | $$$ | €80–100 for a standard double |
| **2ND CLASS** | $$ | €60–80 for a standard double. |
| **3RD CLASS** | $ | €45–60 for a standard double. Guesthouses fall into this category and price band. |

Potemkin pretensions, being filled to the ceilings with goods no-one is supposed to buy. But these shops may yet become prey to international chains. Notwithstanding the arrival of mini-marts in Kumgangsan, thus far WalMart, Tesco and Carrefour have yet to arrive (thank God, Kim Jong Il or anyone) but reports of a Chinese strike in Department Store No 1, with all the portent that carries, suggest these waves are splashing into the heart of DPRK already. China's Zhongxu Group signed a contract in 2004 to run No 1 for ten years with a view to securing, expanding into, and dominating DPRK's retail business.

No 1 is seemingly still in Korean hands, but the idea is there. However, it could be that the DPRK's nascent private retail industry, individual sellers just breaking the state's domination of retail and distribution, might soon enough be bought up or competed to death by private corporations with a speed unparalleled elsewhere in the world.

Available for purchase are some beautiful paintings, excellent embroideries and sometimes the spectacular hand-painted social-realist posters, along with Korea's own fruit-powered rice wines and herbal remedies (mainly ginseng).

## CUSTOMS

The usual restrictions apply regarding narcotics, firearms, live organisms, biochem and hazardous products. Pornographic literature is banned. Don't bring in any texts critical or derisory of the regime. The amount of foreign currency you're able to bring in and out is subject to restriction and local currency can't be taken out.

## TOURIST INFORMATION

Rapid changes domestically (especially regarding power, transport and food) and internationally, the control of information, a reluctance to reprint and very limited indigenous internet coverage, all mean that published information is bitty and usually out of date. In the country the most innocuous questions aren't answered if the questionee doesn't feel empowered to tell you. Your first port of call should be www.fco.gov.uk.

Tour operators and Ryohaengsa (KITC) should be contacted (see page 66). The glossy publications *Korea Today* and *Democratic People's Republic of Korea* are available on the Air Koryo flight in, and in most hotel shops. Many people have written about their DPRK experiences on www.theargonauts.com/index.shtml, www.yunkai.de/stories/northkorea/northkorea.html, www.geocities.com/dprk02/index.htm (an excellently compiled site of text and good photos). More and more blogs about travel in the DPRK are appearing all the time.

A shoal of websites about DPRK travel is at www.budgettravel.com/nkorea.htm, so trawl through them. The CIA Factbook at www.cia.gov/cia/publications/factbook is good for an overall look at the DPRK through CIA eyes.

## PHOTOGRAPHY

You can photograph fairly freely, but your guide might suggest (read, insist) you don't, so don't. Don't take any photos of any military subjects and ask before snapping locals; it may lose the spontaneity of a shot but it will avoid genuine ire, and if they say no, respect that. Many indoor exhibitions forbid photography. Do not sneak photos, especially at the beginning. Going along with the guides' requests builds trust and it's when they trust you that things loosen up.

There is a photography shop that can develop films and does passport photos on the second floor of Pyongyang's Koryo Hotel, while 35mm camera film (usually

200) is available from hotel shops and main department stores. However, parts, batteries and other film essentials are far more likely found in Beijing, although Beijing's dust gets into cameras and developing machines. Restrictions for bringing into the country optical equipment are camera lenses over 150 mm or video cameras with higher than 24x optical zoom and for binoculars or telescopes over 10x power. For the last three, check again with the operator before departing.

## PUBLIC HOLIDAYS

| | |
|---|---|
| **1 January** | New Year's Day |
| **16 February** | Kim Jong Il's birthday |
| **15 April** | Kim Il Sung's birthday |
| **25 April** | Army Day |
| **1 May** | May Day |
| **27 July** | Victory Day |
| **15 August** | Independence from Japan Day |
| **9 September** | Republic Foundation Day |
| **10 October** | Korean Workers' Party Foundation Day |
| **27 December** | Constitution Day |

The country basically shuts down for winter.

## TIME ZONE

GMT plus nine hours, so midday in Pyongyang is 05.00 in London, 15.00 in Wellington and 21.00 in Vancouver the previous day. Years are given in the Gregorian Calendar and the Juche Calendar. The latter marks the years since Juche evolved, ie: 1912, the year Kim Il Sung was born. So, 2000 for example is Juche 88, as 1912 + 88 = 2000, and 2003 is Juche 91, etc.

## ELECTRICITY

110-220 (dual system) 60Hz, flat- or round-pin plugs, but outside Pyongyang's top hotels, power cuts are frequent (even highly regular) and long.

## CULTURAL ETIQUETTE

First and foremost, disrespecting the Great Leaders is the surest way to cause heinous offence to your hosts, be they guides, businessmen, whoever. This will mar your relations with them in the immediate sense and for the rest of the trip. You'll be asked to 'pay respect' to statues and shrines of Kim Il Sung and Kim Jong Il, usually by standing quietly in front of them and giving a solitary nod of the head. Just do it. Sometimes flowers must be brought. Do not disfigure in any way any image of either leader, and leave them high and dry and not screwed up in the bin; newspapers are specially folded to prevent the photos of the Leaders being creased. There have been anecdotal reports of foreigners falling foul of this, chucking newspapers in bins or defacing pictures accidentally or not, and incurring a public dressing down at the least.

However, your hosts will be knowledgeable on a great many worldly matters, and ranging debates about politics and economics may start up. Prevent causing unwitting offence by avoiding overt criticism in favour of suggestions: how things can 'be improved' or 'made even better', if the need is felt to say such things. Koreans are fiercely proud people and there is always the overhanging Asian concept of 'loss of face'. In conversation no-one should be boxed into a corner and

*Ariadne Van Zandbergen*

**EQUIPMENT** Although with some thought and an eye for composition you can take reasonable photos with a 'point-and-shoot' camera, you need an SLR camera if you are at all serious about photography. Modern SLRs tend to be very clever, with automatic programmes for almost every possible situation, but remember that these programmes are limited in the sense that the camera cannot think, but only make calculations. Every starting amateur photographer should read a photographic manual for beginners and get to grips with such basics as the relationship between aperture and shutter speed.

Generally, it is always worth buying the best lens you can afford. The lens determines the quality of your photo more than the camera body. Fixed fast lenses are ideal, but very costly. A zoom lens makes it easier to change composition without changing lenses the whole time. If you carry only one lens, a 28–70mm (digital 17–55mm) or similar zoom should be ideal. It must be noted, however, that, as it stands, you cannot take lens over 150 mm into the DPRK.

For wildlife photography from a tourist vehicle, a solid beanbag, which you can make yourself very cheaply, will be necessary to avoid blurred images, and is more useful than a tripod. A clamp with a tripod head screwed onto it can be attached to the vehicle as well. Modern dedicated flash units are easy to use; aside from the obvious need to flash when you photograph at night, you can improve a lot of photos in difficult 'high contrast' or very dull light with some fill-in flash. It pays to have a proper flash unit as opposed to a built-in camera flash.

**DIGITAL/FILM** Digital photography is now the preference of most amateur and professional photographers, with the resolution of digital cameras improving all the time. For ordinary prints a 6 megapixel camera is fine. For better results and the possibility to enlarge images and for professional reproduction, higher resolution is available up to 16 megapixels.

Memory space is important. The number of pictures you can fit on a memory card depends on the quality you choose. Calculate in advance how many pictures you can fit on a card and either take enough cards to last for your trip, or take a storage drive onto which you can download the content. A laptop gives the advantage that you can see your pictures properly at the end of each day and edit and delete rejects, but a storage device is lighter and less bulky. These drives come in different capacities up to 80GB.

Bear in mind that digital camera batteries, computers and other storage devices need charging, so make sure you have all the chargers, cables and converters with you. Most hotels have charging points, but do enquire about this in advance. When camping you might have to rely on charging from the car battery; a spare battery is invaluable.

If you are shooting film, 100 to 200 ISO print film and 50 to 100 ISO slide film are ideal. Low ISO film is slow but fine grained and gives the best colour saturation, but will need more light, so support in the form of a tripod or monopod is important. You can also bring a few 'fast' 400 ISO films for low-light situations where a tripod or flash is no option.

For the DPRK it is important to stock up on extra digital memory cards and sticks

made to lose face, ie: be forced to apologise, concede defeat or accept criticism (which no-one enjoys anyway). The Korean variant is 'kibun', similar to face, which values keeping personal relations harmonious. You just have to be diplomatic. Watch for the silences or titters. On another note, here's an extreme example of how to get it all wrong:

At the Myohyang International Friendship Exhibition, one gift to Kim Il Sung that stuck out for me was a fanciful corrugated cardboard galleon from a Portuguese before coming as these are not available in the state. Camera film is available at some of the hotel shops and outlets catering to foreign tourists but the limited range and possibly questionable health of the films means that, similarly to digital memory cards, photographers would be best served bringing plenty of their own films. Places to develop films are also few and far between, with one outlet in the Koryo hotel being the longest-standing and most 'trusted' venue for film developing.

**DUST AND HEAT** Dust and heat are often a problem. Keep your equipment in a sealed bag, stow films in an airtight container (eg: a small cooler bag) and avoid exposing equipment and film to the sun. Digital cameras are prone to collecting dust particles on the sensor which results in spots on the image. The dirt mostly enters the camera when changing lenses, so be careful when doing this. To some extent photos can be 'cleaned' up afterwards in Photoshop, but this is time-consuming. You can have your camera sensor professionally cleaned, or you can do this yourself with special brushes and swabs made for the purpose, but note that touching the sensor might cause damage and should only be done with the greatest care.

**LIGHT** The most striking outdoor photographs are often taken during the hour or two of 'golden light' after dawn and before sunset. Shooting in low light may enforce the use of very low shutter speeds, in which case a tripod will be required to avoid camera shake.

With careful handling, side lighting and back lighting can produce stunning effects, especially in soft light and at sunrise or sunset. Generally, however, it is best to shoot with the sun behind you. When photographing animals or people in the harsh midday sun, images taken in light but even shade are likely to be more effective than those taken in direct sunlight or patchy shade, since the latter conditions create too much contrast.

**PROTOCOL** There are restrictions on what can be photographed in the DPRK, and it can be safely assumed that most things military will be off limits. That is not necessarily always the case but ask the guides for advice or if they can get permission; if they say no, respect that. As such, it is not the case that the Koreans demand to examine your film or force you to develop your film (notwithstanding some kind of exceptional circumstance).

In North Korea, as elsewhere, it is unacceptable to photograph local people without permission, and many people will refuse to pose or will ask for a donation. In such circumstances, don't try to sneak photographs as you might get yourself into trouble. Even the most willing subject will often pose stiffly when a camera is pointed at them; relax them by making a joke, and take a few shots in quick succession to improve the odds of capturing a natural pose.

*Ariadne Van Zandbergen is a professional travel and wildlife photographer specialising in Africa. She runs the Africa Image Library. For photo requests, visit www.africaimagelibrary.co.za or contact her on e ariadne@hixnet.co.za.*

printers' union. Somehow, inexplicably, having padded for hours through the incredibly long showrooms in the exhibition's highly sombre atmosphere (the Exhibition is the holiest of holies, enshrining the world's gifts of tribute and homage to the Great Leaders), this little ship cracked me up. The exhibition guide stared at my mirthful writhing in chilled disbelief, while my interpreter haltingly asked, with quiet, incredulous menace, what was funny. I realised I had well and truly pissed in the font, and only another tourist's intervention with a more harmless explanation saved me.

Anon

Your guides are your means to get around, and they need to trust you as you must trust in them. If you're prone to ignore basic manners, antagonising your guides will wreck any chances of more spontaneous endeavours and cloud the trip's atmosphere. Western journalists have made great hay of running away from their guides, and some tour companies have suggested in their literature that tourists can, for example leave their hotels at night without their guides – this book said in its first print that 'Pyongyang is a city where you can wander freely without guides', but did stress,'but do not run off and leave them' – repeat, do not run off and leave them! Tourists without guides get nowhere fast – no-one will take them anywhere and there are very few places beyond a few bars or restaurants to go. The consensus is that there is little to be achieved from abandoning the guides and it could blow back on you, more so them, should any problems arise. Much, much more can be seen and done if you ensure your guides can trust you – they can open doors, you can't, and legging it will mark you out as a worry. That so many journalists write up so much about their exploits of running away from their guides might suggest that, as a result, they end up with little else to report.

The final point doesn't need writing but I'll put it anyway, so don't take offence. The tours can perhaps feel claustrophobic, you're always on the go from here to there and may tire, you're with your guides and fellow travellers for all the hours you're awake, but you're going to the DPRK because you know it is a truly worthwhile, once-in-a-lifetime experience. So try to get along with your co-travellers and hosts or it will ruin a unique adventure.

**IMPORTANT TITBITS** Tipping is not expected but obviously appreciated. If you do tip then do so with great discretion.

Wave people towards you with the palm down and fingers batting back and forth. Don't point. Pour drinks by holding the bottle with both hands, serving elders first. Never sit with your soles pointing at anyone, so sit cross-legged with the feet tucked beneath your thighs, or side-saddle. Women and the young used to sit on their heels as a matter of course, and children would stand up when addressed, something still occasionally seen. Receive business cards with both hands and study appreciatively on receipt before placing in a breast pocket.

Public petting isn't appreciated nor do Korean men take well to Korean women being pawed by anyone, especially foreign men, although it's the women who will incur greater repercussions. One traveller put it this way: 'It's certainly not on the *Sex and the City* scale, but they're not quite the Taliban either'. For women's advances on men, I've no idea. Failure to find the middle ground may be costly.

# Part Two

## THE GUIDE

*Pyongyang*

# 3

# Pyongyang

*39.1° north 125.45° east, Pyongyang City District, capital of the Democratic People's Republic of Korea, Korean peninsula*

Pyongyang, the DPRK capital, is a showcase city, the political, cultural and educational centre of the country, a city built to show and impress the world with the success, progress and fortitude of the DPRK and its people.

The tiled apartment blocks and concrete high-rises strut alongside the city's wide, tree-lined boulevards cutting from titanic state buildings to monuments striking for their powerful shapes and size. Roads stretch arrow straight into the distance, linking monuments and plazas set in alignment over the horizon, across the river, across the city. In sunlight, the streets and squares, without a fleck of dust, can literally dazzle. In rain, the harsh, grey geometries meld into the sky while vast, sweeping Korean-style eaves hurl the rainwater away. Into all this order and space some 200 parks and open spaces have been carefully slotted. Most fume-producing factories have been banished to the city's outskirts. Pyongyang reputedly has 58m² of green belt per citizen – four times the amount prescribed by the United Nations, and in spring its hills heave with green. It is, as Kim Il Sung meant it to be, a city without parallel in Korea, or Asia.

'The capital of our socialist homeland, Pyongyang is the political centre, the centre for culture and education and a wellspring of our revolution' – and a well-ordered wellspring at that. In few parts of the city can be found the higgledy-piggledy mash of streets that comes from the organic growth of other cities, as individual people, firms and authorities fight over space and time; this form of Pyongyang's layout has been virtually obliterated. Every corner of every block has been approved according to one overall, unitary plan, and there is an extraordinary homogeneity in the buildings' design. For the parts and the whole, one design fits all as a handful of factories produce the designs of even fewer design institutes. The same singularity of purpose is visible in all the pictures, placards and slogans round the city, for which and only for which all neon gets used. It is still very much mostly the case that adverts in Pyongyang and beyond do not promote material goods or recognisable brands, but are for promoting the ideals and leader(s) of North Korea's socialism. Pyongyang is a mind-set, an ideal, an idea, the city as the manifestation of the state, the state as the manifestation of the man.

The city limits drawn on the plans are clearly visible on the ground. The grey cliffs of the perimeter high-rise provide a sharp, vertical barrier to the fields and lowlands lapping round the city. Pyongyang doesn't sprawl like other Asian cities, forever absorbing rural–urban migrants. The city's population is stable at around two million because people do not live and work in Pyongyang without permits, which are as valued as the gold dust mined in the city's outskirts. Koreans cannot in fact leave or enter the city without permits, as the checkpoints on the city's perimeter roads verify, and as a result the lack of inter-urban public transport is deliberate: if no-one needs it, why have it?

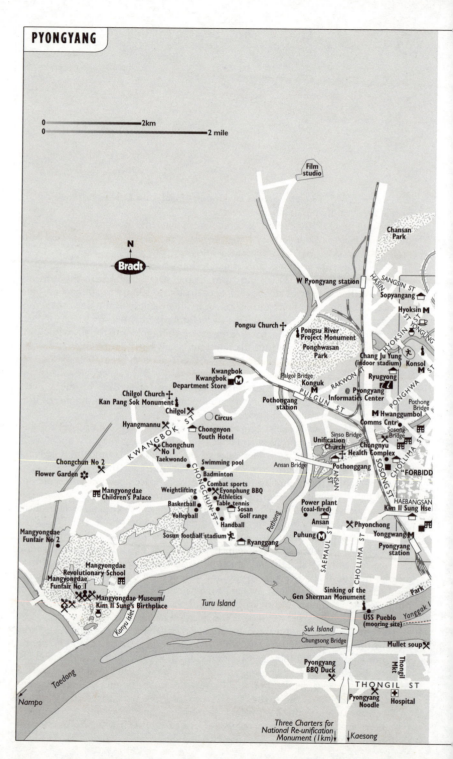

# PYONGYANG

Film studio

Chansan Park

W Pyongyang station

SANGSIN ST

Sopyangang

Hyoksin M

HYOKSIN ST

CHONGUK

Pongsu Church †

Pongsu River Project Monument

Ponghwasan Park

Chang Ju Yung (indoor stadium)

Konsol M

Konguk M

Palgol Bridge

Ryugyong

RAKWON ST

@ Pyongyang Informatics Center

PONGHWA

Kwangbok

Kwangbok Department Store M

PULGUN ST

Pothongang station

Hwanggumbol M

Pothong Bridge

Chilgol Church †

Kan Pang Sok Monument

Chilgol

Comms Cntr

Sosong Bridge

KWANGBOK ST

Hyangmannu

Circus

Sinso Bridge

Unification Church †

Chongnyu Health Complex

CHOLLIMA ST

Chongnyon Youth Hotel

Chongchun No 1

Taekwondo

Swimming pool

Ansan Bridge

Pothonggang

FORBIDD

Chongchun No 2

ANSAN ST

Badminton

HAEBANGSAN

Flower Garden ✿

Combat sports

Weightlifting

Eyonphung BBQ

Athletics

Power plant (coal-fired)

Kim Il Sung Hse

CHONGCHUN ST

Basketball

Table tennis

Sosan

Ansan

Phyonchong ✕

Mangyongdae Children's Palace

Volleyball

Golf range

Handball

Yonggwang M

Puhung M

Pyongyang station

Mangyongdae Funfair No 2

SAEMAUL ST

CHOLLIMA ST

Sosun football stadium ✕

Ryanggang

Pothong

Mangyongdae Revolutionary School

Mangyongdae Funfair No 1

Sinking of the Gen Sherman Monument

Park

Mangyongdae Museum/ Kim Il Sung's Birthplace

Turu Island

USS Pueblo (mooring site)

Yanggak I

Konyu islet

Suk Island

Mullet soup ✕

Chungsong Bridge

Taedong

Thongil Mkt

Pyongyang BBQ Duck ✕

THONGIL ST

Pyongyang Noodle

Hospital ✚

Nampo

Three Charters for National Re-unification Monument (1km) ↓

↓ Kaesong

N

Bradt

0 ————— 2km
0 ————— 2 mile

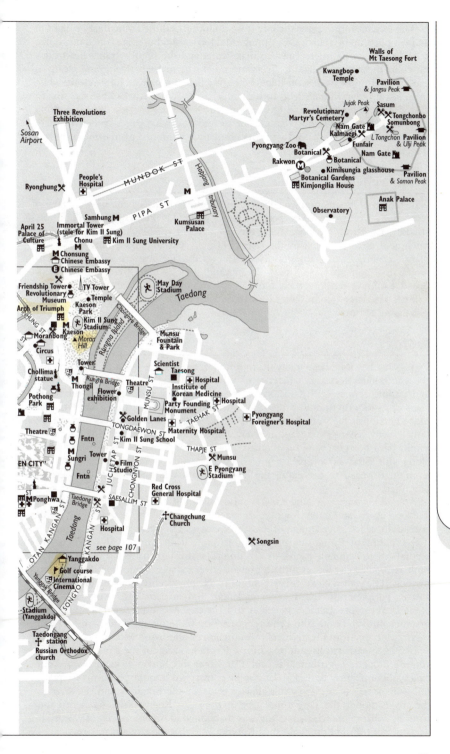

Three Revolutions
Exhibition

Sosan
Airport

Ryonghung ✕

People's
Hospital ✚

MUNDOK ST

Hapjong

PIPA ST

Hapjong tributary

M

M

Kumsusan
Palace

April 25
Palace of
Culture

Samhung M

Immortal Tower
(stele for Kim Il Sung)

Chonu M

Chonsung M
Chinese Embassy

Chinese Embassy E

Kim Il Sung University

Friendship Tower ●
Revolutionary
Museum ✕

TV Tower ●

Temple ●

Kaeson
Park

Arch of Triumph

M

Kaeson
Moranbong M
Moran
Hill

Circus

Kim Il Sung
Stadium

May Day
Stadium

Taedong

Rungna Island

Chongnyu Bridge

Munsu
Fountain
& Park

Scientist
Taesong

Chollima
statue

Tower

M
Thongil
Flower
exhibition

Theatre

Munsu ST

Rungna Bridge

Hospital ✚

Institute of
Korean Medicine

Pothong
Park

Golden Lanes

Party Founding
Monument

Hospital ✚

Pyongyang
Foreigner's Hospital ✚

Theatre

TONGDAEWON ST

Juche Tap

Kim Il Sung School

Maternity Hospital ✚

TAEHAK ST

THAPJE ST

Fntn

Tower

Sungri M

Film
Studio

Film

CHONGNYON ST

Munsu ✕

E Pyongyang
Stadium

"EN CITY"

Fntn

SAESALLIM ST

Red Cross
General Hospital ✚

Ponghwa M

Taedong
Bridge

Hospital ✚

Changchung
Church ✝

Songsin ✕

OTAN KANGAN ST

KANGAN

Taedong

SONGJO

Yanggak Bridge

see page 107

Yanggakdo

Golf course

International
Cinema

Stadium
(Yanggakdo)

Taedonggang
station ✝

Russian Orthodox
church

Walls of
Mt Taesong Fort

Kwangbop ●
Temple

Pavilion
& Jangsu Peak

Revolutionary
Martyr's Cemetery

Jujak Peak

Sasum

Tongchonbo
Somunbong ✕✕

Nam Gate ✕
Kalmaegi ●

L Tongchon
Funfair

Pavilion
& Ulji Peak

Pyongyang Zoo ●

Botanical ✕

Nam Gate ✕

Rakwon

M

Botanical ●

Kimilsungia glasshouse ●

Pavilion
& Somon Peak

Botanical Gardens
Kimjongilia House

Observatory

Anak Palace

The lack of traffic spares the city from pollution and the flying dust brought in and whipped up by vehicles. Incoming rural lorries and buses are hosed down just outside the city perimeters just to make sure, and the regular trams and trolley buses in the city are electric. Everyone mucks in to keep Pyongyang clean, as groups of families are responsible for keeping their immediate locale clean, while brigades of older women tend to the public areas. Water trucks hose the streets. There are very few stalls or vendors and there's little litter because there is nothing to throw away: this is not a consumer society, and what's used gets converted. Watch out for small tools and appliances brilliantly fashioned from drinks cans and the like.

## GEOGRAPHY

'The beauty of its situation well deserves the praises that have been showered upon it by both Korean and European writers,' wrote Dr Philip Jaisohn. The city straddles the River Taedong, where this major waterway (450km long, 20,000km$^2$ catchment area) is joined by the rivers Pothong, Japzang and Sunhwa. The flat plain on which Pyongyang sits is walled in on the northeastern sides by hills, in which coal and gold are mined. Pyongyang, and its manufacturing industries produce mining and construction machinery and products, as well as locomotives, hi-tech electrical goods and IT, textiles and tools, with a burgeoning food processing industry.

## HISTORY

Pyongyang has long been a city of importance, being the second or third city for those interludes in history when it wasn't the capital, and always a vital fortress city and trading centre. DPRK historians are adamant that they've nailed the 5,000 years of history myth onto King Tangun who was in fact a real king and who did indeed establish the walled city of Pyongyang 5,000 years ago. It probably wasn't built exactly where Pyongyang is today, but 500 of an estimated 10,000 dolmen tombs have been excavated around today's city that date back some 5,000 years, along with 150 stone coffins, laden with jewellery and ceramics. There's also much from the Bronze Age, pre-dating the Tangun, with slaves' and slave-owners' graves identified.

A small town grew around 2,000 years ago south of Yanggak Island on the fertile Taedong plains, and under Koguryo a citadel was built on Mt Taesong in 247, with ancestral shrines, government offices and residences in the adjacent Anhak palace. The building of Pyongyang proper soon followed as it moved from Koguryo's second city to being the capital in 427, on order of King Changsu. Pyongyang was built as a walled city that eventually grew to cover today's Central and Phyongchon districts. The walled city consisted of four parts, inner, central, outer and northern, and its perimeter stretched 16km in length and in parts rose over 10m, with crenellated parapets lacing between up to 16 gates. These walls stood in some form or other until the mid-20th century, protecting the miserable streets inside with varying success from the invaders from the north, south and within.

In 598, a sea-borne assault by Chinese forces heading for the city on a punitive venture (not enough tribute was paid from Korea to China) was luckily wiped out by a typhoon. Thirty thousand Tang soldiers marched into the peninsula in spring 661 as their half of the Tang/Silla alliance to defeat the Koguryo, and laid siege to the city. Although the Tang forces gave up the siege, Koguryo was weakened and from its collapse in 668, Pyongyang was abandoned to become a 'city of weeds'. It was not until Wang Kon established Koryo in 918 that the city was reborn.

Wang Kon had Pyongyang reconstructed as a major garrison town to re-establish order in the north, and he contemplated moving the Koryo capital there. The city's administrative and material footprint was reset over the surrounding districts and Pyongyang thrived as second city to Kaesong, both becoming centres of learning from the late 900s with new libraries and academies filled with students from a burgeoning urban population of noble families. But the thriving peace was short-lived. In 1010, the Pyongyang garrison commander General Kang led his troops to Kaesong and deposed the youthful King Mokchong and his nefarious dowager queen mother to install a more suitable monarch. Unfortunately, into the melee from across the Yalu came the Liao, who trashed Pyongyang and burnt Kaesong. This led to the building of a great wall of fortified cities north of Pyongyang by 300,000 men from 1033.

A hundred years later, the threat was from within. In 1135, Pyongyang became the base for the bizarre Myochong rebellion. Led by a prophetic Buddhist monk of that name who attained prominence in the Koryo court, Myochong had been persuading the then king, Injong, to move the court from Kaesong to Pyongyang, arguing that the Chinese Chin needed attacking and that Kaesong lacked 'geomancy', something Pyongyang apparently had in spades. Injong was taken in and a palace and several temples with deities were built in Pyongyang before making it the capital. Then another scholar, advocating peace with the Chin, sat Injong down and carefully explained that Myochong's theories weren't quite aligned with reality. Livid, Myochong set up with his followers a siege state in Pyongyang that took a year to crush.

In 1592, it was in Pyongyang that General Konishi of the Japanese army advancing from the south made fleeting contact with the fleeing Ri court, who over their shoulders exclaimed that they would return. After a final abortive night raid by the city's defenders, Konishi entered a Pyongyang empty of people but full of supplies. The Ri, however, did return that summer, with Chinese and Korean forces encircling Pyongyang, and in February 1593, an army of Buddhist monk soldiers led the city's retaking through the walls breached by heavy artillery. In 1627 and 1637, the invaders came from the north as the Mongols ravaged Pyongyang on punitive raids, but these were the last significant military attacks for nearly 300 years.

The intervening years saw invaders of a different, Christian kind. One 19th-century observer wrote: 'The Koreans of these northern provinces are, in the opinion of the missionaries, far more satisfactory than their southern compatriots. They are more honest and reliable, as well as more enterprising, diligent, and industrious, a view that is borne out by the foreign merchants who have had dealings with them.' And Pyongyang was 'an excellent centre for evangelistic works'.

The city's military significance didn't wane, however, for by the mid-19th century, Pyongyang had around 295,000 households and 175,000 men listed for military duty. It was reserves of such size that the Chinese would call upon decades later in the 1894 Sino–Japanese war, when Chinese armies in and around Pyongyang buttressed the city's forts and walls from Japanese attack. Still, three columns of Japanese troops converged on Pyongyang and routed the Chinese after days of heavy fighting, in which a third of the city was burnt. In *Fifteen Years Among the Top-knots*, Lillias Underwood reported scenes of carnage with one pile of dead troops and horses stretching 'a quarter of a mile long and several yards wide' that lay rotting for weeks, while bodies in the Taedong polluted the city's major water supply. Cholera broke out the following year.

Pyongyang didn't seem to have benefited much from the decades of Japanese rule that soon followed. Most of the schools and hospitals were built and run by

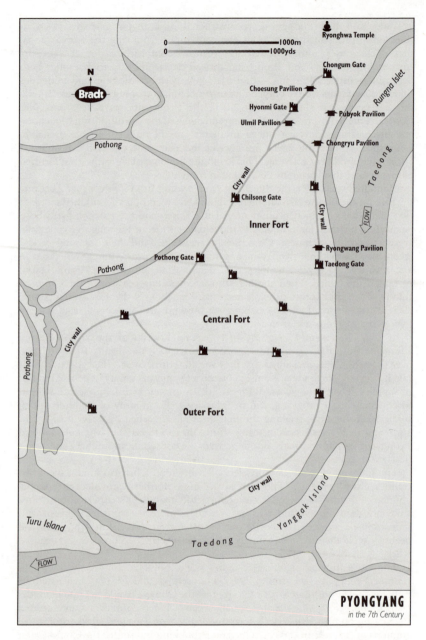

Ryonghwa Temple

Chongum Gate

Choesung Pavilion

Hyonmi Gate

Pubyok Pavilion

Ulmil Pavilion

Chongryu Pavilion

Pothong

City wall

Chilsong Gate

Inner Fort

City wall

Ryongwang Pavilion

Pothong Gate

Taedong Gate

Pothong

Central Fort

City wall

Outer Fort

Pothong

Rungna Islet

Taedong

FLOW

City wall

Turu Island

Yanggak Island

Taedong

FLOW

**PYONGYANG**
*in the 7th Century*

0 ——— 1000m
0 ——— 1000yds

N

Bradt

Protestant missionaries who provided desperately needed relief for the city's poor. In 1939, Jahison wrote that Pyongyang had only one notable thoroughfare that led along the riverbank from Taedong Gate. This was the business district, dominated by Japanese traders, particularly rice and bean merchants exporting to Japan and investment banks charging extortionate rates of interest. Jahison wrote that 'the remaining thoroughfares are extremely narrow and dirty. Most of the houses and shops are more or less dilapidated, while there are no buildings of striking importance.' Mud-plastered thatch-shacks were knotted together by dirt tracks flanked by stinking open sewers running into the river, itself jammed with Chinese junks trading legally and illegally.

Pyongyang was liberated in 1945 by Russian forces and became the capital of the 'temporary' state of North Korea, and some impressive buildings, like the Moranbang Theatre (just!), survive from the few peaceful years preceding the Korean War. During the Korean War, Pyongyang was wrested from both sides' hands during the conflict, while hundreds of thousands of civilians here and elsewhere were killed in American bombing raids that had no palpable effect on the war's outcome: 'Bombing could inflict a catastrophe upon a nation without defeating it' (Max Hastings, *The Korean War*). The *Pyongyang Review* claims that the 428,000 bombs dropped equalled more than one bomb per citizen there. Except for a handful of buildings, the city was truly wiped flat.

**RECONSTRUCTION** The capital of the DRPK had to be rebuilt, quickly, simply. The city was planned around the River Taedong as a 'garden city' with over 200 green spaces, tree-lined roads and riverside walks. Buildings shot up using methods and materials stripped down and honed so that the absolute minimum in skills or resources was needed. Industry and manpower resources, recovering from the war, were faced with a colossal demand for materials and workers, and quantity took priority over quality. You don't have to stand very close to buildings to see that balconies, tiling, vertical and horizontal joints often depart from the plumb-line. Interesting concave and convex patterns appear in prefabricated, hand-finished concrete walls. Window panes have bubbles, bands, fisheye and bottle-glass effects. Spaces exist under doors and their frames.

Still, the buildings of the late 1970s and 1980s are a great qualitative improvement over their predecessors that suffered poor wiring, low water pressure and uneven heating. Heating in many apartment blocks is of the traditional Korean type, under-floor heating (called *ondol*) with hot water provided from the city's thermal power plants. This does cool over a distance and there's no micro-control facility. *Ondol* is the traditional form of heating, with stove-heated air piped under the floor. Stoves are still the major source of heating in modern DPRK flats, such that you can see stovepipes protruding through 18th storey windows. In the taller buildings, unevenly heightened floors and unaligned lift-shafts prevent operational lifts. By day and night, Pyongyang suffers from power shortages, and the low-energy bulbs and fluorescents flicker by day and emit zingy light at night.

But this is to run one's fingers along the mantelpiece of what is ultimately a stunning achievement, and the march of the high-rise stamps onwards. Pyongyang has many traditional single-storey brick and clay huts but are screened from the main thoroughfares by the high-rises out to replace them, so be aware from highpoints and glance through alleys and archways. From the Juche Tower looking east there are many such houses on the fringes of the city, crammed between developments closer in.

Pyongyang is the sister-city to Kathmandu, and was the inspiration for Romania's communist dictator Nicolae Ceauşescu to demolish much of Bucharest and rebuild it as his own civic-sized monument to his glories.

**Design** For the apartment blocks, the homogeneous designs give few architectural clues to indicate a building's age, purpose or occupiers' status, beyond the simple observation that if it's tall and grey it's probably residential, and the taller it is, the newer it is. There are three main types of grand, public buildings. The first is the classically derived grandeurs, all pedestals, pillars and steps like the Moranbang Theatre, or the simplified classicism derived from Soviet-design shops, like

Mansudae Assembly Hall and the Kumsusan Memorial Hall. While the floor space was appreciated, the façades changed from the very late 1960s onwards with the plain Soviet austerity being replaced with the far more ostentatious, traditional Korean-style fronts and sweeping roofs (examples include the Grand People's Study House, Pyongyang International House of Culture, Okryu restaurant). The official architecture was made to reflect the emergence of the DPRK as a power and culture in its own right, cutting its own path in the world, as well as the styles being also technically and commercially affordable to use. Alongside this indigenous design philosophy came arguments advocating how spectacular concrete could be in imaginative hands (Pyongyang International Cinema, Chongryu restaurant, the Ice Rink, Chongchun Street, Ryugyong Hotel, East Pyongyang Grand Theatre, Monument to the Party Founding). The residential developments of Thongil Street, south of Yanggak Islet, and Kwangbok Street in Mangyongdae district, are overwhelming. The May Day Stadium stands alone as a brilliant project in flying steel.

'Let us build our city more beautifully at a faster rate,' the constructors were exhorted. The Pyongyang Maternity Hospital was knocked up in less than nine months before the sixth Party congress in 1980. The Grand People's Study House, 600 rooms over 100,000m², was built in 21 months. Whole streets, like Chollima Street in the 1970s and Pipa and Ragwon streets in the 1980s, were built in months, under the so-called 'Pyongyang Speed'. This was also due to the strictures of the multi-year plans.

**Interiors** The most ostentatious features of any grand building's interior are their vast chandeliers that bear down through floors and stairwells like almighty drill-bits, and paintings of Korean landscapes that cover entire walls. Plastic 'wood' panelling, fake wood, painted metal slats nailed onto the walls, flock wallpaper – all are common features. There are evidently precious few factories producing the fixtures and furnishings. Try and spot the recurring wallpaper and curtain material from the DPRK's own IKEA. Tours focusing on architecture in the DPRK have been run successfully for some time by Koryo Tours in conjunction with the DPRK Architectural University.

## GETTING THERE AND AWAY

By air, you arrive at Sosan airport, a 30-minute drive from the city, and by train at the Pyongyang railway station, two minutes' walk from the Koryo Hotel.

## GETTING AROUND

**METRO** Pyongyang's underground railway, or metro, has two lines running under the main streets on the west side of the Taedong: the Hyokshin Line going under Ragwon and Pipa streets, and the Chollima Line under Podunamu, Kaeson, Sungni and Yonggwang streets. This is important to know as the 17 stations aren't always named by location but by good revolutionary terminology, like Hwanggumbol (Golden Fields), Pulgunbyol (Red Star) and Chonu (Comrade), even though many Pyongyang sites are similarly named. Nor do any available maps show the precise location of the stations and streets, hence those maps available outside of the DPRK are compilations and close estimations.

Aside from being a swift, smooth link across town, the stunning opulence of Pyongyang metro's architecture and the extraordinarily deep stations with their vertigo-inducing escalators are worth a visit in themselves. The Chollima line opened in September 1973, and the metro resembles Moscow's, though some say Pyongyang's is the more beautiful. The escalators take some leisurely minutes to plumb down 200-odd metres, arriving in marble-clad tunnels that bore away from blast doors to blast doors, for the subway doubles as an air-raid shelter for Pyongyang's citizens. The platforms are underground cathedrals to socialism, with their marble pillars, vaults and platform-length murals and mosaics of Korean countryside entitled 'Song of a bumper crop' and 'Builders at the construction of a blast furnace'. The chandeliers are themed by station name, with fireworks at Yonggwang (Glory) and grapes of bumper harvests at Hwanggumbol (Golden Fields). Particularly worthy stations for a look are Puhung, Yonggwang (both of which are firm tour fixtures), Kaeson, Hwanggumbol, Konsol, Konguk and Ragwon. Some of the stations, like Hwanggumbyol, are absolute riots of neon at night (when the power's on). Trains run every five to seven minutes, or every two minutes at peak time, reportedly carting some 300,000 commuters every day. None of this came without a price, however. The Korean National Intelligence Service disclosed in 1999 that during the metro's construction in 1971, over 100 lives were lost when part of an underwater tunnel at Ponghwa station collapsed.

That the stations most often shown to tourists (including Madeleine Albright) are normally Puhung and Yonggwang has given support to a rumour that the metro system has only these two stations, or that these are the only stations 'in operation' with lots of well-dressed actors shuttling like commuters to impress the visitors. The rest of the network definitely exists (the bulk purchase of hundreds of metro cars over the years from Germany and China would make for an absurdly elaborate and expensive hoax, as well as a lot of redundant trains).

Yet there are also rumours of parallel metro lines run exclusively for the top military and government personnel, possibly connecting to a network of underground roads and even a 'square', with an underground line extending all the way out to Sonan airport. The building of underground complexes originated during the heavy bombing of the Korean War and it is highly understandable that the practice would continue, particularly with the US and ROK forces sitting just a rocket's throw away over the DMZ. But the extent and existence of such infrastructure will not be admitted to, let alone added to any tourist itinerary, beyond the metro, no matter how hard you ask.

Plans to link the western ends of the two lines and build a third line crossing the river remain just that.

Cost had been until late 2002 one 10-chon coin (local). It's now 2 won.

For further information try www.pyongyang-metro.com.

## BUSES, TROLLEY-BUSES AND TRAMS

There are extensive trolley-bus and tram connections across the city, but these are usually packed out. Women and children have priority on public transport, with conductors in military-style uniform in control and not to be jostled with if they let you on. Both services are irregular due to power cuts. The trams and most of the trolley-buses are mostly Korean made, now with a few Chinese imports, dodging Russian, Czech and Hungarian petrol buses, and more modern Japanese buses and lorries. For lorries, the situation is a lot of Russian GAZ and KrAZ types, Korean and Chinese copies. On the sides of many vehicles are painted long lines of red stars. Each star shows 50,000km of safe driving, so it appears that some could have cruised safely to the moon and back more than once.

The following are the trolley-bus and bus routes for Pyongyang with roads and landmarks indicated. Where the vehicles go into unmapped outskirts, their general direction is given (eg: north):

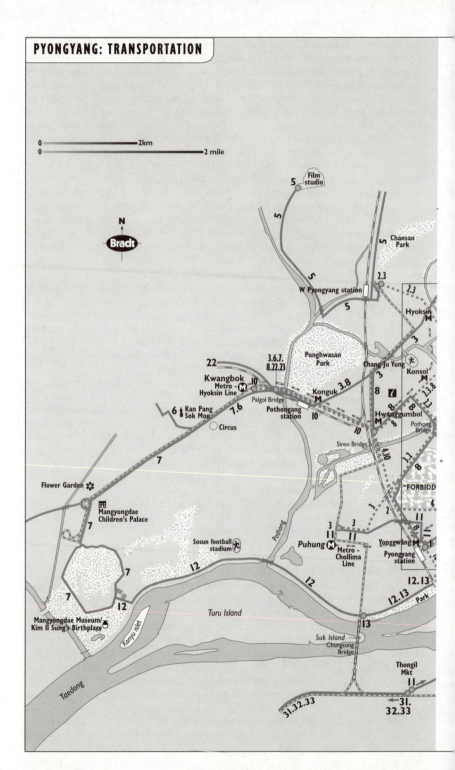

# PYONGYANG: TRANSPORTATION

0 ——————— 2km
0 ——————— 2 mile

**Bradt**

5 Film studio

5

Chansan Park

5 W Pyongyang station

5

2.3

2.3

Hyoksin Ⓜ

3

22

3.6.7. 8.22.23

Ponghwasan Park

Chang Ju Yung

Konsol Ⓜ

2.3.8

Kwangbok Metro - Hyoksin Line

10

3.8

Konguk Ⓜ

8

i

Palgol Bridge

Pothongang station

6 Kan Pang Sok Mon

7.6

Hwanggumbol Ⓜ

8

Pothong Bridge

Circus

10

10

Sinso Bridge

4.10

3.2

7

8

Flower Garden

"FORBIDD

Mangyongdae Children's Palace

3

2

4

7

Pothong

3

3

11

Sosun football stadium

3

11

Yonggwang Ⓜ

12

Puhung Ⓜ Metro - Chollima Line

Pyongyang station

7

12

12

12.13

Mangyongdae Museum/ Kim Il Sung's Birthplace

12

Turu Island

Konyu islet

13

12.13 Park

Suk Island Chungsong Bridge

Thongil Mkt

11

Taedong

31.32.33

31. 32.33

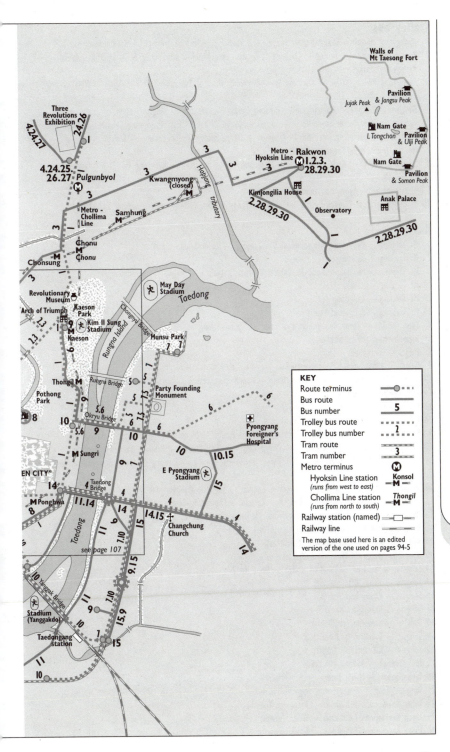

Three Revolutions Exhibition

4.24.26

24.26

4.24.25. 26.27 Pulgunbyol

Ⓜ

3

3

3

Kwangmyong (closed)

Ⓜ

3

3

Metro - Chollima Line

Ⓜ

Samhung

Ⓜ

Chonu

Ⓜ Chonu

Chonsung

Ⓜ

3

3

Hapjang tributary

Metro - Rakwon Hyoksin Line

Ⓜ 1.2.3. 28.29.30

Kimjongilia House

2.28.29.30

Observatory

Walls of Mt Taesong Fort

Jujak Peak ▲

Pavilion & Jangsu Peak

Nam Gate

L Tongchon

Pavilion & Ulji Peak

Nam Gate

Pavilion & Somon Peak

Anak Palace

2.28.29.30

Revolutionary Museum

Arch of Triumph

Kaeson Park

2.3

Kaeson

Ⓜ

Kim Il Sung Stadium

Kaeson

9

Chongnyu Bridge

Rungna Island

May Day Stadium

Taedong

Munsu Park

7

Thongil Ⓜ

Rungna Bridge

5

1

Pothong Park

8

5.6

Okryu Bridge

5.6

9

10

Ⓜ Sungri

9

7

5

1

1

13

6

6

10

Party Founding Monument

Pyongyang Foreigner's Hospital

10

10.15

E Pyongyang Stadium

15

"EN CITY"

14

Taedong Bridge

Ⓜ Ponghwa

8

11.14

14

4

4

15

4

9

14.15 ✝ Changchung Church

14

Taedong

9 7.10

see page 107

9.15

Stadium (Yanggakdo)

Yanggak Bridge

10

11

7.10

9

10

15.9

1

15

Taedongang station

11

10

see page 107

KEY

| | |
|---|---|
| Route terminus | ●━━ ●·· |
| Bus route | ━━━ |
| Bus number | 5 |
| Trolley bus route | ····· |
| Trolley bus number | 1 |
| Tram route | ━╪━╪━ |
| Tram number | 3 |
| Metro terminus | Ⓜ |
| Hyoksin Line station (runs from west to east) | Konsol —Ⓜ— |
| Chollima Line station (runs from north to south) | Thongil —Ⓜ— |
| Railway station (named) | ━◻━ |
| Railway line | ━◻━◻━ |

The map base used here is an edited version of the one used on pages 94-5

## Trolley-bus

1  Pyongyang station – Yonggwang – Sungri – Moranbong – Arch of Triumph – Ryonmotdong
2  Pyongyang station – Sosong – Chollima St – Ryugyong Hotel – Moranbong St – Sangsin – West Pyongyang station
3  Pyongyang Power station – Chollima St – Ryugyong Hotel – Moranbong St – Sangsin – West Pyongyang station
4  Ponghwa – Sosong – Haebangsan – Taedong Bridge – Saesarim – Songsin station
5  Pyongyang Department Store No 1 – Sungri – Okryu Bridge – East Pyongyang Theatre – Munsu
6  Pyongyang Department Store No 1 – Sungri – Okryu Bridge – Tongdaewon – Taehak – Sadong
7  Munsu -Youth St – Rangrang Bridge
8  Friendship Tower – Arch of Triumph – Moranbong St – Ponghwa – Ryogyong Hotel – Pulgun – Kwangbok
9  Ryonmotdong – Ryongsong (north)
10 Kwangbok (Palgol Bridge) Pulgun – Sosong – Yanggak Islet – Rangrang – Taedonggang station

## Bus

1  Mt Taesong – Pyongyang Astronomical Observatory – Mirim Bridge (east)
2  Mt Taesong – Samsin (east)
3  Mt Taesong – Mundok – April 25 Palace – Pipa – Hyoksin – Ragwon – Kwangbok
28 Mt Taesong – Samsok (east)
29 Mt Taesong – Kangdong (east)
30 Mt Taesong – Pongwhari (east)
4  Sopo (north) – Three Revolutions Exhibition – Ryonmotdong
5  Sopo (north) – Film Studio
6  Palgol – Kwangbok – Chilgol
7  Palgol – Kwangbok – Mangyongdae
8  Palgol – Pulgun – Ragwon – Kyonghung – Ponghwa – Pothong Gate – Chollima – Pyongyang Station – Yongwang – Dept No 2
22 Palgol – Wollori (west)
23 Palgol – Kwangbok – Taepyong (west)
9  Friendship Tower – Moranbong – Sungri – Okryu Bridge – Juche Tower – Pangjik – Sanopdong
10 Pyongyang Department Store No 1 – Okryu Bridge – Tongdaewon – Tapje – Taedonggangdong
11 Pyongyang Thermal Power Complex – Koryo Hotel – Yongwang – Taedong Bridge – Songyo Kangan – Chongbaek
12 Pyongyang Station – Yokjon – Pyongchon Kangan – Angol – Mangyongdae
13 Pyongyang Station – Yokjon – Pyongchon Kangan – Chongsung Bridge
15 Rangrang Bridge – Saesarim – Kim Hyong Jik University – Tapje – Taedonggangdong
16 Rangrang Bridge – Pottery Factory (southeast)
34 Rangrang Bridge – Taehyondong (southeast)
35 Rangrang Bridge – Ryokpo (southeast)
14 Songsin – Saesarim – Taedong Bridge – Dept No 2
17 Songsin – Mirim Bridge (east)
18 Songsin – Changchon (south)
37 Songsin – Ripsok (southeast)
38 Songsin – Sangwon (southeast)
39 Songsin – Tokdong (southeast)
40 Songsin – Rihyonri (southeast)
19 Tapje/Taehak – Sadong (south)
20 Tapje/Taehak – Mirim Bridge
21 Sangdangdong – Hyongsanri
24 Three Revolutions Exhibition – Tongbukri (north)
25 Three Revolutions Exhibition – Sunan (north)
26 Three Revolutions Exhibition – Sinmiri (north)

27 Three Revolutions Exhibition — Kanri (north)
31 Chongbaek — Thongil — Wonam (south)
32 Chongbaek — Thongil — Pyokjidori (south)
33 Chongbaek — Thongil — Kangnam (south)

**TAXIS** Taxis are usually 1970s Volvo and 1980s Mercedes saloons (with 'Taxi' on the roofs), ostensibly charging €0.50 per kilometre, also payable in US dollars or Chinese RMB. They don't ply the streets for trade but loiter around the big hotels and Pyongyang railway station, and can be reluctant to go. Tourists will need their guides with them if they want to take a taxi. Phone or get the hotel to call these taxi-centre numbers: ⟍ 33428, ⟍ 45615 or ⟍ 42007. However, round here every Sunday is a 'walking day' – so spare some fuel and see more, and be seen, by walking as much as possible.

**OTHER CARS** Other cars include early Russian Moskvichs and Volgas. More and more newish Japanese saloons and 4x4s are appearing, many being right-hand drive (hence not strictly for export from Japan). The absence of a second-hand car market in Japan means these 'old' Japanese cars are ferried out from Niigata to Wonsan and Rajin/Chongjin.

Also look out for the public announcement vehicles, mini-vans with four massive tannoys on the roof, reminding locals of the orders of the day. Otherwise, Pyongyang's wide boulevards remain blissfully clear; 'Pyongyang is exceptional in that the journey times from one part of town to another are the same at any hour, now as ten years ago,' commented one businessman. Cars are almost exclusively for 'public' use of some kind. If the very few who could afford a car can actually get one, there's the tight supply of petrol to consider, causing drivers of all vehicles to flick into neutral gear as they coast downhill. Spare a thought for the ingenuity and effort needed to keep the older vehicles roadworthy, after millions of kilometres of driving. Parts supplies are irregular (if available at all, considering the age of some). You might see many sitting by the roadside on jacks and/or with the bonnet up, or rolling round on three incorrectly sized tyres.

**BICYCLES** There are few bicycles about (they have registration plates), and no hotels as yet hire them out. One firm, Wanshida, is known to import bicycles from China. Women on bicycles is still a mind-bending concept, so Korean women in Pyongyang are reportedly restricted to riding tricycles.

Most people just walk, and they do not jaywalk! Use the underpass or the arm of the traffic police will befall you. Public transport beyond the city's immediate limits doesn't exist. You can maybe catch a foreigner's Land Cruiser, if you've the permits to get somewhere.

## WHERE TO STAY

You don't have to stay in the top-class hotels, and indeed the DPRK media are always pointing out that the top hotels are already full with visitors, but you will be given the hard sell. Note that none of them, even the high-class ones, have heating in the public areas in winter.

In every instance you can first dial (adding 00850 2 if outside the country) 18111 which puts you through to the operator and you can then either give an extension number of the hotel or the name of hotel. But for international calls many of the hotels also have direct international numbers (or faxes), that run 00850 2 381 xxxx.

## DELUXE HOTELS $$$$

These hotels have guaranteed hot water and electricity. Both the Yanggakdo and Koryo hotels, because they are so tall, make a differential of up to €10 per room cost depending on whether your room is towards the top or bottom of the building.

🏠 **Pyongyang Koryo Hotel** (500 rooms) Changgwang St; ☎ 02 381 4397; f 02 381 4422. Opened in 1985. A little bit south of the city centre & near Pyongyang railway station. 45 floors in twin towers & many restaurants, with 2 that revolve. The hotel's twin towers are a Pyongyang landmark, with comfortable rooms plus bars, pool, billiards & a bookshop amongst other features.

🏠 **Yanggakdo Hotel** ☎ 02 381 2134 f 02 381 2930/1. Opened in 1995, this 47-storey glass prism sits on Yanggak Island in the Taedong River, 4km southeast of the city centre. The hotel is second only to the Koryo in the whole country, & has numerous restaurants & amusements, including bowling, an adjacent putting course, the International Friendship Cinema & a football stadium that makes Yanggak Island an Alcatraz of fun. The Yanggakdo also now has BBC TV in its rooms. Its 'health centre' is run by Chinese from Dandong who offer massage services for around €15 & has an excellent sauna.

## FIRST-CLASS HOTELS $$$

The five-digit phone numbers can be used internationally by first dialing (+850) 18111 then the number, hence they can be used from outside or inside the DPRK.

🏠 **Chongnyon Hotel** (520 rooms) Chukjondong, Mangyongdae District. Cnr of Kwangbok & Chongchun Sts; ☎ +850 2 381 6210; f +850 2 381 3681 Triangular design.

🏠 **Pothonggang Hotel** (162 rooms) Ansangdong, Pyongchon District; ☎ 48301; ☎ +850 2 381 2228/9; f +850 2 381 4428. About 4km west of Kim Il Sung Sq, at the Pothong riverside. Good hotel. CNN shown in its rooms.

🏠 **Ryanggang Hotel** (330 rooms) Chongchun St, Mangyongdae District; ☎ 73825. In the west of the city, where the Taedong & Pothong rivers meet. The hotel has a revolving restaurant.

🏠 **Sosan Hotel** (474 rooms) Chongchun St; ☎ +850 2 381 6212; f +850 2 381 3601. Opened in 1989. At Kwangbok St in the west, 4km from the city centre, this is a big hotel with 30 floors.

KITC has listed on its first-class list the **Angol Hotel** and **Tourist Hotel** (☎ 381 6216), the Angol being 7km southwest from the centre and the Tourist the same distance, but any more information such as number of rooms and indeed precise location has not been forthcoming.

## SECOND-CLASS HOTELS $$

🏠 **Changgwangsan Hotel** (420 rooms) Chollima St, Tongsong-dong, Central District; ☎ 48366. 3km west of the centre, at the Pothong River. Changgwangsan Hotel was previously closed to tourists but since renovation in 2006 is now open to foreigners, although it is somewhat airy & austere.

🏠 **Moranbong Hotel** Moranbong St. The number of rooms and phone number are unavailable but a single there has cost €65.

🏠 **Pyongyang Hotel** (170 rooms) Sungi St, Kyongrim-dong, Central District; ☎ 38161; f 02 381 4426. Opened in 1961 on the west bank of Taedong River & opposite Pyongyang Grand Theatre.

🏠 **Taedonggang Hotel** ☎ +850 1 18111 gets you the operator. Ask for Taedonggang Hotel – when it's rebuilt.

## THIRD-CLASS HOTELS $

🏠 **Haebangsan Hotel** (83 rooms) Sungni St, Haebangsandong, Central District; ☎ 37037; ☎ +850 2 381 6214; f +850 2 381 3569. South of the square, near Taedong Bridge, & the only 3rd-class hotel where foreigners can stay, mostly foreign students. Rooms are clean but not luxurious. Bathrooms with hot water. Weird sentinel tower on one corner.

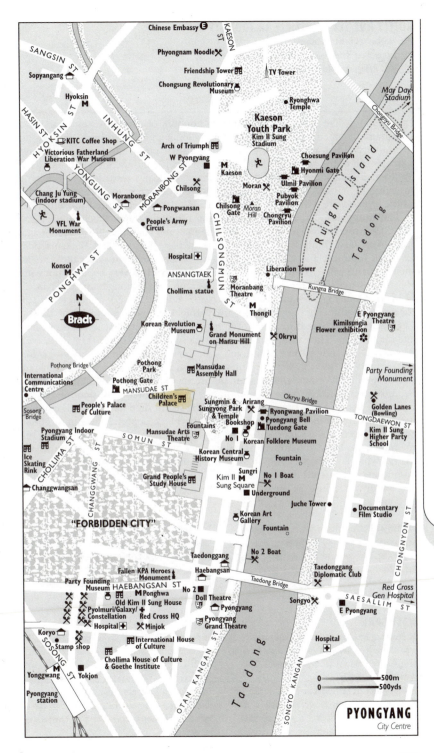

Chinese Embassy ⓔ

KAESON ST

Phyongnam Noodle ✕

SANGSIN ST

Friendship Tower 🏛 TV Tower ⛴

Chongsung Revolutionary Museum 🏛

Sopyangang 🏛

HASIN ST

Hyoksin 🚇

HYOKSIN ST

INHUNG ST

Ryonghwa Temple

Kaeson Youth Park

May Day Stadium

Kim Il Sung Stadium

KITC Coffee Shop

Victorious Fatherland Liberation War Museum

Arch of Triumph 🏛

W Pyongyang 🏛

YONGUNG ST

MORANBONG ST

Chilsong

Choesung Pavilion

Hyonmi Gate

Ulmil Pavilion

Ryongna Island

Chang Ju Yung (indoor stadium)

Moranbong

Pongwansan

Kaeson 🚇

Moran 🚇

Pubyong Pavilion

Chongryu Pavilion

Taedong

VFL War Monument

People's Army Circus

Chilsong Gate

Moran Hill

PONGHWA ST

CHILSONGMUN ST

Konsol

Hospital ✚

Liberation Tower

Rungna Bridge

N

Bradt

ANSANGTAEK

Chollima statue

Moranbang Theatre

Thongil 🚇

Kimilsungia Flower exhibition

E Pyongyang Theatre

Korean Revolution Museum 🏛

Grand Monument on Mansu Hill

✕ Okryu

Pothong Bridge

Pothong Park

Pothong Gate

Mansudae Assembly Hall 🏛

Okryu Bridge

Party Founding Monument

International Communications Centre

Sosong Bridge

MANSUDAE ST

Children's Palace

People's Palace of Culture 🏛

Sungmin & Sungyong Park & Temple

Arirang

Ryongwang Pavilion

Pyongyang Bell

Tuedong Gate

Golden Lanes (Bowling)

TONGDAEWON ST

Kim Il Sung Higher Party School

Pyongyang Indoor Stadium

SOMUN ST

Mansudae Arts Theatre

Fountains

Bookshop

No 1 🏛

Korean Folklore Museum

Fountain

CHOLLIMA ST

CHANGGWANG ST

Ice Skating Rink

Korean Central History Museum 🏛

Sungri

Kim Il Sung Square

No 1 Boat

Changgwangsan 🏛

Grand People's Study House 🏛

Underground

Juche Tower

Documentary Film Studio

"FORBIDDEN CITY"

Korean Art Gallery

Fountain

CHONGNYON ST

Taedonggang

No 2 Boat

Taedonggang Diplomatic Club

Red Cross Gen Hospital

Fallen KPA Heroes Monument

Haebangsan

Taedong Bridge

SAESALLIM ST

Party Founding Museum

HAEBANGSAN ST

No 2 🏛

Ponghwa 🚇

Songyo

E Pyongyang

Old Kim Il Sung House

Pyolmuri/Galaxy/ Constellation

Doll Theatre

Pyongyang

Red Cross HQ

Minjok

Pyongyang Grand Theatre

Hospital ✚

Koryo

OTAN KANGAN ST

Stamp shop

International House of Culture

Hospital ✚

SOSONG ST

Yonggwang 🚇

Yokjon

Chollima House of Culture & Goethe Institute

Pyongyang station

Taedong

SONGYO KANGAN

0 ———— 500m
0 ———— 500yds

PYONGYANG
City Centre

## HOTELS NOT YET ACCESSIBLE TO TOURISTS
⌂ **Ponghwasan Hotel** Moranbong St
⌂ **Sopyongyang Hotel** Opposite Hyoksin metro station
⌂ **West Pyongyang Hotel** Pipa St

# ✂ WHERE TO EAT

Pyongyang is far removed from being London or Bangkok, but bars and restaurants are opening all the time and it is a long, long way from the Pyongyang of not-very-old-at-all, and some offer free dishes, group discounts and loyalty schemes. All of the hotels have their own restaurants, and the top-class ones have quite a few each (some revolve!) but an interesting and ever-expanding selection of restaurants is sprinkled across Pyongyang. In general, expect to pay around €3 for a plate of kimchi, €8 for pre-barbecue beef and €10 for bean-curd soup with rice.

The **Yanggakdo** has a gamut of restaurants round the stairwell behind the foyer bar. Of the two Korean restaurants, **No 1** is small and enclosed, **No 2** is airier and has a river view. Both serve a compromise of basic Western and Korean foods. Enclosed **Japanese** and **Chinese** restaurants sit opposite them across the stairs to the basement, where is the **Macau Chinese restaurant**, a very popular spot with expats – although Koreans are not allowed in – with long opening hours and a menu to match (✆ *02 381 2134 ext 10808;* f *ext 10807;* ⊕*08.30–03.30*); around €12 each for a party of four. The Yanggakdo's warm revolving venue serves its last at 22.00.

**Changgwang Street** has two dozen restaurants and bars that accept foreigners and their money. They all advertise as being open from 12.00 to 15.00 and 18.00 to 21.30, but may not be in practice and some open only for large bookings, for works' units on reward whom you may see queuing outside with their vouchers.

But several more accessible restaurants are there for wining and dining along, behind and around Changgwang and the Koryo. The Koryo's 3rd floor restaurant can, given notice, rustle up shepherd's pie. The stamp shop next to the Koryo has its own restaurant. Several are tucked into the block opposite the Koryo Hotel entrance. Across the Changgwang from the Koryo, heading for the side street on the right, and about 80m down on the left is a gated courtyard. On the immediate left is a white conservatory entrance to a multi-floored **Korean BBQ** (\$\$\$\$) and a **Japanese restaurant**. On the far side of the yard is another Korean venue with karaoke upstairs. Both are open until 23.00.

Look out for:

✂ **Mingjok Siktang** (also known as the National) Next to the Red Cross HQ & Pyongyang University of Medicine, over the road from the Koryo Hotel. Has a fun floorshow most evenings & great ambience. \$\$\$\$

### WEST BANK
✂ **Pyongyang No 1 Boat Restaurant** Usually moors opposite the Juche Tower on the west bank. Excellent BBQs. Can be hired out for events & cruises lazily along the river. \$\$\$
✂ **Pyongyang Boat Restaurant No 2** Smaller than the No 1, this usually moors about 200m south of the No 1, with pink net curtains & a welcoming smile. Serves black beer. \$\$\$

✂ **The Pyolmuri** (aka the Galaxy or Constellation) Changgwang St, 100m northwest of the entrance to the Koryo Hotel. A first in many respects, being the first place to offer pizza, pasta & hamburgers, & it has a good cocktail bar. The Dear Leader has eaten here. \$\$–\$\$\$

✂ **Arirang** 150m south of Okryu Bridge. There's an English menu here with an ostrich BBQ, beer & salad. \$\$\$
✂ **Okryu** Sits in full hip-saddle roofed swing on the Taedong's west bank. Large halls, high turnover of clientele, great in summer for cold noodles on the veranda overlooking the river, but a bit cavernous in winter. \$\$

## AROUND THE CENTRE AND NORTH

**✗ Changgwang Health Complex** Next to the ice rink, has two restaurants, but the one on the terrace is only open in the summer. Both serve the higher end (& higher priced) of Korean fare. $$$$ The nearby ice rink has a restaurant and there is also reputedly a Japanese venue behind the rink.

**✗ Eyonphung BBQ Restaurant** Just off a side road from Photong Bridge. €20 per head including beer & soju – does a good BBQ. $$$$

**✗ Mokran** (Magnolia) Japanese-based Western restaurant in the Pothonghang Hotel, with excellent service & fine wine. $$$$ In this hotel is a standard Korean restaurant that has recently had a makeover.

**✗ Pyongyang Informatics Centre** In the shadow of the uncompleted Ryugyong Hotel. Has a good, if expensive, Korean BBQ restaurant. $$$$ There is also a 2nd-floor restaurant here that serves American-style pancakes. $$

**✗ Moranbang Hotel** Has been revamped & has opened a Japanese-Korean terrace bar; lovely in the evenings. $$$

**✗ Phyongchon Restaurant** Just south of the bend in Chollima St, take the road running east; halfway along is this restaurant. $$$

**✗ The Lotus Restaurant** Noted for its beautiful waitresses who will sing (& graciously be tipped for doing so) ... if you can find it. $$$

**✗ KITC** Has opened its own little coffee shop opposite the Fatherland Liberation war museum. $$

**✗ Moran** In the middle of Moranbang Park. Korean food. $$

**✗ Phyongnam Noodle Restaurant** Kaesong St, opposite the friendship tower. $$

**NORTHEAST** The Pyongyang Botanical Gardens has a Korean place next to its entrance, excellent in summer, open only during the day. To the south side of Jujak Peak on Mt Taesong are four restaurants, named **Kalmaegi**, **Somunbong**, **Tongchonbo** and **Sasum**, but nothing is known.

## EAST

**✗ (Old) Taedonggang Diplomatic Club**. Through its corridors are a few restaurants, including one '70s décor place with a dance floor. Simple servings of soups & salads for up to €12 per person. Open for lunch & until 21.30, & the disco's open until 23.00 on Fri/Sat. $$$–$$$$

**✗ Gold Lane Bowling Alley** 2 restaurants serve draft beer. The stews here are well known. $$$

**✗ Songyo** Opposite the Taedonggang Diplomatic Club. A Korean restaurant. $$$

**✗ Taedongyogwan** Cross Okryu Bridge eastwards, follow Monsudong St straight through a 3-pronged fork, & on the right appears this drum-shaped Korean restaurant. $$

**✗ New Diplomatic Club** In the Munsudong District, in the same compound as the Diplomatic Shop. Serves an eclectic mix of Chinese, Korean, Japanese & Western food. It also has a karaoke bar, but is invitation only.

**✗** There are also the **Munsu** and **Songsin** restaurants to find out everything about!

## SOUTH

**✗ Pyongyang BBQ Duck** On the northwest corner of Thongil St & Chungsong Bridge junction. Excellent food, good service, & popular with the locals. Open until 21.30. $$$–$$$$

**✗ Dangogo Gukjib** Tongil St. Dog meat is the speciality here. $$$$

**✗ Chongnyu Restaurant** Sits on the Pothong riverbank before Sinso Bridge; ☏ 48257. This 4-storey building shaped like a ship serves the usual Korean fare, including sinsollo, with rooms dedicated to particular dishes. $$$

**✗ Pyongyang Mullet Soup Restaurant** On the Taedong's south bank between Chungsong & Yanggak bridges. Fiddly to get to. $$

**✗ Pyongyang Noodle House** Diagonally opposite from the Pyongyang BBQ Duck. Specialises in Pyongyang noodles.

## WEST

**✗ Chilgol Restaurant** Opposite the circus on Kwangbok St.

**✗ Chongchun Restaurant** Kwangbok St, near the Tangsang flyover. A good place to mix it with the working classes. $$$

**✗ Chongchun No 2** Kwangbok St, near the Tangsang flyover.

**✗ Hyangmannu** Kwangbok St, near Tangsang flyover

**✗ West Pyongyang** At the Taedonggang beer factory. Built with bricks from the west of England, this good restaurant now produces 4 types of draught beer & lager (including black beer) that compete with the longer-set home brews of Pyongyang & Ryongsong beer. $$$

## NIGHTLIFE

For nightlife, there's not that much to do. The city was once famed for the wits and other delights of its 'kisaeng girls', akin to the geishas of Japan, but these days they're rather thin on the ground. Most of the hotels now have some form of karaoke, which open until your larynx is frazzled. There's an interesting Egyptian-themed nightclub in the Yangakkdo Hotel basement that's open till the small hours, next to the DPRK's first casino (staffed only by Chinese, ⏰ 14.00–05.00). Atop one of the Changgwangsan hotel's towers is Pyongyang's first disco, still going strong, for foreigners only. During the summer months, and/or when a large show or festival is on, numerous beer tents open around Pyongyang (particularly around the Koryo and to a lesser extent the Yangakkdo) selling drinks and sometimes heated snack foods until the small hours. These two hotels have white-boothed bars selling good, opaque, brown draught beer till midnight, and all the hotels at least have bars doing what bars do in the wee hours.

The Taedonggang Diplomatic Club has a disco until 23.00 on Fridays and Saturdays. The foreign residents by and large congregate at the Random Access Club. But in true Pyongyang style, revealing its location requires an invitation.

But the quietness of Pyongyang at night is another unique attribute; no capital anywhere is as silent or dark. One guest at the island hotel of Yanggakdo leaned out of his top-floor window and heard a baby crying, which he realised was coming from an apartment across the river. If it's a special time of year, or a state visit is on, the main sites are illuminated. If not, tiptoeing through the streets at night in the pitch black is one way to go round town without getting any kind of attention. Sometimes you only know someone's there as you hear voices suddenly going past you. Around Pyongyang railway station is wonderful at night; it's full of waiting travellers, smoking, chatting, playing cards and sleeping, maybe one playing a flute for haunting tunes to waft through the streets.

## OTHER PRACTICALITIES

**SHOPPING** Beijing and some other Chinese cities have vast aircraft-hangar-like covered markets, and Pyongyang now has one, Thongil market, just off Thongil Street. There are scores of stalls and cubicles selling everything from watches and radios to curtains and shirts while another hall has foodstuffs, including exotica like quail and turkey, squelching and spilling all over the shop. Otherwise your ability to buy things is limited to the large department stores, hotel shops and a few other outlets.

**PUBLICATIONS** *Korea* (monthly) and the *Pyongyang Times* (weekly) are multi-lingual publications available from the hotel shops. Much of the available literature in the DPRK concerns the lives and works of the Kims, or foreign affairs reviews like 'The US Imperialists started the war'. Otherwise there are glossy books on Korea's wildlife, and that's it. There is one foreign-language bookshop (⏰ 09.00–18.00, *except Sun & Thu afternoon*) opposite the Pyongyang No 1 store on the same block as the Korean Culture Museum.

**POST OFFICE** The main post office is in the centre, just southwest of Taedong Bridge. The International Post Office is in Haebangsan Street. The International

Communications Centre is in Pothonggang District, opposite the Pyongyang Indoor Stadium.

**CHANGING MONEY** You can change money in the big hotels, some restaurants and at the Trade Bank on Sungni Street, near Kim Il Sung Square. Foreign currencies should be changed in the DPRK to 'the money exchangeable for foreign currency'.

**HOSPITALS AND PHARMACIES** A doctor and a nurse are meant to be permanently based at both the Yanggakdo and Koryo hotels. In the compound of the British Embassy is a UN medical centre that can be accessed in emergencies (✆ *381 7585/ 382 7568*). Note that the following telephone numbers are subject to change:

✚ **Red Cross General Hospital of Korea** East Pyongyang; ✆ 28291, 621 1110
✚ **Pyongyang Friendship Hospital** ✆ 621 6145 (operator)
✚ **Pyongyang First Aid Hospital** ✆ 22758
✚ **Pyongyang Foreigners' Hospital** ✆ 22160
✚ **Kim Man Yu Hospital** East Pyongyang; ✆ 28136, 621 3111

✚ **Pyongyang Maternity Hospital** East Pyongyang; ✆ 621 1125
✚ **Mannyon Traditional General Pharmacy** 1 Ongnyudong, Taedonggang
✚ **Mannyon Pharmacy** 3 Ongnyudong, Taedonggang
✚ **Mannyon Health General Company** 3 Ongnyudong, Taedonggang; ✆ 23048, 31225, 22891

## WHAT TO SEE

Guides and DPRK guidebooks give a lot of statistics: dates of construction, speed of construction, floor space, and the number of tiles, bricks or measurements that have symbolism for the cult of the Kims. The anodyne statistics are also proof of progress. Communist states in the heady decades of success from the 1950s to the 1980s were fiercely competitive among themselves in terms of output and progress, and the proof of a more advanced, more capable workforce was that they could knock up the biggest library in the world in the shortest time.

These statistics also make up for the dearth of other facts. It's quickly apparent that there are far fewer urban anecdotes than those you'd find in London, eg: 'This area used to be a red-light district, and that hotel used to be a brothel and Dickens was once caught there'. The issue is less that of a Year Zero whereupon the communist expunged all the history of the corrupt and wicked past, but Ground Zero, for by 1953 Pyongyang had been levelled by war. Nearly every building, including the 'ancient' ones, were built or reconstructed post-war, and the grander buildings are from the late 1960s and 1970s when the economy could afford more grandeur. In that sense, what you see is what you get. An apartment block is and has always been that, and the purpose for which a government edifice was put up is the purpose for which that building is used today. You might also disagree over what DPRK literature considers to be 'highlights', as the following from the *Pyongyang Review* suggests:

> The Three Revolution Exhibition is a centre for recreation for working people, and for scientific research. It is made up of pavilions, recreation, management, entrance, car park and lawn area, which constitute an ensemble.

**KIM IL SUNG SQUARE** This huge open plaza of 75,000m² of granite, set out in 1954, is seen as the heart of the city, through which the great military and torch parades and mass rallies pass. The other great plazas in front of the cultural palaces around the city are where the local folks swirl and twirl in mass dances on many of the country's national holidays, which are great times to visit. Tourists have not usually

3

been allowed to attend the more formal elements of these kinds of celebrations, such as the torch parades, although it is not unknown, and if you're not in town during such an event, you might perchance be around when the practices for rallies are being held. One visitor to North Korea told me:

> I was in the city one spring, walking back through town quite late, having had a few beers, and happened to see that, for once, the lights were on in Kim Il Sung Square, albeit very dimly. This was rare enough to warrant a look-see and, in a spy-like manner, I peered around the last wall to look out onto the square. What I saw was the entire square with what must have been thousands of people, in lines, in identical positions as they went through some kind of Tai-chi like set of poses. The thing was the only noise was the completely in sync swoosh and shuffle of moving arms and legs, and the breathing, thousands of people all breathing in and out in time. It was eerie, but incredible.

It is as good a place as any to start a tour and will possibly be the first place that you visit. The square is hemmed in by the **Grand People's Study House** to the west and affords a grand vista of the **Juche Tower** east over the river. The simple classical grandeur of the **Korean Central History Museum** (northeast side) and opposite, the **Korean Art Gallery** battle with the Korean-style Study House, while huge placards of the country's flags and weapons add vibrant colour to an austere place.

The Study House truly dominates the square. 'Its architectural ornaments are of light and quiet colours, which contribute to its magnificent yet refreshing appearance. In architecture, it demonstrates the elegance and majesty of the traditional Korean-style building.' The 34 hip-saddle roofs, capped with 750,000 green tiles, rise one above another like unfolded wings of cranes. Built for Kim Il Sung's 70th birthday in 1982, it is the facility that hosts the 'Study-While-Working' educational system for cadres and working people, and can accommodate 12,000 users a day. A huge white statue of the Great Leader sits in the marble-pillared entrance, flanked not by grand stairways but by two modern escalators. Enter the KIS reading room with its half computerised directory, half carded index, and you'll see the music library with the foreign music section – where Koreans can listen to foreign popular music such as Vera Lynn's greatest hits right up to the most modern – The Beatles. Maybe you'll see a language class in action (Repeat after me!) and big reading rooms full of dull, flickering lights to strain the eyes of the library's visitors poring over its 30,000,000 volumes, deliverable on a remote-controlled conveyor. Certainly the lifts are in tremendous demand on Saturdays, and seem to work in a way where 'catch a lift' is appropriate, as they zoom past floors where people are waiting to board. The upper balcony is also used to coordinate the march-pasts and evening torch parades, and you can look out onto the mature metal roofs of the surrounding buildings.

On the east half of the square is the **Korean Central History Museum** (Tuesday to Sunday), a long, detailed tour of the peninsula's history, a lot of which is invasions, resistance and repulsions, feuds and wars between provinces, kingdoms and surrounding countries. It's a complicated tale that's difficult to tell coherently, and the museum could assist visitors' concentration by adjusting the museum's lighting and ventilation. Look out for the world's first rocket batteries and the classic black ball and fuse of the world's first time-bomb.

The **Korean Art Gallery** is well worth a visit. From its excellent reproductions of early Korean tomb paintings, it follows with large (roll mat) screen paintings illustrating court and common life in Korea across time. The guides provide an excellent interpretation of the paintings, from the decadence of feudal Korea up to the real meanings of seemingly innocuous paintings under Japanese rule. The big, bright, socialist-realism paintings on the upper floors are fascinating, especially the 'Sailing Steel Works' that challenges Western notions of what constitutes beauty.

**THE REST OF THE CITY** Now, leave the square by going north along Sungri Street (that splits the square in two), and a block later on the crossroads with Somun Street you'll find the **Pyongyang Department Store No 1**.

> None of the lights were on in the shop when I went there, so only daylight glinting off the polished floor permeated the shop's centre. This meant I could get quite close to the tills (for practically all goods are behind counters) before the shop assistants would see me and wander off.
>
> Robin Tudge

Opposite the No 1 is the **Foreign Languages Bookshop** (⏰*09.00–18.00 Mon–Sat, closed Thu pm*). It's a good place to buy books, pictures, embroideries and other souvenirs as well as maps and occasionally fantastic hand-painted posters. On the corner and riverwards along Somun Street is the **Korean Folklore Museum**. This is a much more manageable three-floor exhibition of the daily lives of Koreans, and the English-speaking guide gives a good account of what work and fun entailed for Korean men, women and children in times gone by.

On the No 1's west side, and accessible via a huge staircase leading down from the Grand Study House, are the hard-to-miss **Mansudae fountains** (firing up to 80m high) providing cooling mists in summer and pools for locals to play in. The fountains front the massive **Mansudae Arts Theatre**, with its spectrum-coloured tower, and in which dance and music performances can be seen by arrangement. In good contrast with the theatre's monolithic simplicity are the more humanly scaled **Sungmin** and **Sungnyong** temples, dating from 1325 and 1429 respectively. The latter was built as a shrine to Tangun and to the founder of Koguryo, Tongmyong. Continuing uphill and northwards to Mansu Hill, a good view of the city to the west becomes visible. Soon, on the left appears the monolithic DPRK building of the **Mansudae Assembly Hall**, with a huge carved national emblem on its façade, surrounded by acres of empty car parks. The Hall, built in the 1960s and revamped in the 1980s, is where the DPRK parliament assembles and votes, and visiting the Hall is really worthwhile but is only possible by arrangement, ie: when it's not in use. Hallways hundreds of metres in length lined with statues of good workers (not aged lords and nobles as in the West) and wall-length paintings beam away from stairwells with chandeliers cascading through them. The main assembly hall is cavernous, with an awesome glazed ceiling and an 18m statue of Kim Il Sung reminding any delegate who had (or has) forgotten quite who is in charge.. Observe the detail of the décor and count the number and location of microphones. Guides take you through the numerous private committee rooms and lounges, with boat-sized oval tables bedecked with towering flower arrangements, these structures sailing on lake-sized deep plush carpets, rooms which would normally be filled with the DPRK's great and the good and all the smoke that goes with top-level decision-taking.

From the Hall, the road tips down then up Mansu Hill towards the **Korean Revolutionary Museum** and what must be Pyongyang's most famous site, the **Grand Monument**. Here is the towering 20m bronze figure of Kim Il Sung, arm out pointing the way forward in front of a 70m-wide mosaic of Korea's spiritual source, Mt Paektu. Flanking the Great Leader are the DPRK and KWP flags carved from stone and lined with 228 bronze figures (5m high) symbolising the anti-Japanese struggle, socialist revolution and construction.

The Korean People erected the monument from their unanimous desire and aspiration to have the immortal revolutionary exploits of the great leader Comrade Kim Il Sung; remembered for all time and to carry forward and consummate the revolutionary cause of Juche which he initiated.

Slogans on the monuments' placards read 'Long Live Kim Il Sung' and 'Let us drive out US imperialism and reunify the country'. A six-figure group on the left banner of the statue plot the overthrow of US imperialism, all imperialism, and the world revolution. The monument and the museum were built for Kim's 60th birthday, and the museum has over 4.5km of display halls of varying interest. Since his death in July 1994, it has become the focus for mourning. The statue in its dazzling glory stands atop a massive plaza, with music softly wafting from the nearby trees. It is an extraordinary, powerful place, and is one of the, if not *the*, most sacred sites in the DPRK. It is as good as an obligatory stopping point for any visitor, from whom the utmost decorum is requested and required (and advised to be followed without question). Koreans visiting the site, and it is a site that wherever North Koreans go in the country they will as likely come here at least once, can be seen to be moved, some to tears. It is obligatory to present flowers to the site, which can be bought from the fountains just down the hill for up from €5 a bouquet but will most likely be arranged by your guides in any case. Photographs can be taken with discretion and the important proviso to observe is that no feature of the statue is cropped from any shot. From the monument, far across the river can be seen the **Korean Workers' Party Monument**, at the end of a broad street aligned with the Grand Monument.

Northwards past the monument run little leafy paths down to Chilsongmun Street, that hugs the hilltop park of Chongnion on **Moran Hill**. First on

Chilsongmun you pass the **Chollima** statue. Chollima is a fabled winged horse that could cover a thousand ri (400km) a day. The 46m-high statue was inaugurated in 1961 and 'symbolises the heroic mettle and indomitable spirit of our people who made ceaseless innovations for post war rehabilitation'. The rebuilding of Pyongyang after the Korean War was said to be carried out at Chollima speed.

> The statue is composed of a worker, a member of our heroic class, spurring the Chollima on to a leap forward with the red letter of the Central Committee of the Workers' Party of Korea in his raised hand and a young peasant woman seated behind him with a sheaf of ripe rice in her arms.

Opposite Chollima is the classical portico of the **Moranbong Theatre**, built in 1946 just after occupation and where the North–South joint conference, followed by the first Supreme People's Assembly (indicating who won that argument), was held in 1948. Rebuilt having been gutted during the war, it is now a great venue for performances of classical music and opera. It's nestled into Moran Hill, the slopes and trees of which provide shade and breeze as you descend to the Arch of Triumph. This road crosses over the road tunnel that bores under Chongnion and on to the Rungra Bridge. Kim Jong Suk nursery is on the left.

Eventually you reach the unmistakable **Arch of Triumph**. Made of white granite, the 60m arch is dedicated to 'the home return of the Great Leader Comrade Kim Il Sung who liberated Korea from Japanese colonialism' and has dozens of rooms in the interior. It was erected in 1982 in one year on the 70th birthday of Kim Il Sung (symbolised by the 70 azaleas, Korea's national flower, that frame the arch). As written in the *Pyongyang Review*, 'Inscribed either side of the arch are the dates 1925–45 covering the period when Comrade Kim Il Sung set out on the 1,000 ri Journey for National Liberation to the time when he returned home in triumph after achieving his aim'. The *Review* continues:

> The three-tiered roof embodies the structural features of the traditional architecture – the pillars, beams, brackets and eaves are formed in a way congenial to modern aesthetic taste.

Taller than the Parisian version we were told – interesting that the architectural styles are so similar! Opposite the arch is the large **Kim Il Sung Stadium**, where the Great Leader made a speech at the 'Pyongyang Mass Meeting' after Japan's occupation finished in 1945. Originally called Moranbong Stadium, it was reconstructed with a capacity of 100,000 and renamed for KIS's 70th birthday. The Japanese had built it as a baseball stadium, but they were the last to use it for that purpose. These days it hosts football games and athletic events, and has been the venue for the Mass Games.

Next to the stadium is a large stone with Kim Il Sung's autograph carved onto it. In the immediate vicinity of the Arch is the West Pyongyang department store (just south of the arch), and the Pyongyang City People's Hospital No 1.

If you continue north on Kaeson Street, the 30m, somewhat chunky **Friendship Tower** arises on the right, celebrating the alliance of China and the DPRK. Built shortly after the Korean War, it is essentially a war memorial to Chinese forces lost in the conflict but a monument that has since been literally and figuratively enlarged upon into a more 'positive' commemoration of Chinese-DPRK friendship, also matching in height the monument built celebrating the Soviet–DPRK alliance.

The tower is bigger and more ostentatious than the more forlorn **Monument for the Fallen Heroes**, which is still what is was, a memorial to the million or so Chinese 'volunteers' killed fighting on Korean soil. Neither site hence figures highly for Western tourists but both are points of poignant and proud homage to

Chinese visitors, many of whom lay flowers in moving memoriam to long-lost forebears, if not loved ones. Opposite is the Chongsun restaurant and the **Chongsun Revolutionary Museum** and further along is the Phyongnam noodle restaurant. Kaeson Street crosses Pipa Street and there appears on the left the **April 25 People's Army House of Culture** (west on Pipa Street), a 'centre of mass cultural education for soldiers of the Korean People's Army and the Working People'. Within the 50m-high, 176m-long building is a cinema and two theatres (one with 6,000 seats). The westward road opposite, guarded by a giant trident called the **Immortal Tower**, dedicated to the onliving spirit of Kim Il Sung, heads to Taesong and Kim Il Sung's mausoleum.

Pressing on north on Podunamu Street, you pass the Ryonmot restaurant on the left towards the **Three-Revolution Exhibition**, about 6km from the city centre. It's a series of massive sheds in 100ha, and an almighty steel globe. The exhibition is made up of various halls such as New Technical Innovations, Light Industry and Agriculture, with exhibits from the ideological, technological and cultural

## MASS GAMES

Almost every year, Pyongyang is host to what has been rightly called the most incredible show on earth, when around 100,000 artistes, dancers, gymnasts, acrobats, martial arts experts, soldiers and children perform in the Mass Games.

Combining scenes of ethnic dances, giddying acrobatics and folk songs, it's a 'compact' story of the DPRK in dance. Everything is celebrated or depicted from the might of the armed forces to how cute children are, the victory of the country in completing the 'Arduous March' to the success of the co-operative farms, the struggle against US imperialism and the strive for Korean reunification; you have to go just for a chance to see 2,000 people-sized eggs running around in sync.

Each scene involves thousands of performers in a stunning feat of choreography, not only in the precision of the dances but in how they all manage to leave stage in a flash in total darkness. Behind the main floorshow is a huge screen showing images created by pixels of coloured card held up by 20,000 students – watching them warm up with a massive test-card before the show is entertainment in itself.

The greater significance of the show is about teaching the collective, and the discipline and surrender to the collective that communism requires, for the slightest mistake by just one operative will ruin the entire performance. This is drilled into the performers as they practise over many months and perform to the watching millions, and is described thus: 'A form of mass physical culture which is combined with physical skills and ideological and artistic value.' The award-winning VeryMuchSo film *A State of Mind* shows some footage from the show but the event obviously has to be seen in its full-size, full-length glory.

The scale of the games makes it a truly national event, directly involving at least one in a hundred Koreans from across the country in the show that it is said some two million Koreans come to see.

Such a scale also makes the event prone to impact from national events, and in 2006 and 2007 the games were subject to some disruption and cancellations due to floods in parts of the country. This is a great shame, especially when the event has also been the facility in recent years for US tourists to visit the country, with special dispensation arranged for these otherwise prohibited visitors. However, confidence is such that there are moves to make the games an annual event.

Seeing the games on a tour can incur an extra charge, with seats costing €50, €100, €150 or up to €300 (although the lowest-priced seats are perfectly good). If you can go, go.

The willowy Pothong River Park is a balmy place to stroll and where can be found long lines of chaps casting lines into the water.

Both banks of the River Taedong from Rungna Island down beyond the Yanggak have raised dykes topped by paths and shaded by trees, making for good walks of the city with grand panoramas and a chance to see the locals relaxing. On the west bank opposite Juche Tower, pedal-boats operate in summer, and the river can freeze thick enough for skating in winter

revolutions. The objectives of these revolutions, a significant political milestone in DPRK policy, are 'to raise the ideological level of the people, equip the economy with modern techniques and to lift the people's technological and cultural level. They are considered essential for successful socialist construction.' The place comes across as a massive expo-centre for DPRK manufacturers, so you get to see loads of what's not in the shops, and if that doesn't appeal then see it as an exhibition of what's considered fascinating.

Pipa Street continues east straight to Mt Taesong. The street gets leafier and hillier along here as the land rolls up to Taesong's base, and where the city begins to peter out you pass **Kim Il Sung University**, a severe-looking complex of buildings for 12,000 serious students (including not a few foreign ones) to do serious study and by God they'll never have worked so hard in their lives nor ever will again. It's Pyongyang's top multi-curricular university of the thirty-odd universities in Pyongyang, that range from Pyongyang University of Foreign Studies to the University of Railways.

Staying at Moran Hill, the hill divides into two parks, Moranbong and Kaeson Youth Park, but the hill's contouring paths lasso the parks together seamlessly. In spring this park drowns in pink blossom and it's a favourite area for strolling lovers. One path leads to the highly prominent **Liberation Tower**, built to commemorate the USSR's assistance in liberating Korea from the Japanese. It is on the hill's southern slope, overlooking the Rungna Bridge and Rungna Islet (itself a park) where the glint of steel from the fantastic **May Day Stadium**'s grand arches soar. This stadium has a seating capacity of 150,000 and is another venue for the truly awesome Mass Games which reached a zenith with the Arirang Festival (see box opposite).

Should you stay on the mainland of Moran Hill, its paths connect a series of old pavilions, gates and sentinel towers that remain from old Pyongyang's fortress walls that protected the city and formed the divisions of its inner districts. Pyongyang's walls were first built between 552 and 586 as the city was then the Koguryo capital and at the height of its prosperity had over 210,000 houses. The walled city went south from Moran Hill, filling the sac of land that rests between the Taedong and Pothong rivers, natural defences for the city. All of the wall's gates and posts have been rebuilt at one time or another, with many rebuilt in the 1710s following a great fire. But before we look at the old pavilions, under Moran Hill are tunnels and caves, where the government functioned during the Korean War.

On Moran Hill's Chilsongmun side is **Chilsong Gate**, known as the 'gate of happiness' or 'gate of love' since the 6th century. On the hill's riverside is **Chongryu Pavilion**, another gate to the walled city. **Pubyok Pavilion** (so named from the 12th century) on the Chongryu cliffs was an annex of the Yongmyong Temple built in 393. Pubyok name means 'floating walls' as if it floats on the river. **Ulmil Pavilion** was originally 6th century, a northern command post, rebuilt in 1714 and named after General Ulmil who defended the place, and is famed for its picturesque location during spring. Just 100m downhill is **Hyonmi Gate**, the northern gate of the walled city during Kogruyu times, named after the black tortoise-serpent god Hyonmi that was fabled as this city district's spiritual defender. On Moran Hill's highest peak is the **Choesung Pavilion**, originally 6th century and rebuilt in 1716. The height of the hill made it the natural choice as the city's central command point. **Chongum Gate** was the southern gate of the Koguryo's northern fort and was rebuilt in 1714. All were part of Pyongyang's Inner Fort, the walls of which traced down the riverbank a kilometre southwards past the Okryu Bridge to **Ryongwang Pavilion** and **Taedong Gate.** Ryongywang dates from the Koguryo period and the Taedong Gate was originally 6th century, as is the eastern gate of the inner fort. One plaque on the gate reads 'Uphoru', meaning a 'pavilion facing a clear stream', and one below it reads 'Taedong Gate'. Next to it is the 13.5-tonne **Pyongyang Bell**, cast in 1726 and used until the 1890s to tell the time and also to warn of danger. In the northern part of Moran Hill is **Ryonghwa Temple**, a 20th-century construction where worship is allowed and is now graced by the 5m-tall, seven-storeyed pagoda, an 800-year-old, Koryo period pagoda that has, for all its granite weight, managed to move around quite a lot since its first location at the (disappeared) Hongbok Temple. The pagoda is covered in reliefs of Buddha and is topped by a carved lotus flower bud.

On the northern side of Moran Hill is speared the hard-to-miss, 150m-tall **Pyongyang television tower**. It is in the same cocktail-cherry design as Moscow's lunatic Ostankino TV tower, and from where the DPRK started broadcasting in colour in the 1970s. Daring the ascent in the shabby elevator will be rewarded with a rather good (yes, revolving!) restaurant. The tower site is accessible by a path on the north side.

Head back down south through the park and to Okryu Bridge, a modern, wide-arched concrete construction, from where Mansudae Street can be followed westwards all the way to **Pothong Gate**. This was the west gate of the walled city, first built mid-6th century under the Koguryo, and rebuilt several times since, most recently after the Korean War. It now marks the Pothong Bridge crossing into Pothonggang District, a heart-shaped area moated by two arteries of the Pothong River. From here the Pothonggang Pleasure Park curves northwest and is a beautiful venue for walking amid willow trees, confirming Pyongyang's moniker as 'city of willows'. Pyongyangians are seen relaxing and fishing all along the river. Compared with other Asian cities, Pyongyang is exceptionally quiet at most times of day, but the thin and lazy Pothong is charmingly gentrified and serene. The park's paths can be followed as they curve northwest, past Mansu Bridge and the adjacent dome of the People's Army Circus, towards the **Victorious Fatherland Liberation War Museum** on Yonggung Street. This is a brilliant museum, with halls of compellingly arranged documents and artefacts from the Korean War, its build-up and aftermath. It's impossible to take it all in in a day, but along the way are fabulously intricate models and dioramas, that help to inspire a feeling of shame that such a devastating war can have been so largely forgotten in the West. Up a rounded stairway is a spectacular 360° revolving panorama of a battle. In the basement are the remains of numerous southern and American vehicles, boats and aircraft, juxtaposed with the intact Korean People's Army machines responsible for blowing them up and bringing them down (well you would only have the enemy's wrecks to display, wouldn't you?). If you wonder how the US tanks, DPRK aircraft, British Bren carrier, torpedo boat et al got down there, they were put in place first and the building built on top – making them very permanent exhibits. There are the remains of American reconnaissance craft intercepted since the Korean War, and the gruellingly written confession of one US helicopter pilot whose handwriting suggests what broke him to spill all beyond his name, rank and serial number.

Behind the museum, across the Jongsong Bridge into Pothonggang District, is the **Monument to the Victorious Fatherland Liberation War 1950–1953**, erected in 1993 'on the occasion of the 40th anniversary of war victory'. The setting consists of a 150,000m² white stone-flagged park with ten group sculptures in dark bronze depicting various battles on sea, land and air. It is dedicated to the 'Korean People's Army and Korean people who defeated the US imperialists and its allies in the Fatherland Liberation War'. On a sunny day, the contrast of the dazzling white floor and the nearly black sculptures is eerily impressive. The **'Victory' Sculpture** is the monument's focal point, its bronze sculpture representing a soldier shouting 'hurry', at the top of his voice, in the direction of the nearby Ryugyong Hotel. From every viewpoint can be seen the great unfinished **Ryugyong Hotel**, a vast pyramid stabbing the sky that was simply a hotel too far. It stands as an empty, unclad shell, and has done for years, with no date set for completion. Its 105 grey-brown storeys topped by five revolving (what else?) restaurants have space for 3,000 rooms and the building's planned facilities would have warranted it as a district in its own right. The guides roll their eyes when asked about this magnificent folly. Another site on the Pothong River's western artery is the **Monument to the Pothong River Improvement Project** and further west is **Pongsu Church**, built in 1988 when Changchun church was built. Officially, Pongsu has a head minister, a vicar and a bevy of elders, deacons and deaconesses and a congregation of 300 and is undergoing an expansion paid for by South Korean Presbyterian churches. Foreign residents have attended services there.

Heading south from Pothong Gate along Chollima Street, it seems that the road broadens out and the buildings are given more personal space to flaunt themselves, lined up along the Pothong and taking in the sun. You pass the huge traditional Korean-style **People's Palace of Culture**, a labyrinth of rooms and halls for the 'ideological and cultural education of the working people', and in front of which grand public dances are held on national holidays. Next to it is the **Pyongyang Indoor Stadium**. Spacious roads break west to cross the Pothong by the Susong Bridge (just over which is the silvery tower of the International Communications Centre) and Sinso Bridge. Just before Sinso is a knot of buildings including the Changwang Health Complex, Ragwon department store, Chongryu restaurant and the **Ice Rink**, the 12 supports on its conical shape resembling skates.

Continue south on Chollima Street until it intersects with Sosong Street and follow the rail tracks to **Pyongyang railway station**, where you may have first arrived or perhaps will leave the country. The clock overlooking the square is said to be the time-standard for all the DPRK. The entrance door on the left is for foreigners, entering through the right door will lead to your swift exit back through it. The station, with its impressive arch, pillared colonnades and impressive octagonal lantern atop, was first built by the Japanese, but was obliterated in the War and rebuilt in the 1950s. The copse of trees in Station Square is full of waiting travellers at all hours of the day, who choose not to peruse the wares of the Pyongyang station department store on the opposite corner nor follow Yongwang Street towards the river, taking in the simple classical design of the **Chollima House of Culture**, where the German Goethe Institute now has a reading room, the bad day for modernist architecture creation of the **International House of Culture** and the sweeping fancy of the neo-Korean **Pyongyang Grand Theatre**.

Now, in front of the classical portico of the **State Theatrical Company**, you can go west along Haebangsan Street past two post offices to the **Party Founding Museum**. This schoolish edifice was a Japanese company headquarters before 1945, whereupon it became the HQ for the Party's Central Committee immediately following 1945, and has the hallowed rooms and residence where Kim Il Sung mapped and slept upon the Party's future. It also contains the pond in which Kim

Jong Il's younger brother drowned when the Dear Leader was a child. You're walking in the grounds where the state germinated, just over the road from the 'Forbidden City' where the state lives today. In the area between Changgwang, Chollima and Jebangsan streets is what many foreigners refer to as Pyongyang's own 'forbidden city', a compound where many of the top echelons of North Korean society work and live, with roads heading into the complex blocked by security checkpoints of guards manning a chain barring the entry point, and surrounded by long strips of metal fencing. You'll quite often see saloon cars cruising in and out of this city-within-the-city and well-dressed types walking in and out, but your chances of getting in, like your average North Korean's, don't exist. This is the best-known of the large gated communities that exist in Pyongyang and in other parts of the country, but none appear on any official DPRK maps nor have any indications in name or symbol, and the surrounding roads and areas on maps can be (as in this case) somewhat moulded to underplay the size of the compounds. However, it is clearly visible on Google Earth. Return to Sungri Street dog-legging past the **Monument to Martyrs of the People's Army** and you're going back towards Kim Il Sung Square, or cross the Taedong Bridge to the city's eastern half.

**East Pyongyang** This side of town is quieter and there's less to see. The Taedonggang and Tongdaewon districts of East Pyongyang are home to the city's diplomatic quarter, a dozen universities and a few hospitals, including the top-flight 1,500-bed **Pyongyang Maternity Hospital**. Some have claimed this was built to dispel the myth that pregnant women were banished from the city but it would seem to be a somewhat dramatic response to a persistent rumour. Some tour itineraries now have visitors taking a wander through the hospital. Just off Saeserim Street running from Taedong Bridge is the **Changchun Catholic Church**, the first Christian house of worship to be built in the DPRK when completed in 1988 in time for the 13th World Student and Youth Festival the following year, to show the world that religion was not banned in the DPRK, although the wall surrounding it does not impart that much freedom of association and there is no resident priest. The building's simple design, colours and layout are very similar to the Pongsu Protestant church which was commissioned at the same time.

Perhaps you can load up at the Taedonggang Diplomatic Club or the Songyu restaurant opposite, both on Taedong Bridge's east end. Then head along Juchetap Street for the **Juche Tower** dominating the eastern riverbank. This 150m stone-clad tower, with a 20m, 45-tonne metal flame flickering atop it, was built, as its name suggests, to celebrate the Juche philosophy of self-reliance as expounded by Kim Il Sung and developed by Kim Jong Il. The two words Ju and Che appear in large form on the east and west sides. The sides' tiers add up to 70, Kim Il Sung's age in 1982 and for that birthday the tower was built, while each stone is for a day in his life.

At the east base is an open shrine to dedications to the Juche idea, containing over 500 tabulets from around the world given in deference to the man and his idea. The entrance to the tower is down the steps on the southeast corner. Pay €5 entry then head through a long tunnel, with guide, before climbing into the lift that in its minute climb passes the floors of no known purpose up to the plinth of the flame from whence a very impressive view of the city is available. This guide dodges photos with a boxer's skill, and has a very good memory for faces. Coke was available from one of the karaoke rooms along the tunnel.

The statue fronting the tower onto the river has three people, intellectual, worker and farmer, holding their tools aloft into the KWP insignia, and looking out onto the 150m-high fountains blasting out of the Taedong. Behind the tower across Juchetap Street is the Korea Documentary Film studio where all things

Deriving from the Dendobrium genus of the orchid family, Kimilsungia is a tropical perennial with deep pink flowers, cultivated in Indonesia and named after Kim Il Sung in 1965 when he visited the country: 'The Indonesian president said that his respected excellency (Kim Il Sung) had rendered great services to mankind and deserved a high honour. The Indonesian president was so firmly resolved that Kim Il Sung could no longer decline his offer.'

Kim Jong Il received his own species of Kimjongilia, a blood-red bloom of tuberous begonia, in 1988 from a Japanese botanist, Kamo Mototeru, 'in the hope of achieving amity and friendship between Japan and Korea'. Both plants have inspired songs, won international competitions, and are cultivated countrywide for local shows and an annual festival for Kimjongilia flowers held in Pyongyang in February.

The flower shows are held at a special venue on the west bank, just south of the Rungna Bridge.

Juche are produced. Further north along this road is a tall, plain building with a deep bronze tint that's noticeable only for the large KWP sign on its roof. This otherwise innocuous high-rise is the **Kim Il Sung Higher Party School**, where Korea's brightest and best get trained in ruling the country.

Then further north along Juchetap come the peculiarly sculpted **Central Youth Hall**, with its anvil and armadillo roofs, and the slide machine of the **East Pyongyang Grand Theatre**. Around 3,500 people can pack in to see music or revolutionary opera here. Midway between these two buildings is a symmetrical street, and you realise it's in perfect alignment with the Mansu Grand Monument west across the river and the **Monument to Party Foundation** to your east just across Munsu Street. This staggering piece of work was erected in 1995 to celebrate the 50th anniversary of the Korean Workers' Party: a hammer, sickle and calligraphy brush grasped in the hands of a worker, farmer and intellectual. The sculpture's 50 granite-faced metres mark one metre for each of the Party's 50 years. The belt uniting the three tools has bronze reliefs lining its interior, emblazoned with the slogan, 'Long live the Workers Party of Korea, the Organiser and Guide of the Victory of the Korean People!' The inscription on the pedestal refers to the development of the Party from the roots of anti-imperialism. Venturing to the very northern end of Munsu Street you come upon a waterpark and funfair – although I have not personally visited either venue and have not heard from anyone who has.

## FURTHER OUT OF TOWN
**Korean Film Studio** Far out into Hyongjesan District, about 10km due northwest of Kim Il Sung Square, is the other great factory of the DPRK's view on the world, the Korean Film Studio. With nothing to note on the way to this massive Korean Hollywood (except the Railways University) it's a must-see, churning out such thrillers as *Daughter of the Revolution*. You'll likely watch old melodramas being filmed and tour through reconstructed feudal villages which give a good insight into ancient Korean life, so it's partly a moving museum (although the crops grown in the village are for real). Note the German town, pre-revolution Chinatown and the totally decadent Seoul city, awash with US- and Japanese-run brothels, go-go bars, casinos and all so decadent that they don't eat dogs but pamper them. Despite having to pay to take photos (of the actors at least), the studios are well worth visiting to experience the dream world within the dream city.

The number 5 tram ventures there from West Pyongyang railway station.

**Mt Taesong** Beyond the sprawl, about 10km northeast of the city centre, are Mt Taesong and its hills. The road with **Kim Il Sung University** and **Kumsusan Memorial Palace** (see page 126) continues to undulate eastwards, crossing the Hapjang River, which seems to be a border for town and country.

Physically, Mt Taesong is one peak, Jujak (192m), surrounded by a series of vegetation-covered summits capped with small pavilions, while many small lakes pock the valley that curves around Jujak and its surrounding peaks. A series of paths weaves the lakes and hills together and make for a good afternoon's walking in balmy air, finding amid the scant ruined walls of **Fort Taesong** viewpoints over distant Pyongyang. The peaks were linked by a fort wall from the 3rd century, and the fort was bolstered for Pyongyang's defences after the Koguryo moved their capital to the city in AD427. Fort Taesong's walls reached 9.2km in length, and of its 20 gates, the most prominent 'survivor' is the **Nam Gate**, rebuilt in 1978.

Looking from the bus terminus at Taesong's southwest foot, on the left is **Pyongyang Central Zoo**. It may have 600 species of all breathing things, many of which were gifts to Kim Il Sung, but it's a zoo in the very, very traditional sense. Attractions include Korean tigers in a seriously miserable cage, elephants penned in by spiked plates on the floor, and a collection of cats and dogs. Only the unconvincingly escape-proof baboon pen merits much more attention – that and a turkey, two-and-a-half bears (well, one of them has only one arm) and the giant German rabbits – they were not all eaten as the press said they were – although people do eat rabbits.

Opposite the zoo are the **Botanical Gardens**, of note for any of the 5,000 species there. The chance to see Kimilsungia and Kimiljongilia out of season is possibly the best reason to visit, and to investigate what's being bred in the gardens' 'experimental' section. The gardens also have some ancient tombs, possibly of Koryo origin. The gardens are next to the **Taesongan Fun Fair**, with a charming Buddhist temple within its grounds (open on request) and beyond that, past a handful of restaurants lies the main path for the pavilions of Jangsu and Sumon peaks around Jujak.

These are all light distractions compared with Jujak's crown, the **Revolutionary Martyrs' Cemetery**. Unless driven to the top, you pass through the large Korean-style gate and ascend a breathless flight of 300 granite steps up to a road (where the van otherwise stops), then the cemetery begins on a shallower slope up to Jujak Peak. Between a large medal and a huge crimson granite flag are interred over 200 leading figures from Korea's resistance to Japanese colonial rule. By no means did all of those interred here die during that struggle; some were killed during the Korean War, many would die of old age years later, but they are the ones Kim Il Sung had most dedication to, and he had the cemetery built in the mid-1970s in commemoration, castigating himself for what was until then an oversight of respect. A bust of Kim Il Sung's wife is before the flag. Many were scarcely adults when they fell fighting the Japanese and in the War. Now their bronze busts look out onto Pyongyang as somber music is piped around them, in what is an exceedingly austere but very moving setting. It is expected that you pay respects at the medal and the flag. (Another cemetery holding the remains of 400 of the DPRK's great and the good is off the road from Sonan airport.)

Exiting left of the flag, there appears a road heading back to the bus terminus and another path heading for the peaks.

Buses 1, 2, 3, 28, 29, 30 terminate at Mt Taesong. Only the 3 is useful in running into central town along Hyoksin, Pipa and Mundok streets. Back at the terminus, the number 1 trolley-bus trundles southeast for a mile, past **Pyongyang Astronomical Observatory** and another 500m to the Koguryo's **Anhak Palace**. It must have been a major sight to behold, for within its four walls (each measuring

By the 1860s, the Ri court was deeply alarmed that despite the prohibition and persecution of Christianity and its followers, Koreans were still converting by the thousand. The Tonghak rebellion of 1864 further shook the court and it boded that any more foreign proselytisers would get very short shrift.

So it was ill-timed that in August 1866, the armed steam-schooner the *General Sherman* should steam up the Taedong River, ostensibly to broach trade with Korea, but on board was the young Protestant missionary, Robert Jermaine Thomas. The *Sherman* had been a trader used by both sides of America's Civil War, following the end of which the *Sherman* was pressed into service in east Asia. Captain Page piloted the ship into Korea but it was evidently Thomas that called the shots. The *Sherman* was first greeted by an emissary for Governor Park Kyoo Soo of Pyung-an, who told Page, Thomas and the other Westerners aboard (including the ship's owner) that trade with Korea was illegal, but that provisions would be provided for the ship's departure from Korea.

Nonetheless, on Thomas's insistence, upon the emissary's departure the *Sherman* continued upriver towards Pyongyang, where heavy rain and high tides allowed the ship to sail an unusually deep river and get to Turu Islet, near Mangyongdae, from whence Thomas proselytised and his companions tried to trade with locals. Deputy Commander Lee Hyon Ik of the Pyongyang garrison was sent to the ship to convey the king's displeasure at the *Sherman*'s further intrusion. The Koreans now heavily suspected that this was less about trade than about Christian evangelism, and a testy confrontation was imminent when, upon the call-out of the Pyongyang garrison, Lee found himself taken hostage as the ship turned. However, the wet weather had abated, the tide was turning, then fog sealed the futility of the ship's escape and it ran aground. Accounts differ as to whether the Pyongyang garrison or the *Sherman* fired first. Keeping Deputy Commander Lee as a hostage to forestall any attack while the *Sherman* turned may have provoked the garrison to attack, but the *Sherman* may have opened fire to seal its getaway before running aground, or to repel boarders afterwards. Either way, the garrison attacked with fire-rockets and cannon, and the *Sherman* returned cannon fire on anything that moved, civilian and military alike. After four days' battle, on 2 September, Korean turtle-boats were tied together, set afire and pushed towards the *Sherman*. All the Westerners and the ship's Asian crew that had escaped gunfire or the fumes of the burning ship were caught, executed and mutilated. Thomas apparently followed his Bible riverward from the burning ship's deck, and was captured. Whether he died the brave martyr or was slain begging for his life is not clear. The USS *Wachusett* was sent the following year to investigate the incident, but little was learnt except that the *Sherman* had indeed been destroyed. In spring 1868, the USS *Shenandoah* reached the Taedong River's mouth where Captain Febiger received an official acknowledgment that all the *General Sherman*'s crew were dead. The *Sherman*'s destruction was cited as but one 'depredation against Americans' that justified a punitive attack on numerous sites and forts by American forces in 1871: the incident and its repercussions also justified to the Ri that politeness was ultimately wasted on these foreign devils and their duplicitous ways, and stelae were put up nationwide that read 'Posterity should remember that unwillingness to fight the intrusion of the Westerners means reconciliation, and that insisting on negotiations for peace mean selling the country'.

622m and 6–12m high) the remains of 52 buildings, most linked by lengthy cloisters, have been found amongst gardens and waterways.

Over Taesong's west side is the **Kwangbok Temple**, tucked up a small valley and with a handful of monks still seen to practise their religion. The site, if not the buildings, is one of Pyongyang's most ancient, for a temple has been here since AD392. However, the original burnt down in 1700 and its replacement was razed during the Korean War, hence the gleaming one you see today, built in 1990 following the 1989 World Festival of Youth and Students.

**Mangyongdae** Following the river road down to Mangyongdae you may see the USS *Pueblo* moored around Yanggak Bridge. This Cold War trophy is now a floating museum.

In January 1968 the 850-tonne spy-boat USS *Pueblo*, with Captain Pete Bucher and 82 crew members, left Japan supposedly on an oceanographic research mission but really to conduct electronic surveillance off the DPRK coast. The North Koreans had recently expressed their heightened irritation over spy-ships loitering in its waters; indeed in January 1967 North Korean battery fire from their shores had sunk the American patrol-boat *PCE-56* near the DMZ, but their threats of an even more vigorous response weren't heeded. Surely, though North Korean planes and boats buzzed the *Pueblo*, its captain and crew considered they were safe (the US insist that it was never closer than 15 miles from the DPRK, ie: in international waters), until one North Korean vessel approached to board it. Bucher ordered the *Pueblo* to weave away at speed, but the *Pueblo* received gunfire from the north. In the ensuing chase and boarding, one crew member was killed and several were wounded. Realising that the *Pueblo* was outpaced and outgunned, Bucher surrendered the ship. A haul of secret documents and equipment, neither destroyed nor dumped in time, fell into North Korean hands, later gleefully shared with the Soviets. More importantly, they had 82 Americans captive to torture and with which to torture President Johnson's administration for 11 months. The weight of American commitment in Vietnam (1968 being a year of heavy casualties for the US there) precluded more aggressive attempts to get the crew returned. The crew's captivity was harsh and only improved upon the signing of confessions. The crew were ultimately handed back, with the remains of the dead crew member, through Panmumnjom on 23 December 1968, but the equipment remained. The North Koreans kept the *Pueblo* in Wonsan until the late 1990s, then moored it in Pyongyang next to a monument celebrating the 1866 burning of the *General Sherman*, although this is not a permanent mooring. Guiding people around the *Pueblo* is a veteran of the incident and there is now a self-guiding torpedo to marvel at and a DVD of the incident to buy and play over and over.

Mangyongdae District is the westernmost area of Pyongyang city, filling the banks of the River Pothong's western artery. Two boulevards, **Kwangbok Street** and **Chongchun Street**, divide and rule this area in their roles as open galleries for the art of concrete architecture. Kwangbok Street, finished in 1989, is described as a city in its own right, with 25,000 flats racked and stacked along this 6km-long, 100m-wide strip. Beginning at the Pothong's Palgol Bridge, Kwangbok has the hexagonal spaceships of the **Circus** on its west side. Here you'll see a fun mix of high-wire acrobatics and grotesque parodies of American troops and South Koreans. Tickets to the circus is (on a tour) an extra of € 10. Kwangbok ends in the embracing arms of the **Mangyongdae Students and Children's Palace** and its bronze-coloured 'Chariot of Happiness' amid sculptures from numerous tales told to children by the Great and Dear Leaders. Many of the various 690 rooms are for group classes where children learn the violin, accordion, dance, public speaking, tae kwon do, boxing, etc, and a tour should prelude an electrifying, technically razor-sharp 90-minute show of music and dance by the children trained at this DPRK version of 'Fame'. Extended visits to the Palace for observation only can be arranged. Halfway along Kwangbok, Chongchun or 'Gymnasium' Street undercuts it. A series of nine sports halls, each dedicated to one sport, line this road down to the Angol flyover on the Taedong. Each hall's design apparently represents some facet of their nominated sport, but unless you're going to watch one, the buildings are bizarrely impressive enough, some being able to take up to 5,000 spectators, built as they were for the 1989 World Festival of Youth and Students (although originally planned to host the 1988 Olympics that in the event was awarded to Seoul). At the Taekwondo Hall tournaments can be attended or even courses arranged. Just off Chongchun is a professional shooting range where €1 gets three bullets in .22 rifles or pistols, making for a great evening's entertainment of shooting things. There is also a golf driving range off this street.

Continuing northwest along Chongchun beyond the large junction where it crosses Kwangbok are two sites of interest. First, on the right, 350m from the junction, is a park and statue dedicated to Kim Il Sung's mother, Kang Pan Sok, a Presbyterian deaconess. The same distance further on the same side is the Chilgol Church, built in 1992, which is dedicated to her.

You may traverse Kwangbok and Chongchun going to or from the **Mangyongdae Revolutionary Site,** where the Great Leader was born and spent his first few years. Otherwise, you may hug the road on the Taedong's west bank down to Mangyongdae, spying the huge thermal power plant to the east belching fumes skywards.

Just before Mangyongdae, you'll notice that the river has split around the rather large Turu Islet and its satellite islets. Here it's thought that the American missionary trader USS *General Sherman* was beached and destroyed in 1866. Official histories credit the burning of the ship to Kim Il Sung's great-grandfather Kim Ung U, but the story's details swirl in debate (see box on page 123).

**Mangyongdae Shrine and its environs** Follow the Taedong's west bank southwards and the landscape becomes rapidly green and rural. Some 12km south of the city centre, just before the River Sunhwa empties into the Taedong, is a site of nearly religious significance, the former village of Mangyongdae. Here Kim Il Sung was born and spent his childhood, and the handful of tiny thatched huts where his parents and grandparents tilled the land are now enshrined. They form the centre of some well-trimmed parkland to which throngs of Koreans are taken on Party, factory and school tours to pay homage. The huts sit beside the small lotus pond, and are surrounded by small sites of significance, including the graves of Kim Il Sung's forebears. The full, official history of Kim's forebears is within the **Mangyongdae Revolutionary Museum,** 100m from the huts. On the lotus pond's opposite bank is a line of trees, each donated by visiting leaders from the communist bloc, a reminder of the world of comrades that has so recently disappeared. Mangyong hill has a small pavilion atop it, and has two sites where Kim Il Sung studied and another where, according to legend, he wrestled with a larger foe and won.

Fighting through the throng of **Mangyongdae Fun Fair**'s reported 100,000 daily visitors, you'll find the grenade throwing ground and machine gun stalls as well as fifty other amusements visible from the fair's gondola and monorail rides that link the two halves of the fair, and an impressive corkscrew rollercoaster. The fair is open on most holidays and some weekends. You might also get to see the DPRK's own little Eton, **Mangyongdae Revolutionary School,** just over the hill from the shrines. Here are trained the 'children of revolutionary martyrs to be political and military cadres. Kim Il Sung Higher Party school and Pyongyang Communist University [just east of the Koryo Hotel] train Party workers or give reorientation to them' (*Pyongyang Review*).

The refreshingly untouched **Ryongak Hill** sits about 4km north of Mangyongdae. On the edge of town, it's largely unvisited and appeals for being what it is, a hill set in greenery with a few forgotten sites around it. The Koguryo-dynasty Pobun Monastery and the Ryonggok Academy, dating from 1656, are to be found there. At 292m, Tae peak is the highest on Ryongak and gives splendid views of the city.

**South Pyongyang** Chollima Street beams southwards to Chungsong Bridge, the westernmost bridge in central Pyongyang, which crosses the Taedong and attaches to Ssuk Islet on its easternmost point and shortly after reaching the Taedong's south bank the road crosses the east–west-running Thongil Street, a breathtaking, massive, modern boulevard finished in 1993, lined with scores of concrete apartment blocks. If the shock of the new does not appeal, Pyongyang's BBQ duck restaurant is to the northwest of the junction with Chongsung Bridge Street, and the Pyongyang Noodle restaurant to the southeast. Going east along Thongil on the north side is the entrance to the large Thongil market which is open to foreigners seeking anything from foodstuffs to Chinese electricals. Beyond the market towards the riverfront is the Pyongyang Mullet Soup restaurant.

Continuing east along Thongil, again on the north side, set back a couple of hundred metres is placed the beautiful, brand new Russian Orthodox church, also known as the Church of the Life-Giving Trinity, and is the first in North Korea. A stark white building complete with gold onion domes, it was consecrated in mid-2006 by numerous Russian political and religious dignitaries.

Thongil then bends northeastwards, becoming first Chungnyon, then Munsu Street that beams through the east side of the city.

**Tomb of King Tangun** The 5,000-year-old bones of the mythical King Tangun were identified in the early 1990s, an event so ground-shaking that 'Comrade Kim Il Sung was so please [*sic*] he asked dear Comrade Kim Jong Il if it was true'. At the base of Mt Taebak in Munhung-ri, Pyongyang, Tangun's tomb was reconstructed and opened in October 1994 (reflected in the number of stones used to rebuild the tomb), a nine-tiered granite pyramid without a point at the end of two colossal flights of steps. Inside, in polished wooden coffins are kept the remains of Tangun and his wife, guarded by a stone tiger, the 'biggest in the world' at 3.5m height. The steps to the tomb are flanked by statues of Tangun's sons and ministers, while another monument celebrating the reconstruction stands between the two flights. Followers of the Taejong religion, a Korea-centric religion built around the deity of Tangun, can now worship at the site, which also receives two pilgrimages on 2 October and 15 March every year, so the tomb has been awarded profound spiritual and political resonance.

**Kumsusan Memorial Palace** Kim Il Sung's final resting house is the Kumsusan Memorial Palace. Set in 100ha of trees, this was formerly where Kim Il Sung lived, worked and entertained and its interiors are lavish, so it is not a monolith built around a mausoleum but was refurbished to make it one. The cuboid mausoleum where Kim Il Sung lies in state is similar in design to that of Lenin, Mao and Ho Chi Minh, with a vast, dazzling plaza in front of it making it Pyongyang's other Kim Il Sung Square (much bigger in fact: the two halves of Kim Il Sung Square total 300m east to west, whereas the mausoleum's plaza is almost 500m at its longest). But it is not normally open just for people to turn up – Fridays and Sundays are 'open' days but notice must be given. Koreans like it if you do ask to be taken, although it is more likely for you to receive an invitation off the bat if you are part of a delegation, or resident.

If you do go, you are expected to dress smartly, ie: long trousers, shirt and tie, for men. The visit involves travelling along miles of moving walkways and being metal-detected and your shoes automatically cleaned and dust blown off you. You bow as you walk around the body, but not at the head or feet, before going into a room where are held the accolades and honours from other dignitaries such as Nikolae Ceauşescu and Colonel Gadaffi.

From the centre of town the road leading there begins opposite the classical façade of the April 25 People's Army Palace, and what appears to be an almighty trident stabbed into the road is a stela on which is an inscription in red to remind the populace that Kim Il Sung's spirit shall forever be with them – this is the master copy of stelae scattered across the country, built following the great man's death in 1994.

*Kim Il Sung Square*

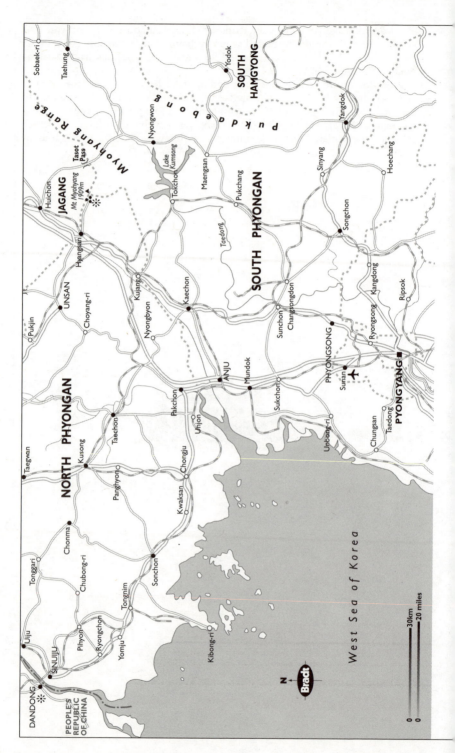

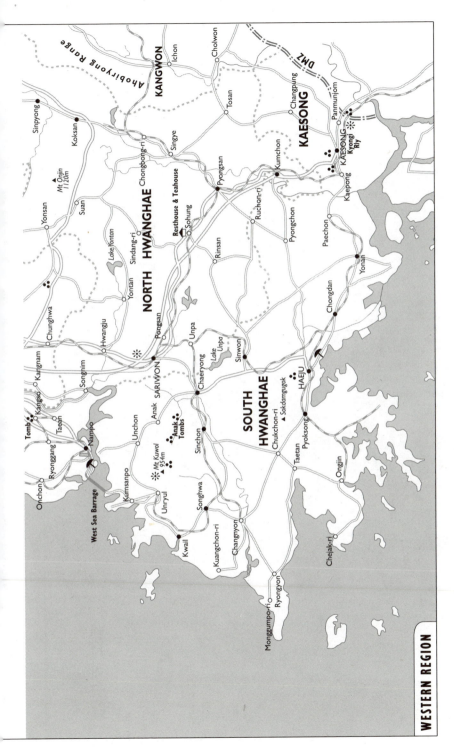

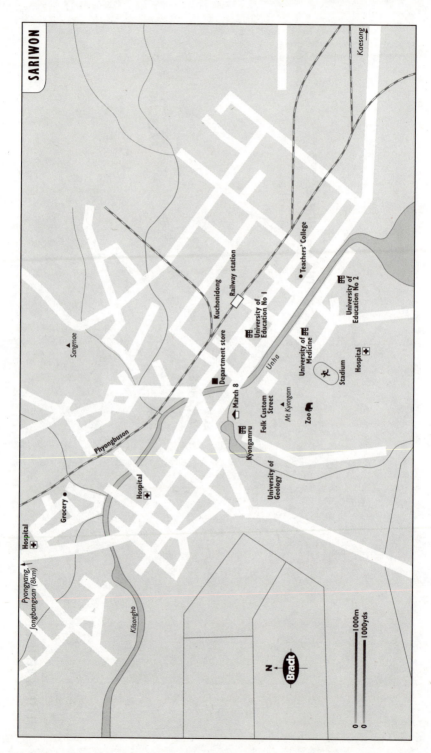

SARIWON

Kaesong

Pyongyang,
Jongbangsan (8km)

Hospital

Grocery

Hospital

Kilsongho

Phyongbuson

Sangmae

Kuchonidong

Railway station

Department store

March 8

Kyongamru

University of
Education No 1

Unha

Teachers' College

University of
Medicine

University of
Education No 2

Folk Custom
Street

Mt Kyongam

Zoo

Stadium

Hospital

University of
Geology

N

Bradt

0        1000m
0        1000yds

# 4

# Pyongyang to Kaesong and Panmunjom

*Pyongyang to Kaesong, three hours by train and 90 minutes by road. Pyongyang to Sariwon 50km, Pyongyang to Kaesong 161km*

Going to Kaesong from Pyongyang by road involves cruising down Thongil Street, a monolithic housing development completed in 1993. The road rises up and under the extraordinary '**Three Principles Monument**', a 30m granite statue of two women from both Koreas leaning together over the highway. The monument's longer title is the Monument to the Three Charters for National Reunification, unveiled in 2001, although at the time inter-Korean relations were beginning to sour. The two women in traditional dress and symbolising the two Koreas, are holding aloft the symbol of the charter. Its symbolism is accentuated by its location on the road towards the ROK. The Army Film Studios are quite near this monument. Through the checkpoints, and 9km from Pyongyang, is the country's only turnpike, indicating Wonsan 191km and Kaesong 152km. As you cruise to Kaesong you observe the farms and the long slogan boards planted in the fields, then you can admire how well tended the verges are on the road itself. Most of this highway, like the rest, is as straight as a runway, but the turns get sharper as the landscape gets hillier going south. And yes, the roads are always this quiet, although they didn't used to be: 'In this country, in which sumptuary laws prevent the humbler classes from travelling on horseback, and where wagons and steam roads are unknown, the roads are lively with numerous foot passengers,' wrote Griffis, listing pupils, pilgrims, pompous functionaries on horseback, travelling players, picnickers, postal slaves on the pony express, pack-horsed merchants, beggars, refugees of war and weather, and 'men dead of hunger in times of famine'. But the well-trodden roads did not support ye olde motel industry: 'The country is very deficient in houses for public accommodation. Inns are to be found only along the great highways, and but rarely along the smaller or sequestered roads. This want arises, perhaps, not so much from the poverty of the people, as from the fact that their numerous proverbial hospitality does away with the necessity of numerous inns.' If a household hadn't the food to replenish a traveller, the travellers would be invited in anyway to cook their own.

## SARIWON

*38.3° north, 125.4° east; capital of North Hwanghae Province*

Forty minutes' drive from Pyongyang is the North Hwanghae Province seat of Sariwon. The city skyline is broken up by heavy and light industry factories strewn between the Kyongam and Sangmae hills, and although you may be attracted to the **Sariwon Orchard,** noted for its 'Sariwon Grape', or be seduced by the allure of the **Sariwon Potassic Fertiliser Complex**, there's little of interest in an otherwise attractive town. It's easier to breathe in the **Jongbang**

**Mountains** 8km north of the city, which were decreed as a park (Jongbangsan Pleasure Ground) by Kim Il Sung. On the mountain slopes is the **Fort of Jongbangsan**, which actually laps up to the Jongbang tunnel of the Pyongyang–Kaesong highway. It was a good enough site for the fort to be rebuilt in the mid-1600s and within its 12km walls can be found the remains of its main armoury, garrisons and bits of 48 long-destroyed temples. The buildings of the Buddhist temple Songbul still stand, although they've been rebuilt many times since 898.

A recently built addition to Sariwon is a Folk Customs Street, open for business in 2007, 'to show the traditions and customs of the Korean nation to the youth, students and working people' and high hopes of interest for tourists too, with its murals depicting old arts of traditional games like tug o' war and wrestling and crafts like kimchi-making. Unless there is a festival or occasion where this site is in full use, there is little point in seeing it. Behind is a track up Mt Kyongam, which gives a view over the town.

Drive 30km due east from Sariwon via Chaeryong and you'll come to Sinchon, with the **Sinchon Massacre Museum** which, in customary micro detail, tells of an appalling atrocity committed by the US forces during the Korean War. The museum charts the massacre of over 35,300 civilians in and around Sinchon – men, women, children and babies. In a building much like a provincial boarding school are held the remains of 5,605 patriots, 400 mothers and 102 children killed in the massacre. Extremely graphic paintings depicting all manner of killings and torture hang alongside tortuous black and white photographs of the real aftermath. It is not for the faint-hearted.

Some 16km north-northeast of Sinchon is Anak, and it is between Anak and Sinchon that the three UNESCO-listed tombs of Anak lie, but arrangements need to be made to see these.

## 🏠 WHERE TO STAY

🏠 **March 8 Hotel** (29 rooms) At the foot of Mt Kyongam. 2 2nd-class and 27 3rd-class rooms available. $–$$

Otherwise, press on 30km further from Sariwon towards Kaesong until you reach the **Sohung Tea House**, where you can 'recover from fatigue and enjoy the nature' and have some tea. As well as the usual ginseng, embroideries and paintings, it might have a load of ostrich eggs in stock (€5) for there is an ostrich co-operative farm somewhere nearby. The ostrich farm, which also supplies ostrich meat to some of Pyongyang's eateries, is open for visits. You could also pick up a CD-ROM about dogs.

The road has finally quit trying to avoid the hillsides and by now just bores straight through them. The tunnel entrances have precariously supported concrete obstacles, waiting to fall in the path of any invading tank or tourist bus. Evidence of a far older invasion is some 28km before Kaesong, just before Ryunggung Tunnel. On the left at the bottom of a hill are a series of **dinosaur footprints**, 30 great plate-marks from 180 million years ago, found during the road's construction.

Eventually, you pass through the mist of the last seeping tunnel and a long flank of apartment blocks appears on the left, your vehicle curves right round under the highway and onto Thongil Street, the other end of the one you left Pyongyang on. The street darts down and up a hill to a bronze statue of Kim Il Sung, who hails your arrival into Kaesong.

*37.55° north, 126.3° east; city and area under central authority*
This former capital of Koryo is really a pleasant and interesting place to pass a couple of days. Most of the sites are within walking distance of each other and the city has the broad boulevards of Pyongyang but none of the traffic (!), giving the city a relaxed air that you wouldn't expect so close to the DMZ (only 8km away!). Except for those lining the thoroughfares off Thongil Street, the buildings are low-storey and leave the surrounding hills to provide the shelter.

Kaesong means 'castle gate opening' and the city had long been a significant fortress city before King Wang Kon made it the capital of Koryo in 932, deeming it best located as a centre for the Koryo kingdom. In the next 400 years, Kaesong grew and prospered not only as the kingdom's political centre but one of great commerce and learning. Buddhism was made the official religion and Kaesong its heart, as the aristocracy poured money into monasteries, temples and schools of learning. Although no longer the capital, the city remained a significant commercial centre and military staging post throughout the Ri dynasty, and became a centre for the cultivation and trading of the great medicinal cash-crop, ginseng (*Koryo insam*), still a highly prized crop produced locally today. Until World War II, visitors noted a bustling business town, a great centre of the grain trade, with various mercantile guilds and roaring businesses in sesame oil, paper products, tobacco pouches, umbrellas and sheetings for walls and windows, and imports from Britain and Japan. Kaesong was fortunate to be set in a 'no bomb' zone that exempted it from the attention of US carpet-bombing, but it didn't escape the effects of the Korean ground war. The first armistice talks were held here in June 1951 before being moved to Panmunjom. In 1955, Kaesong was declared to be under direct central authority, and now constitutes one city and three counties.

Today, the city's main commodity is ginseng, with good trade in rice, barley, and wheat until recently. The city's also known for its embroideries and porcelain, textiles, and heavy industry, but there's more dust and rust here than in Pyongyang. Little remains of the city walls that once circled 15km around, its scores of temples and monasteries are largely vanished, and its population, at 335,000 is a sharp fall from its height of 800,000 under the Ri. Floods in recent years have damaged the city's surrounding farmland, and look out for any food-aid sacks with the stars and stripes on them. However, an industrial complex is planned for foreign investors, particularly those from the ROK, and the city's tourist potential is to be built upon as part of the forthcoming Kaesong Industrial Zone.

Between Kaesong and the DMZ is an expanding industrial park being built by the South Korean megalithic conglomerate Hyundai Asan, where South Korean firms are outsourcing production to the skilled but low-cost northern workforce. This park is not on the tourist itinerary and it has had negligible visible economic impact on Kaesong city itself (although the three planned golf courses will probably become a fixture), but is worth noting.

The US$180 million project is being built in several phases, with apartment complexes, hotels, restaurants and an amusement park all planned to in effect create a new industrial city with 150,000 workers from North and South Korea toiling to produce some US$15 billion worth of goods a year. Buses run workers from Kaesong and managers from Seoul daily.

Bids outnumbered allotments by 10 to 1, and by early 2007, 22 South Korean firms employing over 12,000 in shoe-making, textiles and light industry had set up shop, with non-Korean companies invited to do the same the following month.

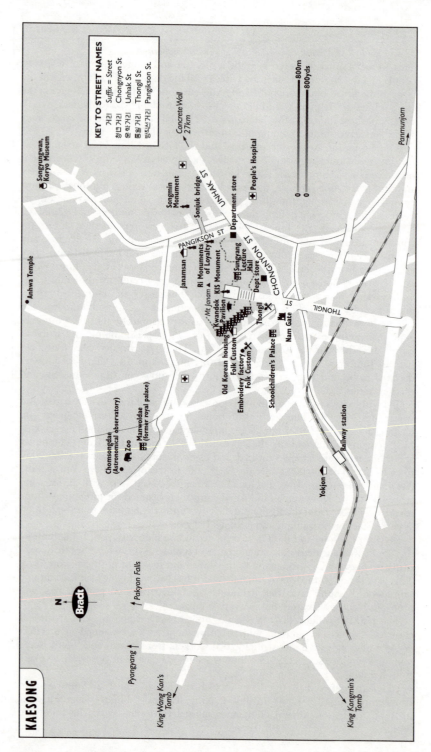

# KAESONG

**KEY TO STREET NAMES**

거리 Suffix = Street
청년 거리 Chongnyon St
윤학거리 Unhak St
통일 거리 Thongil St
방직서거리 Pangikson St.

Songyungwan,
Koryo Museum

Anhwa Temple

Songmin
Monument

UNHAK ST

Sonjuk bridge

People's Hospital

Department store

PANGIKSON ST

Janamsan

Ri Monuments
of Loyalty

Sungyang
Lecture
Hall

KIS Monument

Mt Janam

Dept store

CHONGNYON ST

Kwandok
Pavilion

Thongil
ST

Old Korean housing
Folk Custom

Nam Gate

Embroidery factory
Folk Custom

THONGIL

Schoolchildren's Palace

Chomsongdae
(Astronomical observatory)

Zoo

Manwoldae
(former royal palace)

Railway station

Yokjon

800m
800yds

0

0

Concrete Wall
27km

Panmunjom

N
Bradt

Pyongyang

Pakyon Falls

King Wang Kon's
Tomb

King Kongmin's
Tomb

134

Although preceded by Rason and Sinuiju as foreign investment zones, Kaesong's is far the most successful since the plans were finalised in 2000. It makes a metaphorical parallel to the speed with which the DPRK economy is shifting from a mostly autarkic state-run communist economy towards an open-trade, capitalist basis, with the accompanying shift in mind-set to accepting individualist inspiration and entrepreneurship, even if it be from those dreaded more successful brothers from the South. The Dear Leader reportedly asked Hyundai Asan to draft special regulations for the Kaesong industrial estate saying 'North Korean officials have made a futile attempt at this,' according to NKchosun.com.

The massive investment from the ROK government and companies also indicates how closely inter-Korean relations are developing, physically tied by fibre-optic telephone cables, power lines running from South to North and the road and rail links augmenting happier lines of invasion. Investors piling billions of dollars into an industrial park right on the flashpoint of a future war suggests they are not banking on their investments being obliterated anytime soon, despite the war of words between the DPRK and US. In the industrial park, money talks. Unfortunately there is not much evidence yet of any pecuniary benefits filtering back to Kaesong itself.

## WHERE TO STAY AND EAT

🏠 **Foreigner Hotel and Restaurant** At Puk Gate, by the Pakyon Falls.

🏠 **Kaesong Folk Hotel** (50 rooms) Traditional one-storey houses built aside a stream during the Ri dynasty, & furnished as such. Absolutely charming place, with little courtyards set in the city's old quarter, great fun. Also has restaurant. $$

🏠 **Janamsan Hotel** (43 rooms) Next to Mt Janam up the road from Sonjuk Bridge. Also has restaurant $$

🏠 **Yokjon Hotel** Opposite Kaeson railway station. Class unknown.

✗ **Thongil Restaurant** At the foot of Mt Janam. Serves local cuisine like *pansnaggi, insam takgom,* Kaesong *posam kimchi,* Kaesong *yakbap.*

✗ Right opposite the Folk Hotel is a charming **courtyard restaurant** serving not only cold noodles but also the multi-dish.

**WHAT TO SEE** Overlooking Kaesong is the pine-tree-covered Mt Songak, with the smaller Mt Janam 'kneeling before it like a cute child to its father'. But it's around the latter hill that Kaesong centres, and Mt Janam is all the more dominant with its crown of bronze, in the form of Kim Il Sung, gesturing to the south. At night the statue is the lucky recipient of the city's only regular power supply, with the huge searchlights illuminating the statue and setting its shadow against low cloud. By day, the 17ha of leafy slopes around it include a revolutionary museum, a monument and 'on-the-spot guidance' from the Great Leader. It's good for views of the city's old quarter. To the statue's left is the **Kwandok Pavilion**, built in 1780, where archery was practised in feudal times:

> The chief out-door manly sport in Corea is, by excellence, that of archery. It is encouraged by the government for the national safety in war, and nobles stimulate their retainers to excellence by rewards. At regular times contests are held, at which archers of reputation compete, the expense and prizes being paid for out of the public purse.
>
> William Eliot Griffis, *The Hermit Nation,* 1882

Cut into the eastern slope of Mt Janam is the charming **Sungyang Lecture Hall**. Confucianism was taught in this private hall, where lived the Confucian official Jong Mong Ju in the dying days of Koryo (he was assassinated on the Sonjuk Bridge). On a north–south axis, the school buildings were in the front and those annexes for sacrificial rites in the rear of the site, while to the east and west lie the dormitories.

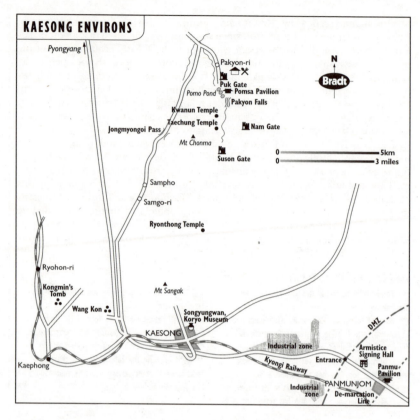

## KAESONG ENVIRONS

Pyongyang

Pakyon-ri

Puk Gate
Pomo Pond     Pomsa Pavilion
Pakyon Falls

Kwanun Temple
Taechung Temple          Nam Gate
Jongmyongoi Pass
Mt Chonma
Suson Gate

N

Bradt

0 ————————————— 5km
0 ————————————— 3 miles

Sampho

Samgo-ri

Ryonthong Temple

Ryohon-ri

Kongmin's
Tomb
Wang Kon

Mt Sangak

Songyungwan,
Koryo Museum
KAESONG

Industrial zone

DMZ

Armistice
Signing Hall

Entrance          Panmu
Pavilion

Kaephong          Kyongi Railway

PANMUNJOM

Industrial
zone     De-marcation
Line

All around Mt Janam's base are narrow-as-a-man alleys of single-storey, clay-brick houses, with gently sweeping roofs and an old-world appearance that both charms and appals. Though not all the roof tiles can be accounted for, it's fortunate that these densely packed houses are no longer thatched.

There's an unmissable neo-Korean edifice, the **Kaesong Schoolchildren's Palace**, for 3,000 children to engage in after-school activities.

From Koryo times, Kaesong had been a great castle city, with a royal palace stashed within an inner and outer castle. The southern gate to the inner castle, **Nam Gate**, has been reconstructed and dominates the crossroads just off from Thongil Street. Originally built in 1391, it stood as the southern gate of Kaesong's inner castle until it was destroyed during the Korean War. The gate houses the **Yonbok Temple bell**, made in 1346 for Yonbok Temple and moved to the gate in 1563 when the temple burnt down. Weighing 14 tonnes, it's covered with figures of tortoises, crabs, dragon, phoenix, deer, and images of the Buddha, and the two dragons on top of the bell indicate 'intrepid spirit'. The bell can be heard 4km away.

Bishop (see page 224) wrote that the road was lined with monuments to good governors, magistrates, faithful widows and pious sons. Very few such sites remain, but walking east along Chongnyon Street, possibly the same road that caused Bishop to call Kaesong a 'one-road town', you come to a bridge and a road going left. A hundred metres up here on the right is **Sonjuk Bridge**, a tiny stone crossing built in 1215 that now has a small fence round it and another crossing next to it. Ri Song Gye assassinated Jong Mong Ju, a civil servant and loyalist to the Koryo dynasty, on this bridge in 1392. Where Jong's blood fell, it stained the bridge (visible today?!) or from the blood grew bamboo. To commemorate the incident, a descendant of Jong fenced off the bridge in 1780.

Jong's loyalty is also celebrated at the **Songmin Monument** just beyond the bridge, erected in 1641 along with two monuments, one to the memory of the government official Gyong Jowho who was killed with Jong. Loyalty to the Ri dynasty inspired the monuments set across the road from the bridge, with two large stelae set on the backs of tortoises. The left dates from 1740 and King Yong Jo and the right from 1872 and King Ko Jong.

At the base of Mt Ogwan is the **Koryo-era Ryongthong Temple**, or rather the rebuild that was completed in 2005, a joint effort between UNESCO and South Korean Buddhist groups.

A renowned Buddhist priest of the 11th century, Ui Chon, founded the sect of Buddhism in Korea and at one time resided at the temple which became a centre of Buddhist learning. It burnt down at the end of the 16th century and its pagoda was buried. That the temple dated from the Koryo era makes its current location near the DMZ all the more significant, with Koryo being the first unified Korean kingdom, and the temple being rebuilt with cross-Korean co-operation. The temple was built to look circa mid-11th century by the Koryo Art Studio.

**Songyungwan** This large education complex of 20 buildings was founded in AD992 as the Kukjagam, the highest educational institute for the civil service as Kaesong was directed towards being the intellectual heart of Koryo as well as its political capital. The children of Koryo and later Ri aristocracy attended the school to learn the Confucian ways of administration and sacrifice. Renamed Songyungwan from 1308, it was expanded but burnt down during the Japanese invasion of 1592 and was rebuilt ten years later. The main buildings are on a typically Confucian north–south axis, with a pleasure ground for archery and swinging over the west side. Since 1987, the site has been home to the **Koryo Museum**, a good little museum with a thousand pieces of pottery, iron work, prints and relics from the Koryo dynasty, with readable presentations of life in those times, and some thousand-year-old pagodas rescued from Hyonhwa, Hungguk and Pulil temples, all overlooked by 500-year-old ginko trees and a 900-year-old Zelkova. East of the museum are two mounds of a tomb that are worth investigating.

On the southern foot of Mt Songak, 2km north of Nam Gate, sits the site of the Koryo royal palace of **Manwoldae**, dating from the AD900s, with a part of the Kaesong Outer Castle, and the Chomsongdae astronomical observatory in most use between 1024 and the late 1300s. The Koryo Museum has more on the observatory.

A fleeting excursion could be made to Anhwa Temple, 4km from Nam Gate and built in AD930 on the mid-slope of Mt Songak. Here studied Wang Sin, a cousin of King Wang Kon. Obaek Hall's thousand Buddhas protected it from the ravages of war, and the seven-storey pagoda survived too.

## OUT OF TOWN

**King Kongmin's Tomb** Fourteen kilometres southwest of central Kaesong is the charming tomb of the 31st King of Koryo from 1352. King Kongmin was a skilled painter and draughtsman, and when his wife died in 1365 he designed two tombs side by side (construction completed in 1372), the right one housing his wife and the left he entered upon his death in 1374. The statues are of military and civil officials. The 'older' military figure is on the outside, better able to defend the king from attack through his veteran experiences, and the older civil officials are nearer the tomb than the youthful assistants, as maturity guarantees better advice to the king. The tiger outside the tomb is representative of the Koryo ancestry and the sheep of his wife's Mongol descent.

**Wang Kon's Tomb and the Pakyon Falls** Just over 3km due west of Nam Gate in Haeson-ri, on the road to Pakyon Falls is the **Tomb of King Wan Kon** (AD877–943), the founder of Koryo. He was born into a wealthy farming family and his father held great influence as a local aristocrat and landowner. Wan Gon served as a civil servant from the age of 20 and achieved high rank. His coup d'état in June 918 overthrew the Thaebong state and founded the Koryo, inheriting Koguryo's remnants and bringing Silla and Paekche under the rule of Kaesong. He died in AD943 and they built his tomb there, with lawns carpeting up to it. Statues of officials and animals, stone lamps for burning incense, an offertory table and images of 12 guardian gods all guard the tomb. But it is a bit new – possibly renovations were over-enthusiastically done.

**Pakyon Falls** Moving north from the tombs, the road gets grottier and tighter as you head up through the Jongmyongsa Pass and down into a valley of *insam*. You're en route to Pakyon Falls, a delightful waterfall 24km from Kaesong, tucked into a sharp valley fort on Mt Taehung.

As you turn right through the village of Pagyon-ri, there appears on the left a monument to the falls. Then there appears Puk Gate, a large edifice that fronts the Taehungsan Fort surrounding the falls. The fort, established before Koryo, was beefed up to defend the new capital Kaesong, and along its 10km of lacing walls still stand the Nam and Sosan gates. Puk is flanked by a hotel and restaurant.

Passing through the gate and past some large ponds, you come to the falls, dropping 37m down from Pakyon pond. To the right is the **Pomsa Pavilion**, dating from Koryo times, that gives a good view and a sit-down. A kilometre further up the valley from the pond is the beautiful **Kwanum Temple**, built when the fort was expanded. With its seven-storey pagoda, it's a fabulously tranquil location that could inspire the most agnostic to concede that, living in such settings and high architecture, the Buddhists were possibly on to something. Nearby is Kwanum Cave that was blessed with two marble Buddhas in AD970 by the temple's high priest.

Another 2km upwards is the private school where Wang Kon's son studied in AD921. The old temple of Taehung that was here burnt down. Later the school building was converted into the temple it is today. This is set dead in the centre of a reserve for the white-bellied black woodpecker, which could be spied from the paths around Taehung Temple that lead to the fort's remaining gates.

## PANMUNJOM AND THE DMZ

Many moons ago there was a road linking Kaesong to Seoul. The road crossed the River Sachon, a tributary of the River Rimjin. People built a bridge with logs and boards and named it Panmun, but rains would wash the bridge away and prevent anyone from crossing, so an inn was built for delayed travellers called Panmunjom (board-framed shop) that lent its name to the village built here. The village itself was wiped from the map during the Korean War, but the name survived and it's now known as the venue for the Korean Armistice Talks. It's here that the 'US imperialists bent the knees down before the Korean people' when the US 'gave up' in 1953, and is the epicentre of the De-Militarised Zone (DMZ). The actual division line of Korea is the Military Demarcation Line (MDL) that snakes across Korea from the mouth of the River Rimjin in the west to the east coast Walbisn-ri, and the DMZ is a 4km-thick buffer straddling the MDL. The DMZ is anything but demilitarised, and is one of the most heavily guarded, heavily mined frontiers in the world. This isn't surprising as a combined total of 1.5 million Korean and 40,000 American soldiers would clash along this frontier, and the DMZ bristles

On 23 June 1951, nearly a year after the Korean War had started, Soviet delegate Yakov Malik suggested that both sides should try peace negotiations. The DPRK's forces had nearly succeeded in uniting the country, as had the United Nations Command (UNC) coming back the other way. A week later, UNC General Ridgeway got word that the communists might be favourable to armistice talks, which were arranged, unarranged and rearranged for Kaesong. The decision to move the talks from Kaesong to Panmunjom in September 1951 was the easiest decision reached by the communists (consisting of the Korean People's Army and the Chinese People's Volunteers) and the UNC, and it totally dominated discussions for two weeks. The agenda finally decided upon was to agree what a ceasefire meant, how it was to be implemented, where (which involved drawing a demarcation line while fighting continued) and what to do with prisoners of war (POWs). Two years of long, tedious and tortuous negotiations followed, while talking peace took second place to another day's fighting that could tip the balance in a side's favour. Both delegations, the communists led by Korean General Nam Il, and the UNC by Lieutenant-General William K Harrison, engaged in time-wasting tactics and talks descended into vitriolic slanging matches, with the most colourful language coming from the communists. As soon as a point of conduct or principle of a ceasefire was agreed, one side accused the other of violating it and raised hell if they didn't storm out, resuming negotiations by letter days or weeks later.

The repatriation of POWs took the most debate. The UNC declared they held up to 132,500 POWs, and the communists held around 11,400 UNC and 7,150 ROK troops (a disputed figure), with fierce debate over how a POW would be defined. The lists lengthened as fighting went on and shortened as dribs and drabs of POWs were repatriated through Panmunjom. The communists demanded their POWs be repatriated whether they wanted to or not, which the UNC insisted was a matter of free choice. Thousands of POWs on both sides were slain after capture and others held in camps so foul that prisoners grew sick and died while their captors looked on. Nam Il and Harrison signed an armistice on 27 July 1953. Accusations of violations of the armistice have flown from all sides every other week since.

with artillery and troops ready to let rip at the drop of grenade. As you are driven in and out of the area, try and spot as many disguised sentry points, pill-boxes, tank-traps, machine-gun and artillery posts as you can. Having said that, the atmosphere is overall surprisingly relaxed, especially compared with the Friendship Exhibition in Myohyangsan, and while here more than anywhere permission for photos is needed, the officer guiding you will yay or nay with a friendly bat of his hand.

**DMZ WILDLIFE AND THE PEACE PARK** So little actual human activity for good or ill goes on in the DMZ (for obvious risks of being shot or blown up) that wildlife, particularly endangered species, have been seen to thrive in this fenced-in strip of land. It is unsurprisingly difficult for any ologists to get in and check what hops amid the mines, but Manchurian crane, ringtail pheasant, spot-billed duck, black-tailed gull, white-naped and red-crowned cranes, and the black-faced spoonbill have been sighted, as have bears, wildcats, leopards, deer and Siberian tiger in the hillier parts, as well as freshwater turtles, terrapins and butterflies. The DMZ has become such a haven for species that are endangered elsewhere that plans are afoot to turn this buffer zone to keep the peace into a 'peace park', to protect a substantial

On the lane to the Bridge of No Return, southwest of the huts, occurred a bizarre incident on 18 August 1976 that became known to the US side as the 'Panmunjom Axe Murders'. A group of ROK and US soldiers arrived near the bridge to prune a large poplar tree obscuring the view of two proximate UNC checkpoints. Captain Arthur Bonifas with First Lieutenant Mark Barrett and a Korean officer oversaw the task as a group of Korean People's Army (KPA) soldiers arrived. The KPA officer demanded the pruning be stopped; when it didn't, the KPA soldiers attacked the group with axes, knives and clubs, killing Bonifas and Barrett and injuring ten more. The KPA claimed that the tree pruning was a cover for provocative attacks on KPA checkpoints. Over the next few days, tensions ran high as the KPA shot at patrolling US aircraft while both sides readied for further bloodshed. The US response was Operation Paul Bunyon early on 21 August. US and ROK infantry and artillery trained their guns on KPA positions as US air-force bombers readied from across Asia and the US scowled the skies. A US 'task force' completed the pruning. The Americans now call the JSA 'Camp Bonifas', and the JSA was summarily divided, with the Bridge of No Return going into the southern half. The KPA built themselves a new bridge in three days, calling it '72-hour Bridge'.

slice of the peninsula's biodiversity. Nelson Mandela has put his name to the scheme that supporters are asking the United Nations to endorse. The park would symbolically convert the DMZ from a symbol of division into one of peace and unity. However, in an ironic twist, the haven is being threatened by those same forces of reconciliation; rail and road links across the DMZ will require the area's de-mining, and may destroy these fragile habitats. For updates about this plan, visit www.dmzforum.org.

You may lunch in a resthouse on the way in to the DMZ. Gritty rice.

**What to see** The entrance to the DMZ is 8km south of Kaesong, and the first building at the entrance is the **General Lecture Room**. Its small shop sells a masterpiece book of propaganda about the Americans and their lackey puppets. It's here also that, over an impressive map of the area, you meet your Korean People's Army officer, who leads you around the DMZ sites.

The officer (and any others needing a lift) board your vehicle at the entrance gate, through which is a little lane kitted out with an amazing array of anti-tank traps, from block-obstacles, drop-down barriers, ditches and moats, leading towards the **Armistice Talks Hall,** a pretty little hut with a small stele outside. This is 1km into the DMZ and is where the Korean War Armistice Talks were held. It took a year of fighting from 1950 for both sides' armies to grind to a halt pretty much back where they'd started, and talks began in June 1951 in Kaesong itself. Two more years passed in which hundreds of thousands of lives were squandered while talks continued in this hut, in what is now an eerily quiet part of the world.

Next to the Armistice Talks Hall is a large, light-coloured building with a dove on the roof, the hall where the armistice was **signed** on 27 July 1953, and the chairs, tables and flags are all preserved there. Here is a museum with the usual impressive display of enlarged photos, documented 'proof' of US aggression and maps of the war, but it's mostly in Chinese.

**The Panmun Pavilions and the Joint Security Area** About 1km southward from the Armistice Halls, you cross the 72-hour Bridge over the Sachon River into the **Joint Security Area** (JSA). The JSA radiates 400m around a row of blue and white huts in which armistice talks continue to this day. From the DPRK side, you approach the huts from behind the elevated Panmungak Hall, an austere, Soviet-style building flanked by the carved signature of Kim Il Sung. Opposite Panmungak on the ROK side was once only a small, raised pavilion but now there is also a remarkable building fusing hi-tech modern materials and traditional Korean building style. Between these two architectural emblems of Korea is a tidy row of huts straddling a thin concrete path indicating the military demarcation line between North and South, and the huts are seemingly all that staple the two states together. The hut you will enter is the **Military Armistice Commission Conference Hall,** still used by the Military Armistice Commission and the Neutral Nations Supervisory Commission. In the middle of the hall is a table, across which are strung microphone leads, indicating the demarcation line in the hall, and it's at this table that representatives from the UNC, Korean People's Army and Chinese Volunteer Army sit and thrash out how each side is upholding the armistice, not always in the most cordial fashion. It's also been used for negotiations with the Red Cross and Olympic committee. However, tourists can orbit the table and thereby technically cross into the ROK, but do not touch the microphone leads and do not try to cross the concrete demarcation line outside (one Soviet defector made it in 1983). In the hall there's also a list of participatory countries in the Korean War against the DPRK side that the guides refer to apologetically as you may well come from one of them.

The JSA itself used to be pocked with equidistant United Nations Command and Korean People's Army checkpoints, for, until 1976, both sides had free run of the JSA and jointly maintained its security. This changed in September that year following the bizarre Panmunjom Axe Incident (see box), and the JSA was divided into North and South.

At various points along the road to the JSA, you can see the two flags of Korea flying atop vast masts opposite each other. The DPRK flag mast is in the **Panmunjom-ri co-op farm,** a series of brightly painted apartment blocks that comprises the northern half of a divided village, the southern side of which is Taesong-dong where the ROK flag flies. The ROK call the northern coop 'propaganda village', claiming it has no purpose but to broadcast high volume abuse at Taesong-dong. ROK literature contrasts the villages with ROK photographs of Taesong-dong showing a beaming, happy population that are regularly helped in the fields by smiling soldiers, before darkness falls and the 23.00 curfew begins.

Elsewhere along the DMZ you can see an 8m-high concrete wall, the **Wall of Division,** in the southern half, built from 1976 to 1979 by US forces along nearly all the DMZ. Going due east for 27km from Nam Gate you will eventually get to a good viewing point, to see this coldly impressive Korean wall.

**VISITING FROM THE ROK** On the DPRK side you'll be spied upon by UN troops with binoculars and may be dazzled by the flash photography of a tour group from the other side, mainly Americans, ROK citizens and Japanese who might otherwise never have a chance of stepping into the DPRK. Panmunjom is only a 90-minute drive from Seoul, and day-long bus tours running from Seoul can include commentaries on the area's history and visits to the tunnels that the DPRK dug under the demarcation line into the South to sneak fully armoured attacks on Seoul. A series of monuments to the 15 countries' forces dot the route into the DMZ, and should you stray past a sky-blue obelisk saying DMZ you know where you are. Tours do not run every weekday and not on holidays, so check with operators.

## Tour operators

**Korea Travel Bureau** 1465-11 Seocho-Dong, Seocho-Gu, Seoul, Korea 137-073; ☎ +82 2 585 7072 4; f 82 2 585 1187; e tour@ktbinc.co.kr; www.go2korea.co.kr, www.ktbtour.co.kr. One-day tours are around US$90. You must bring your passport on the day, your hair must not be unkempt & your

safety in the DMZ cannot be guaranteed.
**Panmunjom Travel Centre** Lotte Hotel, 2nd Flr (Main Bldg), Chung-Gu, Sogong-dong, Seoul City; ☎ +82 (0) 2 771 5593 5; f +82 (0)2 771 5596; www.panmunjomtour.com

*Co-op farm on the way to Kaesong*

# 5

# Nampo, Mt Kuwol and Haeju

From Mangyongdae, follow the 'Youth Hero Motorway', so named for having been built by the young, as the road tacks alongside the Taedong River, 55km southwestwards to reach Nampo city. This route passes through one of the DPRK's most industrialised areas, and passes the **Chollima Steel Complex** and the **Taean Heavy Machine Complex**, both sites having great significance as landmark points of technology and scale in the progress of DPRK's post-war strategies of reconstructing and advancing heavy industry.

Another road goes from Pyongyang past the tombs of **Kangso** and **Tokhung-ri** (outside Taepyong) and then **Kangso** town where the 7,000m, 18-hole **Pyongyang Golf Course**, built and financed by Japanese-Koreans for Kim Il Sung's 75th birthday, awaits to give the golfing experience that no golfer could ever miss (a round passing for around €65). Legend has it that the Dear Leader played a round here and scored 18 holes-in-one (quite a record and even more quite a drinks' bill), but the legend is rumoured to actually be one of Western origin. Hmmm. There is another 9-hole course next to the Yanggakdo Hotel and a driving range off Chongchun Street in West Pyongyang – more courses are being built in Kaesong).

The area around Kangso is also noted for its numerous springs of mineral water which helps the 'function of secretion, absorption and motion in the alimentary canal, accelerates the formation of bile and excretion, increases the amount of urine and promotes the excretion of stones in the urinary canal,' according to KCNA. When it is not being bottled and shipped to Pyongyang, the water is the bedrock (as it were) of spa treatment centres in the area, where the waters have bucked contamination from industry and facilities are open for visitors to bathe in mineral waters.

Around and south of Nampo is the DPRK's main agricultural area and the region is best noted in Korean lore for its apples, although in recent years both the water and the fruits have been imperiled by increasingly intermittent rainfall.

## TOMBS

Across Korea have been found thousands of tombs, forts, walls, gates, relics and settlements in varying states of repair, a great many of them dating from the Koguryo period (37BC–AD668). The most exceptional of these sites have intricate mural paintings depicting. customs and other less salubrious goings on in Koguryo court and country life. Koguryo also included parts of China, and UNESCO estimates that there are around 10,000 Koguryo tomb sites in China and across Korea, but only 90 or so have such wall murals.

Of those that have been long known, many have suffered the withers of time as well as ransacking and robbery over the centuries, most recently under the Japanese (who might have been expected to have some respect for these sites), plunder that can 'never be covered up … they will certainly be made to pay for their crimes despite the flow of time,' KNCA commented half a century after the events.

But many of these tombs, especially around Pyongyang and to the southwest, are undergoing restoration and renovation, nay, total reconstructions – some sites have been spruced up with 'authentic' statues that are just tat, but others are worth seeing.

Of greatest note are the three tombs of Kangso, the Royal Tomb of King Tongmyong and three tombs in Anak (16km north-northeast of Sinchon and due west of Sariwon). They are all on a list of 63 Koguyro tombs in Pyongyang, Nampo and South Hwanghae, collectively known as 'the complex of Koguryo tombs', that UNESCO designated as World Heritage Sites in 2004, along with several Koguryo forts and remains in northeast China. Such is the prestige of this ancient kingdom that UNESCO's listing was partly ascribed to be a bid to force the two communist countries to 'share' their common past and stop rewriting it with a view to getting one over the other.

Of the Anak tombs, No 3, that of a provincial king, is notable not only for its paintings and size (seven chambers) but more for a rare inscription that allows the construction to be dated to 357AD.

Other sites at Susan-ri, Yaksu-ri and Taechu-ri (in an area around the Kangso tombs, 20km west-southwest of Mangyongdae) can be walked around. The tombs at Anak, Kangso and Tokhung-ri can be entered, but only with some advance preparation and for a price – the downside to the preservation is the associated cost of 'unsealing' the tombs for visitors, and the charge for visits within the tombs was last quoted at €100 per person per tomb.

## NAMPO

*38.4° north, 125.2° east, 55km west of Pyongyang, South Pyongan Province, Taedong River estuary, West Korea Bay*

In that Inchon is Seoul's city on the sea for trade, so is Nampo for Pyongyang, being on the mouth of the Taedong River and only a short scoot or sail from the capital.

With a population of nearly three-quarters of a million, Nampo is to most intents DPRK's second city, where cargoes for Pyongyang are unloaded, ships are built and repaired in the state's largest shipbuilding facilities, copper is smelted, electrodes, textiles and glass products manufactured, and many a living eked out by fishing on the West Sea (or to non-Koreans, Yellow Sea) – all a very fortunate array of activities as there is really not that much else to do in the city.

In fact for centuries the only activity was fishing, not a bad thing to do with the West Sea, rich in shellfish, sea bream, croakers, lizard fish, prawns, cutlass fish, horse mackerel, squids, flounders and blue crabs, being hooked, trapped and netted by Koreans, Chinese and Japanese for some time, although this is becoming a bit of an issue, causing bullets to fly. There is also said to be oil under them there sea waters.

At the turn of the 19th century Nampo's location at the mouth of the Taedong River realised greater significance as the village grew into a naval-trading town. Post-1945 the government of the DPRK directed Nampo's most spectacular urban and industrial growth and in the mid-1980s was built the gargantuan West Sea Barrage.

South Korean companies are already operating textile factories, an electronics complex is under construction and an industrial park twixt Nampo and Haeju, is on a similar scale to the Kaesong project.

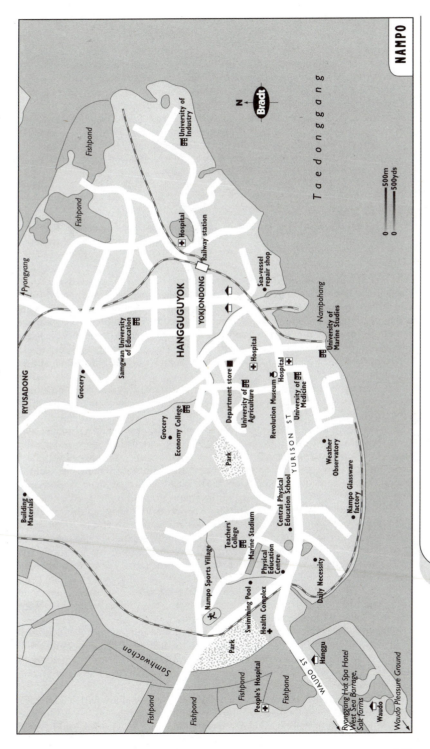

NAMPO

5

Taedonggang

0 ———— 500m
0 ———— 500yds

↑Pyongyang

RYUSADONG

HANGGUGUYOK

YOKJONDONG

University of Industry

Fishpond

Fishpond

Fishpond

Hospital

Railway station

Sea-vessel repair shop

Nampohang

University of Marine Studies

Samgwan University of Education

Grocery

Grocery

Economy College

Department store

University of Agriculture

Hospital

Revolution Museum

Hospital

University of Medicine

YURISON ST

Park

Weather Observatory

Building Materials

Nampo Glassware factory

Central Physical Education School

Teachers' College

Marine Stadium

Physical Education Centre

Daily Necessity

Nampo Sports Village

Samhwachon

Swimming Pool

Health Complex

Park

People's Hospital

Fishpond

Fishpond

Fishpond

Fishpond

Fishpond

WAUDO ST

Hangu

Ryonggang Hot Spa Hotel West Sea Barrage, Salt farms

Waudo

Waudo Pleasure Ground

145

**WHERE TO STAY**

🏠 **Hanggu Hotel** (109 rooms) Waudo recreation ground. $

🏠 **Ryonggan Spa Hotel** East of Nampo, 80km from Pyongyang. Stone cottages & enough mineral water to bathe in.

**WHAT TO SEE** Sights to see in Nampo now include a tour of the **sea-vessel repair shop** and of late the city's **orphanage** has been open to visitors, and the **Nampo Glass factory** is where all of the sexy neon in Pyongyang and elsewhere is produced. The city's other features include the 1970s' buildings in **Nampo Sports Village** and the **Waudo Pleasure Grounds** of Wau Islet and Wan Peak. Going west through the city, great plains of solar salt farms (as opposed to mines) roll right out to the point where 6km west of Nampo begins the **Nampo West Sea Barrage**.

The barrage is the main point of any tour, a massive feat of civil engineering, through which all vessels to Pyongyang pass, through three locks able to take ships up to 50,000 tonnes in size.

It was built as a one-fix solution to many problems – to control the tides and allow Nampo port to operate without ships being beached; to prevent periodic large-scale flooding from Nampo all the way to Pyongyang (as happened with fatal consequences as recently as 1969) and protect the farmland by the same token, a critical area of agricultural output for DPRK; and further to that, to serve as a massive single-fix structure to revitalise the region's agriculture.

This involved reclaiming some 500,000 acres of land for farming from wetlands and lagoons, to back up a 130 square mile, 2.7 billion cubic metre reservoir and a 70km canal built to irrigate the farmlands of South Hwanghae with river water now protected from ebbing salination, and not least to provide hydro-electric power to feed large-scale fertiliser factories to feed the farms and increase rice and grain output several-fold.

The barrage opened in 1986, crossing the 8km-wide estuary, costing an equivalent of US$4billion over its five-year construction, and not a few lives from the three KPA divisions employed in building it.

Obviously such vast-scale projects will have as vast impacts, not necessarily all of them positive, with the loss of wetlands and the halting of tidal flows impacting on the river and coastal estuary's abilities to cleanse themselves, particularly of industrial pollutants that by and large pipe unchecked into the waters, impacting marine health and fish stocks.

It is not clear the extent to which the barrage has alleviated the DPRK's agricultural problems. It may be reluctantly noted that Nampo has in the past half-decade been a major point of import, along with Haeju, for hundreds of thousands of tonnes of humanitarian foodstuffs and fertiliser, principally supplied from the ROK.

The monument at the barrage's northern entrance celebrates the sacrifice of the KPA and others who built it, and the Pi Islet Pavilion which overlooks the barrage shows a stirring video of its construction.

Otherwise, the Nampo beach resorts are well known and liked by Koreans and foreign residents, and it's worth getting an afternoon's frazzling on the sand if dwelling in this part. In addition, or else, you might prefer mineral water to salt water. At the Ryonggang Hot Spa Hotel are provided baths filled with local spring water that are 'rich in bromine and radon'. This is a charming retreat of little stone lodges near Sindok, 80km from Pyongyang on the Youth Hero Highway. Other spa sites listed, but of which little is known, include Susan Spa, Chongsan Spa and Lake Thaesang. The town of Kangso has similar mineral springs' facilities, a source of life in contrast with Kangso's other hearth of interest, the Koguryo tombs.

**UNRYUL** The southern end of the barrage connects with Unryul County, on the northwest coast of South Hwanghae Province.

Unryul's dominant industry is iron ore extraction and processing, for which the Unryul conveyor belt, almost as long as the sea barrage, was built and is worth a look for the sheer scale of this great black tongue of rock. In Unryul town, diversion may be made to the **Unryul Revolution Museum**, dedicated to Kim Il Sung's father, Kim Hyong Jik. From there speed onwards to the town of Kwail in the so-named county, where fruit farms cover most of the cultivated land, especially around **Songgok-ri**. The farms and mines crop up amid the shallow, afforested slopes and trickling streams sliding away from the Mt Kuwol range of peaks and hills that commands the district.

## MT KUWOL

*38.3° north, 125.2° east, South Hwanghae Province*
Mt Kuwol is a gentle, handsome range of peaks, hills, waterfalls and spas, with a healthy sprinkling of temples and hermitages, roped within a nature reserve covering 110km². Its name is taken from the ninth month of the lunar calendar, when the area's natural blooms are at their most radiant. The mountain and its nature reserve have fallen off the tourist radar (for foreign tourists at any rate) in recent years, and not all of the sites are accessible. But it is worth seeing, even if just passing through, and noting what could be seen.

The highest peak is the 954m Sahwang peak, followed by O at 859m, Insa at 688m and then Inhwang and Juga peaks. Sahwang is looped by the remains of the 5.2km **Kuwol Mountain fort**, built during the Koguryo dynasty (277BC–AD668) and expanded under the Ri (1392–1910). The fortress gates on all but the northern side are still visible. Also around Sahwang is the **Samsong Pleasure Ground**.

The site is sprinkled with relics such as fortresses, temples, historical houses and tombs, related to the early development of Korea as well as to the origins of Buddhism.

The faded beauty of the 9th-century **Woljong Temple**, rebuilt in the 15th century, hides in the southern Jol Valley, east of Asa peak. The restored **Samsong Temple** was originally dedicated to Korea's spiritual founder, Tangun, and during Koryo times the temple added Tangun's father and grandfather to its rolls of reverence.

The mountain of **Sokdamgugok** (nine valleys of pools and rocks) sits on the River Sokdam, 12km north of Haeju. In the Unbyong Valley (namely, the finest among nine valleys) sits the 15th-century Sohyon Academy, where the famous scholar Li Ryul Gok taught, and the names of Sokdamgugok's various peaks and valleys are themed along with the celebration of all things peaceful, quiet and meditative, from the Munsan (best place for reading), Kwan Rock (horsehair hat), Chwilyong (a flower-patterned blind), Chohyop (fishing place) to the Kumtan (stream murmuring like Komungo).

An official nature reserve since the 1970s, Mt Kuwol is supposedly visited by half a million tourists each year, being a short belt from Pyongyang, but despite being listed as one of the five celebrated mountains of Korea, along with Paektu, Kumgang, Myohyang and Jiri, Kuwol has been an irregular entrant on Western tourists' itineraries this century. In 2003 however it was listed as a UNESCO Biosphere Reserve, mostly to protect a 'typical forest ecosystem of Korea which survived the damages of the Korea War', according to a report from the DPRK State Academy of Sciences. It's an area of interest for its mix of pristine and rehabilitated forest, mostly temperate, broadleaf stuff, *Abies nephrolepis, Picea jezoensis, Eichornia umbellata, Castanea crenata, Pinus koraiensis, Fagara schinifolia*, etc. Its range of ecosystems from 900m-high ranges to wetlands, includes the coastal Unryul Migratory Birds Reserve estuaries; black-faced spoonbill, Chinese egret and red-crowned crane are found in the wetland dominated by *Suaeda japonica, Phragmis communis* and *Carex dispalata*. In the biosphere reserve is also one of DPRK's most important rice producing areas, although most of that is 'transition area' and therefore open to use. Within the reserve is also one of the North's most important rice production areas and the base is rich in medicinal herbs such as ginseng and *Forsythia ovata*.

## HAEJU

*38.05° north, 125.45° east, 140km south of Pyongyang, capital of South Hwanghae Province, located on Haeju Bay, Korea's West Sea. Population 236,000*

In contrast with Nampo's more recent resurgence, Haeju has been in decline after centuries of prominence as a trading port with China and also as a scholars' town of Buddhist learning, in keeping with the fact that in 983 it was made one of 12 civilian-run regional capitals under the Koryo King Seongjong. Little would interrupt these two strands of the city's business for many of the intervening years up to the late 19th century, whereupon it would become noteworthy to history more by default, being the birthplace of one of the leaders of the 1894 Tonghak rebellion, Kim Gu, and Ahn Chung Gun, the assassin of the Japanese colonial governor Hirobumi Ito in 1909.

In the early 20th century the city's trading position was somewhat sidelined by the building of the Seoul–Sinuiju railway. The area became a hotbed of intra-Korean fighting in the run-up to the Korean War,

In the years preceding the Korean War, Haeju was host to the Kangdon Political Institute, which trained guerrillas and political officers for infiltration and sabotage raids into ROK, with several thousand troops being trained in activities further south in the months preceding June 1950, although Kim Il Sung reputedly closed the academy as it was being run by a potential rival from South Korea.

What with being just 3km from the 38th parallel, and so part of or proximate to the stalemate battle lines of the late Korean War, Haeju was possibly inevitably going to be in the thick of it.

It was the first city taken by ROK forces in a counter-attack in June 1950, and thereafter became a major through route for refugees fleeing the conflict from both directions, while the city was repeatedly strafed, bombed and shelled by British, US, Australian and Canadian carrier-borne aircraft and ships at various points throughout the Korean War, with tens of thousands killed, mainly civilians.

Post-war, with the DML redrawn more like a wiggly and heavily mined 38th parallel, Haeju found new favour by being the DPRK's only west coast port not

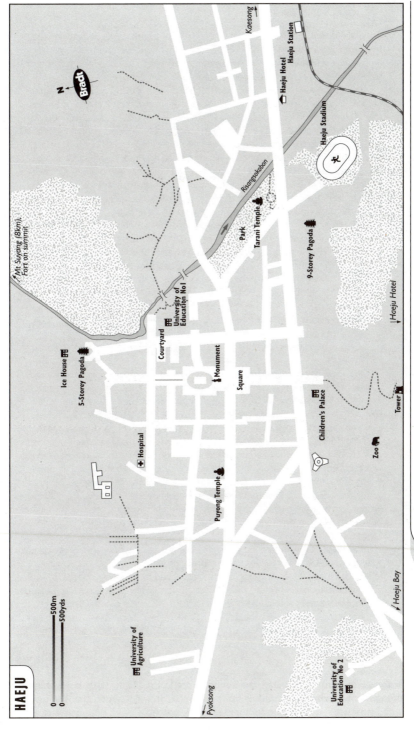

# HAEJU

0 [====] 500m
0 [====] 500yds

N

Bradt

Mt Suyang (8km),
Fort on summit

Ice House

5-Storey Pagoda

Courtyard

University of
Education No1

Hospital

Monument

Square

Puyong Temple

University of
Agriculture

Pyoksong

University of
Education No 2

Children's Palace

Zoo

Tower

Haeju Bay

Risongsokobon

Park

Tarani Temple

9-Storey Pagoda

Haeju Hotel

Kaesong

Haeju Hotel

Haeju Station

Haeju Stadium

For all the diplomatic and economic rapprochement that has gone on between the two Korean states since the late 1990s, in spite of tensions over the DPRK's nuclear ambitions, the West Sea (or Yellow Sea to non-Koreans) has been the venue for some bitter spats between the Korean fishing and naval fleets.

The DMZ division extends into the West Sea by way of the Northern Line Limit, or NLL, as drawn on the map by the UN after the Korean War and as a boundary foisted from outside it is not a line the DPRK has ever accepted. Naval boundaries can be inadvertently crossed at the best of times (as British sailors off Iran know all too well), and such a watery line between two states on the cusp of war is bound to lead to trouble, especially when under the line lie hundreds of thousands of blue crabs, a crustaceous bounty worth around US$30,000 a tonne and of value in both Koreas as well as sold profitably to China and Japan, that has led fleets of fishing boats backed by flotillas of navy craft to cross the line both ways daily, particularly during the peak crab season of May–June.

In 1999, several ROK sailors were wounded and 30-odd DPRK sailors killed when a torpedo boat was sunk in the first armed naval clash between the Koreas since 1953. A ROK navy boat was sunk in 2002 with numerous dead on both sides; and the ROK navy fired shots at northern fishing boats the following year.

Various theories have surrounded the skirmishes, which in the press beyond the DPRK have largely blamed that state for it, irrespective of what actually happened on the seas.

The shoot-outs have been seen as a politically metaphorical tool for DPRK dissatisfaction with other issues, such as moves to normalise diplomatic or economic relations between the US and DPRK, or moves to talk about intra-Korean family reunifications.

One explanation offered at the time of the 1999 shoot-out was the DPRK military seeking to express its dissatisfaction with the DPRK leadership over a visit to Pyongyang by US envoy William Perry, as improved relations with the US would ultimately imperil the need for a large military. Indeed, the state needed to reaffirm its political and ideological sovereignty in a kickback against the seduction of capitalist corrupters (about better US relations, family reunifications, rapprochement with the ROK, anything) in their own somewhat oblique manner. An alternative explanation was that Perry also visited Japan and ROK to discuss the regional situation, upon which DPRK thought 'well if you're going to talk about me I'm going to give you something talk about!' Joint military exercises being planned by the US and ROK were another given excuse, compounded by the US having successfully bombed out the Milosevic regime and apparently a similar plot was being planned on the Peninsula.

Most theories revolve around the DPRK needing aid to survive and usually only getting it when it lets rip. In addition the DPRK is unhappy with the NLL and so sought to kick up a fuss in its usual non-diplomatic manner and start shooting about it.

That last theory may be the closest to the truth. South Korean boats unfortunately strayed into a part of the sea where jurisdiction is hotly contested by its northern neighbour and the bullets ultimately flew. Such is the booty of a boatload of crabs, which themselves don't respect borders, that both sides will risk bullets and shells for them.

to freeze in winter. Industry was added to trade for Haeju with large chemical and cement production facilities built post-war, and it is stated that the city is a noted producer of semi-conductors. The city's airfield is a KPA gig and is where more than a few dodgy operations against the South Koreans have been launched.

But for the longest time, the city's position on the cusp of the DRPK's bread basket province of South Hwanghae, and the (once) bounteous West Sea for fish, has meant that much of the city's trade and later industries have been involved in agriculture, fish products, food processing and exports. Indeed these trades had earned the city the moniker of 'city of rice and fish' with rice being markedly cheaper to buy than in other Korean conurbations.

However, this has also made for stark contrast with the food crises affecting DPRK and according to Good Friends: Centre for Peace, Human Rights and Refugees reports, Haeju is still suffering harshly from malnutrition as floods as recently as 2006 adversely affected transportation, power production and industry and farmland, leaving many people on low incomes facing tight food supplies and resulting high prices for rice and grain.

Hopes for Haeju's industrial rejuvenation mostly rest with Hyundai's proposed investment in the city's port facilities and the building of rail links to Haeju, along with a large-scale, ten-year redevelopment of the city and its industries, focusing mainly on textile, shoe and toy manufacture.

## WHERE TO STAY
**Haeju Hotel** (42 rooms) On the edge of Haeju Sq. $

**WHAT TO SEE** Because of Haeju's undulating fortunes, the city is very rarely open to foreign visits, and the War and subsequent rebuild has left not much of Haeju's illustrious past to be seen. There are a few remains of the **Puyong Temple** in town, the **Cheonwang** (Heavenly King) monument that dated from Koryo times and an arbour called the **'Sami Arbour'** from the Ri dynasty.

Possibly it's best to start from **Mt Suyang**, an impressive mound that rises up to 946m in height and the peak of which sits about 7km northwest of Haeju's centre.

At the foot of Mt Suyang is the **Five-storey Pagoda**, built from granite during the early Koryo period, and close to it is the gaping arch of the **stone ice house**, once faced with loam and peat, being first built around 1000 and rebuilt in 1735, and the **Koryo Sami Pavilion**. Another temple, the Haeju Temple, is often mentioned in local literature although has long disappeared, and it may be here that was once a statue of the Great Buddha with a magical stone in its forehead that glowed red every time Japan threatened to invade. The Puyong Pavilion has been restored to its original state, a government report on the restoration of sites says, but its location is not verified.

Changdae Peak is on the southern side of Mt Suyang and is very close to Haeju's northern edge. Here sits the **Koryo Fort**. Within its 8km of walls, which in parts rise up to 7m in height, 14 command posts and gates of the barracks are identifiable, and the fort was in successful usage up to at least 1894 when it repulsed an attack by the Tonghak army. From Suyang's southeast side flow the waters of the **Suyangsan Falls**, falling some 128m in all, being split halfway through the descent by a large pool.

The area is also dotted with statues and slogans commemorating the 'Great Leader'.

It's 54km north from Haeju to the resthouse of Chaeryong town, and another 20 to Sariwon, from where you can go back south to Kaesong or loop up back to Pyongyang. A road running directly eastwards to Kaesong exists, via the spa towns of Yonan and Paechon, but the accessibility of this route is tenuous.

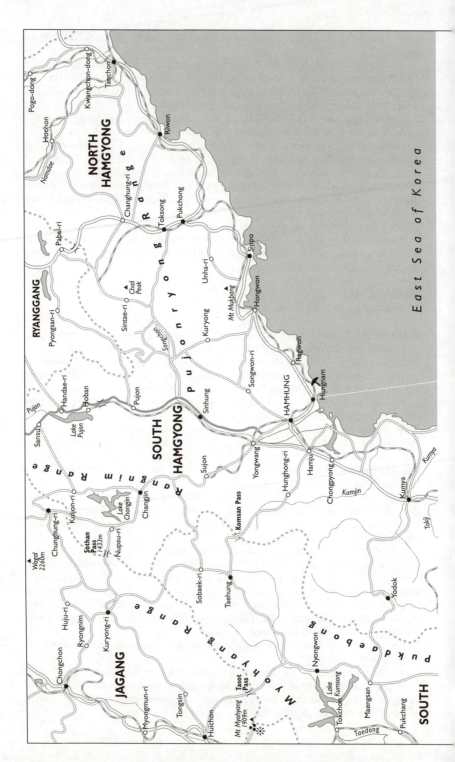

East Sea of Korea

NORTH HAMGYONG

RYANGGANG

SOUTH HAMGYONG

JAGANG

SOUTH

Taichon
Kwangchon-dong
Pogo-dong
Hochon
Namdae
Riwon
Pabal-ri
Changhung-ri
Toksong
Pukchong
Pyongsan-ri
Chail Peak
Sintae-ri
Unha-ri
Sinpo
Kuryong
Mt Mukbang
Hongwon
Handae-ri
Hoban
Pujon
Sinhung
Songwon-ri
Ragwon
Sansu
Lake Pujon
HAMHUNG
Hungnam
Pujon
Sujon
Yongwang
Hunghong-ri
Hamju
Kuljon-ri
Lake Changjin
Changjin
Chongpyong
Kumjin
Kumya
Chunghung-ri
Sothan Pass 1433m
Nupsu-ri
Komsan Pass
Tokji
Wagal 2260m
Huju-ri
Kuryong-ri
Sobaek-ri
Taehung
Yodok
Ryongnim
Nyongwon
Chongchon
Myongmun-ri
Tongsin
Tasot Pass
Mt Myohyang 1909m
Huichon
Maengsan
Lake Kumsong
Tokchon
Pukchang
Taedong

Puiryong Range

Rangnim Range

Myohyang Range

Pukdaebong

Songchon

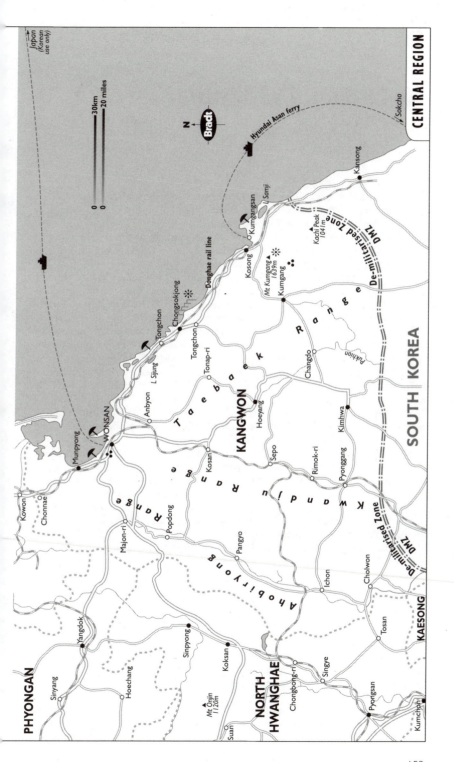

PHYONGAN

Sinyang

Hoechang

Yangdok

Kowon

Chonnae

Majon-ri

Popdong

Anbyon

*L Sijung*

WONSAN

Munpyong

Tongchon

Chongsokjong

Tongchon

Tonap-ri

Kosan

Sepo

Pangyo

Sinpyong

Koksan

*Mt Onjin 1120m*

Suam

Chongbong-ri

NORTH HWANGHAE

Singye

Kumchon

Pyongsan

Tosan

KAESONG

Cholwon

Ichon

Pyonggang

Rimok-ri

Kimhwa

Changdo

Hoeyang

KANGWON

Kosong

Kumgang

*Mt Kumgang ▲ 1639m*

Kumgangsan

*L Samji*

Kansong

*Kachi Peak 104 m*

Pukhron

De-militarised Zone

DMZ

SOUTH KOREA

De-militarised Zone

DMZ

Sokcho

*Hyundai Asan ferry*

Donghae rail line

*T a e b a e k   R a n g e*

*K w a n d j u   R a n g e*

*A h o b i r y o n g   R a n g e*

N

30km

20 miles

0

0

*Japan (Korean use only)*

153

# 6

# North from Pyongyang to Mt Myohyang

*40.05° north, 126.2° east, 150km north of Pyongyan. Chagang, North and South Pyongan provinces meet around it. Weather: January –11.6°C, August 23.7°C, average 8.3°C. 1,300mm rain, mainly in July and August*

Kim Il Sung put it quite succinctly: 'You can see scenic beauty everywhere in our country, but Mt Myohyangsan is particularly well known from ancient times for its wonderful and exquisite geographical features and idyllic scenery.'

Mt Myohyang is a fabulous pocket of peaks and forested valleys in the centre of the country. Its temperate climate makes it a worthwhile visit in all seasons, although in July the windless slopes make it a humidity trap. Mt Myohyang (meaning 'mountain of a single fragrance', which is that of the juniper covering the area) is one of five of Korea's holy mountains, with a famed 1,000-year-old temple at its heart that drew pilgrims for centuries. The DPRK state has reconfirmed the holiness of the area by siting the extraordinary International Friendship Exhibition here.

It takes four hours by the very early morning train from Pyongyang, with the dawn lighting the route along the way, although the site is most easily and usually accessed by road – a 160km drive from Pyongyang via Anju, or 150km via Pyongsong and Sunchon. Away from Anju is **Paekchang Pavilion** and the nearby **Namhung Youth Chemical Complex** on the River Chungchon, which the road follows for a long way. Either way, both roads converge at Kaechon and go through Kujang. Where the River Myohyang meets the River Chongchon, there is a sharp turn-off (to avoid a sharp finish to the road) towards Hyangsan town that is the gate to Sangwon Valley though the town has little else to say for itself. Eight kilometres past Hyangsan Barrage is the pyramidal Hyangsan Hotel and the valley proper begins.

Myohyang mountain is like a wet hand resting on a table, with four valleys running up between the fingers and thumb to the knuckles, or peaks. The River Myohyang runs along the fingertips towards the River Chongchun, and from the road tracing the river begin all the valley walks, some taking a morning, some all day. Myohyang is very much a staple of any tour to DPRK and is really not to be missed. As with many of the other great sights, Hyundai Asan has some plan in the pipeline to develop Myohyang – so see it sooner rather than later.

## WILDLIFE

Wild goat, musk deer, hare, badger, racoon, wild boar and flying squirrels occupy these parts, and leopards and bears occasionally forage in the deciduous forests from the valleys beyond. The thick tree canopy up to 1,000m is structured by 200 species of trees, including Korean maple, many Asiatic oaks, pakdal, Aceraceae, Korean spindle tree, ash, agaric, Asian hazelnut, Chinese sumac, Japanese red pine and Asian white birch. Bark-climbing fern and a multitude of moss, lichen and bryophytes thrive in the humid micro-climate, as do 460 species of herb, with medicinal poppy and aconitum. Azalea, apricot and wild cherry blossom bombard the valley with colour in spring, and magnolia, clove tree and guinguecostatus take over in summer. Blue bird, grosbeak, Korean crested-lark, oriole, Korean scops owl, goldfinch, grey wagtail, woodpecker and cuckoo take in the scene from the skies and char, silver fish, rainbow trout, eel and Moroccan oxycephalus view from the streams.

##  WHERE TO STAY

**Hyangsan Hotel** (228 rooms) 5km from Hyangsan town on the Myohyang River. 15-storey pyramid with all manner of amusements: brilliant foyer with waterfall & the hotel is capped by a revolving restaurant that doesn't quite succeed with the night views. Serviceable décor. This is in all probability the hotel you will stay at. The hotel also offers massages. $$$

**Chongbyong Hotel** (22 rooms). 15mins from the station by car. Small & cosy looking. $

**Chongchon Hotel** (33 rooms) 5min by car from the railway station. Neo-Korean grandeur. $–$$$

## WHAT TO SEE

Just across the River Myohyang, 1km from the Hyangsan, are two huge traditional Korean-style buildings burrowing into the mountainsides, housing the **International Friendship Exhibition** dedicated to the world's gifts for the Great Leaders. On the left of a classical edifice is Kim Il Sung's building, and the right one is for Kim Jong Il. From the moment you see the guards with their silver-plated machine guns, be on your best behaviour, and cast your gaze upon the concrete beams and rafters decorated with Kimilsungia and azaleas. You may (with gloved hands) be allowed to open the four-tonne, bronze-coloured doors of the Kim Il Sung exhibition, doors that open so easily it 'makes you feel mysterious', according to local literature.

Inside, it's hats off, cameras into a kiosk (no, no photos, no negotiation) and baggy cloth socks covering your shoes as you pad around the exhibition's 100 rooms. Be on your best behaviour. It contains 71,000 gifts of homage to the Great Leader, starting with a large room with his statue and a map showing the country and 'rank' of the gifts. You will be asked to bow before the figure of Kim Il Sung, positioned coming down a path from Paektu to greet you (not doing so would simply cause gratuitous offence). Among the gifts and tributes given in honour of Kim Il Sung by global dignitaries over the decades are some bequethed by no less than Billy Graham. Look out for them in the hall where Kim's statue stands. Then, off corridors that disappear into the distance, and between groups of Korean tourists who swiftly disappear from view, you tour long, windowless rooms of gifts, categorised by continent and arranged chronologically. Time-lights buzz on and off from room to room, as you marvel at Mao's and Stalin's railway carriages (Mao pays homage to Kim Il Sung!), a stuffed crocodile drinks' tray holder, fossil-topped tables, Kalashnikov-shaped vodka bottles, gold tanks. It's a pantheon of the great and the dead from lost worlds of politics and style. This enormous collection is like a vast collage of gifts charting the chronology and reach of DPRK foreign relations, as gifts from some countries begin and finish. It's observable how by the early 1990s the gifts become more discreet in the Kim Il Sung Hall, but by the late 1990s improved relations with the ROK saw Kim Jong Il blessed with some excellent consumer durables among 40,000 other gifts.

Crossing the river, it's some 4km left to the Hyangsan, or a few hundred metres right into the Sangwon Valley to find the historically holy **Pohyon Temple**. The Pohyon Temple was founded in 1042 by the monk Kwanghwak, and was named after the saint that guards the morals of Buddha. Half of its original 24 buildings

Religious groups have been the conduit for much of the DPRK's less reported diplomatic efforts, and one of the more outstanding (albeit under-reported) examples of such diplomacy was the invitation of Billy Graham, the righteous conservative American evangelists' evangelist, to the DPRK in spring 1992 and again in 1994. Graham could be seen as the epitome of the mind-set of invasive American missionary Christianity that the DPRK government had reacted so virulently against, yet invite him Kim did.

The trips were great successes. On the first, Graham described Kim as 'very warm and friendly' and said he had 'learned to appreciate Korea's long struggle to preserve its national sovereignty'. The esteem in which Kim held his visitor may be reflected by the proximity of Graham's gift to the Great Leader's figurine in the Friendship Exhibition. In addition to getting on so well with the Great Leader, Graham gave talks at Kim Il Sung University, where a religious studies programme was established in 1989, and also addressed congregations at the then very new churches in Pyongyang, as well as delivering a message from the Pope.

In 1994, as the DPRK's suspected nuclear programme was cooking up a possible meltdown in regional stability and a military altercation with the US looked all but inevitable, Graham returned in a diplomatic effort to defuse the tensions, and war was averted.

Of course, as we all know, the nuclear issue resurrected in 2002, only this time instead of a deal being breached the region has had to endure half a decade of clanking threats, talks and stomping around. That said, in 2006, South Korean church leaders and businessmen persuaded Californian pastor and evangelist Dr Rick Warren, author of best-selling books on divine Christian living, that the DPRK was happy to receive him, with the invite coming just as DPRK missile tests were chucking rocket fuel on its nuclear fire. Dr Warren's invite also included the chance to preach to 15,000 Koreans in Pyongyang in 2007, the first public outdoor Christian service north of the DMZ in half a century. An extraordinary gesture in itself, the event was part of the 100th anniversary of the Pyongyang Revival, a near-miraculous event when in 1907 Pyongyang became the epicentre of a resurgence of Christian spirituality that enshrouded the peninsula. What better occasion for the DPRK to revitalise its Christian connections into the ROK and US – indeed, it was the year the US and DPRK stand-off stood down. The Lord moves in mysterious ways ...

were levelled during the Korean War. Prior to then, the temple housed 60 monks, a fifth of whom were students. Substantially fewer monks await as you enter into Pohyong through the 14th-century Jogye Gate. Beyond this sits a monument to Kwagnhwak and another monk Thamil, founder of the Ansim Temple, and embedded among 1200 characters relating their lives are bits of bomb shrapnel.

You then have your sins cleansed as you pass through the Haethal Gate that marks the crossing from the mortal into the Buddhist world. The Boddhisattvas of Pohyon (the moral guardian) and Munsu (the guardian of wisdom) inhabit this gate. Four guardians of the Buddha check you for heathen status as you cross through the final, largest gate, Chonwang, dating from 1042. Beyond is the courtyard of Manse Pavilion with its nine-storey pagoda, 6m of granite and with its lotus-covered pedestal indicating its Koryo heritage. In Manse were kept the one-tonne bell and drums struck for prayer every morning. Behind Manse is the Koryo-dated octagonal 13-storey pagoda, nearly 9m tall, and there sits Taeung Hall, Pohyon's main temple room. This was the grandest building from 1042 to be destroyed during the War. It was rebuilt with its stunning paintings and carved detailing.

Decades ago, at around 03.00, the valley would shake with the reverberations of the temple gong being struck in the darkness. This was the first call to prayer of the day, and would be overlapped by the throaty chimes of the bell that hung in Manse Pavilion. The monks striking these instruments sang Buddhist hymns in low, monotonous incantations. The one beating the gong would move to striking the large bell, then the drum and then a large wooden fish before leaving the temple to join a score of monks in another hall who had congregated in the passing half-hour. Lights burnt before the altar, and monks, some dressed in black and others in white, sat cross-legged in a semicircle, intoning hymns in high-pitched voices. They then stood and raised their hands in prayer to the Buddha, bowing and kneeling so their foreheads touched the floor, repeating this as they filed to another altar before resuming their seating and their prayer. The whole sequence would be repeated several times a day.

Next appears **Manse Hall**, a residential building originally built under the Ri and rebuilt in 1875, either for the messengers or the head of Pohyon Temple. The **Kwanum Hall** is an original Pohyon edifice and in this heated setting was most Buddhist doctrine taught. The 1794 **Suchung Temple** commemorates the Army of Righteous Volunteers who fought in the Imjin war against Hideyoshi, with the great priests Samyongdang, Choyong, and Sosan, the leader of tens of thousands of monk soldiers that liberated Pyongyang. Every spring and autumn, memorial services are held here to their memory.

On the far side of the temple complex is the newly built, traditionally styled archive for the 80,000 blocks of the Tripitaka, a massive containment of Buddhist scripture and literature from the Koryo and Ri dynasties and considered a world treasure.

The first books of Buddhist scriptures, 6,000 volumes, were made in the 10th century, followed by another 4,770 volumes. All the prints and printing blocks were destroyed in 1231 during the Liao occupation. Exiling itself to Kanghwa Island from 1236 to 1251, the Koryo court spent its time productively, remaking the entire text in 80,000 blocks of magnolia, pakdal and birchwood. Each block measures 50 x 23 x 4cm with 22 lines of 14 letters per line, with a lacquer protection. Scholars come from far and wide to review the blocks and the scriptures. Nearby is the Bell House and Korea's largest bell at seven tonnes.

## WALKING

There are three main hikes that can be done in one day or less: up the Sangwon Valley, up the Manpok Valley and up to Piro Peak. The Sangwon Valley route totals 14km and starts a little way west of the Pohyon, at the monstrous mushroom shapes of stupas in the monks' graveyard.

**SANGWON VALLEY** Near the westernmost stupa is the large rock of Sangwon Gateway, which you pass under towards the collided rocks of Kumgang Gate. Past here is the Kumgang Pavilion overlooking Kumgang Falls, and 1km on are the misty Taeha Falls. It's only half as far again to the spectacular Ryongyong Falls, cascading 84m from the Ryong (dragon) pool, preceding the Sanju Falls and Pavilion. Inho rock sits up to the left of Ryongyong Falls, and the pavilion up there has great views. Carry on up to the stepped Chonsin Falls (86m) that overlook the charming Koryo-era Sangwon Hermitage (rebuilt in 1580). The Su Pavilion here has the legendary milk of Buddha that cures all ills. Walking 2km onwards, rising 500m, you come to Nungin Hermitage, the highest in Myohyang at 1,000m, rebuilt in 1780. Chilsong Pavilion and Chonsin Pavilion are located very close to Sangwon Hermitage. Then it's only another 1km to Popwang Peak at 1,389m. From Popwang Peak it's possible to trace the knuckled ridge about 10km to Piro Peak, a three-hour jaunt but watch the winds.

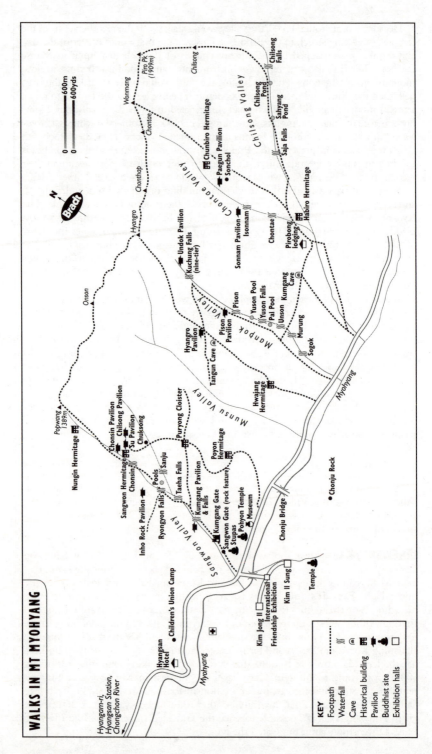

# WALKS IN MT MYOHYANG

**KEY**

| | |
|---|---|
| Footpath | |
| Waterfall | |
| Cave | |
| Historical building | |
| Pavilion | |
| Buddhist site | |
| Exhibition halls | |

N

Braich

0 ___ 600m
0 ___ 600yds

Piro Pk (190m)

Wonmang

Chilsong

Chilsong Falls

Chilsong Valley

Chilsong Pond

Sahyang Pond

Saja Falls

Chontae

Chunbiro Hermitage

Paegun Pavilion

Sonchol

Chontae Valley

Habiro Hermitage

Chonthap

Chontae

Pirobong lodging

Isonnam

Sonnam Pavilion

Hyongro

Undok Pavilion

Kuchung Falls (nine-tier)

Unson Kumgang Cave

Unson

Yuson Pool

Yuson Falls

Pal Pool

Murung

Pison

Pison Pavilion

Sogok

Onson

Hyangro Pavilion

Tangun Cave

Manbok Valley

Hwajang Hermitage

Munsu Valley

Popwang (1389m)

Nungin Hermitage

Chonsin Pavilion

Chilsong Pavilion

Su Pavilion

Chuksong

Sangwon Hermitage

Chonsin

Sanju

Puryong Cloister

Poyon Hermitage

Pools

Taeha Falls

Inho Rock Pavilion

Ryongyon Falls

Kumgang Pavilion & Falls

Kumgang Gate

Sangwon Gate (rock feature)

Stupas

Pohyon Temple

Museum

Chonju Rock

Chonju Bridge

Myohyang

Sangwon Valley

Children's Union Camp

Myohyang

Hyangsan Hotel

Hyangam-ri, Hyangsan Station, Chongchon River

Kim Jong Il

International Friendship Exhibition

Kim Il Sung

Temple

Coming straight down from Popwang, from the back of Sangwon Hermitage is the Chuksong Temple, built in 1875. A 2km diversion tumbles down to the Puryong Cloister and its massive sweeping eaves dating from 1700. From Puryong is a path back to Kumgang Pavilion, about 800m away, and another path taking a more direct route down to the valley floor, taking in the Poyon Hermitage on the way.

**MANPOK VALLEY** Roughly 4km from the Hyangsan Hotel along the River Myohyang is Manpok Valley, with a 6km round trip drenched in waterfalls. First, 500m along the way is the Sogok (prelude) Falls that prelude the valley's 'symphony of falls'. It's then 250m to Murung Falls, where eight brothers used to rest here after collecting firewood. On to Unson Falls, then the Pal pools where fairies used to frolic. Onwards to a bridge spanning the 66m Yuson Falls (fed by the Yuson Pool above them) that break from a sheer slope amid the trees into eight pools. A steel handrail goes up to the highly protrusive Changes Rock, and it's 300m to the twin Pison Falls that drop some 46m. Then past Pison Rock and Pison Pavilion, it's 1km to Kuchung (Nine-Tier) Falls and Undok Pavilion. Seven hundred metres down west of here is Hynagno Pavilion and the nearby Tangun Grotto, where legend says was born the founder of Korea, Tangun. Down from there appears the 30m-wide Mujigae (rainbow) rock, a rainbow that the fairies rode down to earth. It's 2km downhill to the Koryo Temple of Hwajang Hermitage, and then you're back on the road.

**PIRO PEAK** A third hike goes up to Myohyang's highest peak, the 1,909m Piro Peak. Starting 5.5km from the Hyangsan, it's 9km up the Chontae and Chilsong valleys and along to Piro, with stunning views from the knuckled ridge leading to it.

First, past Pirobong lodging for travellers, it's 2km up to Habiro Hermitage, originally 16th century (rebuilt in 1882), where the Chontae Valley and Chilsong Valley streams meet. From here are two routes, one going directly to Piro Peak up Chilsong Valley, the other up Chontae Valley to Wonmang Peak and along.

**Chontae Valley** Up Chontae, it's 400m to Chontae Falls and 200m more to Isonnam Falls, then the three-pillared Sonnam Pavilion. Paegun Pavilion sits at 1,200m, 2km from Habiro, and nearby is the heavenly (drinkable) spa of the 'sachol' spring. Behind Chunbiro Hermitage is Paegun Rock, affording a bird's-eye view. Alpine flora found here include thuja, sabina (*sargentii nakai*) and cloves. Wonmang rock is 2km up, at 1,825m, third to Piro and Chilsong peaks.

**Chilsong Valley** Up Chilsong Valley, it's 2km to Saja Falls and another 2km to Chilsong Falls, and then 6km to Piro Peak, from which point the whole world is yours and on the finest days can be seen the West Sea of Korea.

**RYONGMUN AND PAENGRYONG CAVES** Ryongmun Cave is an amazing grotto of cavernous halls with vaults soaring 40m, populated by stalactites and stalagmites and separated by long pools. Discovered in the 8th century, it's been used as a hiding place for refugees evading the numerous wars that have swept the peninsula (hence the many marked fireplaces), and to stash Buddhist images and other treasures from greedy local chieftains. A lone Buddhist monk spent 18 months down here among the bear skeletons. In the rainy season, the waters rise to make pools big enough for boats to traverse over long distances. It's 2km all the way through, and is situated 30km east of Hyangsan town, 1.5km from Unhung-ri. Seventeen kilometres further east, 5km beyond Taephung-ri, is Paengryong Cave, smaller but no less full of giddyingly weird limestone protrusions and damp chambers populated by damp dwelling spirits.

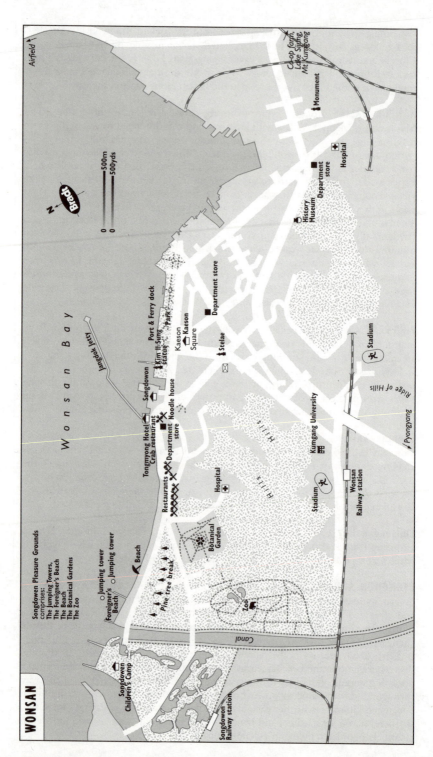

WONSAN

Songdowen Pleasure Grounds
comprises:
The Jumping Towers,
The Foreigner's Beach
The Beach
The Botanical Gardens
The Zoo

Songdowen
Children's Camp

Songdowen
Railway station

Canal

Foreigner's
Beach ○ Jumping tower
○ Jumping tower

Beach

Pine tree break

Botanical
Garden

Hospital

Stadium

Zoo

HILLS

Kumgang University

Stadium

Wonsan
Railway station

Ridge of Hills

Pyongyang

Stadium

Wonsan  Bay

Jangok Jetty

Tongmyong Hotel
Crab restaurant
Restaurants
Department
store
Noodle house

Songdowen

Kim Il-Sung
statue

Port & ferry dock

Park

Kaeson
Square

Kaeson

Stelae

Department store

Department
store

History
Museum

Department
store

Hospital

Monument

Co-op farm,
Lake Sijung,
Mt Kumgang

Airfield

N

Bradt

0        500m
0        500yds

# 7

# East Coast Central: Pyongyang to Wonsan

*39.1° north, 127.28° east, 200km east of Pyongyang, capital of Kangwon Province, Gulf of East Korea*

The two-hour drive to Wonsan via Koksan takes in few sites. **King Tongmyong**, founder of the Koryo kingdom, has his reconstructed tomb 25km from Pyongyang, and 15km further on you pass the **Hugu-ri**, with early Palaeolithic remains and a nice cave.

The road winds and coils up tighter and tighter round conical hillsides, until it breaks out onto a large, lush plateau hemmed in by slopes.

About 110km from Pyongyang, **Sinphyong Resthouse** appears on the shore of a small reservoir in steep-sided hills that in autumn become canopied by blazing red maple trees. Sinphyong's current expansion and healthy stock of good liquor and champagne. The main talking point of the resthouse is a great vat of snake-wine, which is as it sounds, a snake fermenting in rice wine, a brew that is a speciality of the county and is renowned for its positive qualities for your appetite and sexual prowess. It's deceptively potent stuff: you can imbibe a lot and think you're mildly inebriated, only to find hours later you're absolutely smashed out of your mind and incapable of any ardour whatsoever.

From then on it's dripping tunnels and grand bursts of paddies until finally the Sea of Japan comes into sight and you sweep into **Wonsan**.

## WONSAN

*39.2° N 127.4° E capital of Kangwon province*

With a population of 331,000, Wonsan is at the centre of this well-populated strip of coast and is the connecting hub from Pyongyang northwards to Hamhung city; it also acts as the gateway to the Kumgang Mountains in the south. The surrounding land is the most fertile in the province, and under the soil, gold is mined.

As the Kangwon provincial capital, Wonsan is a major port for trading goods with Russia and Japan, and ferry boats to Japan loiter along the quays. Served by ten universities and colleges, the city's industries include fishing, rice processing, oil refining and brewing (particularly rice wine), and the manufacture of ships, locomotives, textiles, chemicals. Since the 19th century, the city's been well known for its leather and fur goods. Wonsan's connections to the forested, mountainous north meant it was the first point for many hunters, whose appetites for game were provoked by the large bear and tiger skins treated and traded through the city. Now visitors come for Wonsan's access to Kumgang and the beaches all along this coast. The city's tall, wide boulevards branch like spokes from the hub of a stela commemorating Kim Il Sung, and connect to big open spaces. It is a handsome, tidied reflection of the hills and beaches surrounding the city and the sea breeze blows coolly through it all.

**HISTORY** The city has existed here since the early Koguryo period and was named Wonsan under the Koryo, and was for centuries a trading settlement with incoming junks anchoring in its natural harbour.

By the 1880s, Wonsan was one of three ports being run by the Japanese (who called it Gensan) and had around 15,000 inhabitants, with two small settlements, one for the 700 Japanese inhabiting the city (with their own police force), and the other for other foreigners, mainly French, Russian and British. There was also a small Chinese population, filling minor official and entrepreneurial roles and selling imported goods, and staffing their own small police force as a counter to the Japanese. As the Chinese and Japanese both ran the country, Captain Cavendish couldn't tell 'which race the inhabitants hate most'.

It was under Japanese colonialism that Wonsan underwent unprecedented urban growth, as its role in exporting commodities to Japan grew and the city's major industries were founded for producing and shipping cheap manufactures to Japan, and a railroad hub for Japanese goods and men into Korea. These same port and shipping facilities made Wonsan ideal as a Japanese navy operations base during World War II. Five years after that conflict's end, US marines landed here to a reception of South Korean soldiers as the UN forces pushed back the Korean People's Army in late 1950, but the city was retaken by the North in the coming winter. Ground fighting and bombing had levelled the city by the middle of 1953, and all that you see has been built since then. Wonsan was where the USS *Pueblo* was taken in 1968 and where it was moored for decades as a museum, before being moved to Pyongyang.

**GETTING THERE** Ferries from Japan come to, and direct flights to Wonsan have been proposed from, South Korea's Gimpo as part of the Kumgangsan development 110km south down the coast, but, as it is, the only practical way to get there is by road from Pyongyang.

## 🏠 WHERE TO STAY

🏠 **Kaeson Hotel** (164 rooms) On the seashore opposite Haean Square. $$

🏠 **Tongmyong Hotel** Located where the Songdowon beach & base of the artificial Jangdok Islet meet.

Flower-shaped, perfectly serviceable with billiards & a bookshop. $$

🏠 **Songdowon Tourist Hotel** (83 rooms) Songdowon pleasure grounds. $

## ✗ WHERE TO EAT

The seafront roads running on both sides of the Tongmyong Hotel are lined with restaurants. Recommended are two places right opposite the Tongmyong: there is a large eaved building named **Korean Noodle House** with stairs going up, but at the car-park level is a doorway going into a much smaller, cosier place with two rooms, one with baking *ondol* heating. Here a slap-up steamed crab feast for four is about €25. Arrange in advance.

**WHAT TO SEE** Wonsan's concrete cityscape is bolted to a backdrop of steep hills that screen in the natural harbour and give the city its name of 'Folding Screen'. The high-rises that fire out of the hillsides resemble the Chongsokjon rock formations further south down the coast. Wonsan's port proper is bracketed by the **Songdowon** pleasure grounds to the north and the southern Kalma peninsula resort of **Myongsasimni** and its 4km of beaches.

The **Songdowon** begin just beyond the manmade Jangdok jetty, with the seafront road flanked by sandy, segregated beaches on one side and a gamut of restaurants on the other. You stroll along towards a forested area, watching locals hurl themselves from rusting water towers or lolling on the beach.

Songdowon is dominated by a deep windbreak of pine trees, some 700 years old, in which are hidden a **zoo** and **botanical gardens** (with stores of Kimilsungia and

Co-operatives are units of up to 300 households that jointly own and run the land. Each co-op is controlled at the kun (prefecture) level, that sets output targets to be met by the co-op. Produce is traded and sold for external goods like tractors and fertiliser. In the co-op the farmers own their own houses but work in units on the land, in specialised work teams, like the rice-work team, or the cow-work team. Similarly assigned teams can compete for speed and output, with results posted up in the village square so all can see who's leading and by how much. At the end of the crop cycle or year, those more than fulfilling their targets are rewarded in cash and kind, those failing lose payments.

Each day, members of co-ops gather at around 08.30 after a signal bell to receive instructions for the day's tasks. Lunch is at noon, held at home or in the communal hall, with dancing and music groups. During the ten-minute breaks per hour are 'news reading meetings'. At each day's end the work is evaluated and points are put in farmers' Labour Notebooks according to the work done. This ultimately affects their level of pay. They then go to the communal bath-house, cinema, political meeting or home, unless they're needed for other 'voluntary' tasks of irrigation building or factory work; otherwise they tend to their own plots. Farmers have small private plots for bees, pigs, chickens and rabbits, which can be sold. This element of private ownership differentiated the DPRK's collectivisation programme from China's that happened almost concurrently in the 1950s, for China had much greater emphasis on communal living and state ownership. Where surplus has allowed, in recent years there has been an increasing number of farmers' markets appearing across the country, as a private supplement to state rations. However, with regard to the problems of food supply still afflicting the country, the number of farmers' markets remains limited.

Kimiljongilia – see box, page 121) that makes for a good half-hour's ambling around. Within the woods is a tree that Kim Il Sung once commented on, requiring it to be fenced off. The woodlands also shroud a mudbath centre with electric plates. Locals picnic and dance in the clearings amid the pine trees. An aged canal abruptly cuts the windbreak and the beach, across which is **Songdowon International Children's Union Camp**. It's a nice three-star hotel built in 1993 with lots of activities and events for up to 1,200 children, but don't visit unless children are there or you're touring a Holiday Inn without guests.

Along the quay are supposedly boats that can do small trips of the coast down to Tongchok, but this hasn't been verified. Following the coast beyond is a neighbourhood pretty much reserved for the great and the good.

The waterfront running southeast of the Jangdok jetty, beyond the two hotels, is the main point of embarkation and loading of ships goes on, and it is here that cargo ships and ferries from Japan moor up.

These vessels break up the sea view from the kilometre or so long, wide park that runs all along this waterfront, dominated at the northwest end by a statue of the Great Leader, and a formal series of geometric paths and junctions grid down to the other end, dotted with small pavilions and statues. The broad plaza of Haean Square fronts onto this park.

About 2km due south of the Tongmyong (as the crow flies) are burial mounds, behind Ai Su Dok University, but not much about them is known. They could be the Old Castle of Tokungen which holds the tomb of the founder of the Chosun dynasty. The road heading southwest, which you'll take if going on to Kumgang or the co-operative farm just out of town, will also pass an obelisk high on a hill just over 3km southwest of the hotel. Anyone is welcome to identify this structure.

There is also the Myongsasi peninsula, a long, bone-shaped outcropping that makes up the eastern wall of the bay in front of Wonsan. Local tourist maps have placed a line of beaches along its bay side, as this book did in its first edition; however, further research suggests that accessibility for tourists is doubtful as the peninsula has a substantial airfield at its base, protecting a complex of large, palatial buildings dotted towards its turkey-headed end. Who goes there, and what do they talk about? Other reported sites include an airfield and an 'experimental station for marine products', so go see those three-eyed fish.

Well worth a look is the **co-operative farm** 7.7km south of the city centre. Cross the last bridge on the edge of town, turn right, then turn left at the next big stele 6km later. This idyll of rustic harmony and model of co-operative farming (see box below) has been frequented by Kim Il Sung and Kim Jong Il, which suggests why it's on the tour map, and it's interesting to see to what ends the finest stone is put.

Try to cadge a drag of a local's newspaper cigarette. You may get to 'drop in' on a farmer's household to meet some very well-mannered children, although their songs may be interrupted by broadcasts from the radio high up the wall. This may be your only chance to visit a house of this kind in the country, and these are good quality, well-made houses, shown by their tiled roofs. You won't see any houses with thatched roofs. Older houses used to have wooden chimneys wrapped in thatch, but the air from the stove would have lost all sparks as it was piped under the floor in the *ondol* heating. Many of the poorest rural dwellings didn't have raised floors for *ondol*, and were built on the earth, so were notoriously dirty. Cattle and pigs were brought in to protect them from tigers, and the floors were veritable bug farms, such that travellers would barricade themselves in with fresh straw, hoping this would prove impenetrable to bugs during the night.

Unless made of concrete blocks, today's single-storey houses are built as they were from clay brick coated with cement, with gardens fenced in by split bamboo. As you enter (and take off your shoes!) there's an obvious lack of furniture, beyond the shelves and cupboards against the wall. Very little clutters the smooth, lacquer-papered floor, except a low table and floor cushions brought out for eating meals. As you sit and notice the heated floor, don't forget not to point your soles at anyone. These houses often have no more than three rooms, including the bedroom and kitchen, so the third room is multi-purpose, for entertaining, studying, eating, and listening to the announcements from the radio. Two gleaming pictures of the Great Leaders will hang high somewhere. The rooms are not divided by doors but maybe by screens. In the kitchen you'll see large earthenware pots for *kimchi* and holding dry comestibles. Having been duly entertained by the wife and her children, it should be time to bid farewell and get back on the way to Kumgang.

# 8

# Wonsan to
# Mt Kumgang

The road from Wonsan to Kumgang sails alongside the railway across a green sea of paddies before tacking right onto the shoreline, racing the electric fence all the way to the DMZ. En route there are many modern stelae on the roadsides, the inscriptions of which the guides can translate, and cranes keeping an eye over the fields and lakes.

Around 37km from Wonsan is **Tongjong Lake**, formerly a seawater bay, and the beach of Chona Port. Ten kilometres further south is **Lake Sijung**, which the road and railway keep separate from the sea. On the lake's shore is a small, very hot guesthouse specialising in mud treatment and massage. The mud at the bottom of the lake is formed by a rich, thick layer of rotting God-knows-what, but very likely contains the carcasses of carp, sardine, mullet, lobster, clam, abalone, eel and snakefish that otherwise harass the row-boats floating from the guesthouse. This mud is heated up and packed onto your bits so that its nutrients may seep in and sooth your inner ills. It also pongs and can be too well heated, but a soak in the stuff helps cure numerous skin complaints, bronchitis and heart trouble. Although the bedrooms can become like ovens at night, it is a tranquil, pleasant place to stay with a good little restaurant and a bar more or less willing to sell alcohol late into the night.

The guesthouse is about a kilometre north of a private beach, entered through a reception pavilion that provides towels and showers for a nominal fee and sells the good booze (it's an area popular with Russians). The little islets dotted along it can almost be walked to across the beach's long shallows, in which the holidaying Koreans scour for shellfish and will share with you. Agree to any drinks the Russians might offer you.

Further on, the town of Tongchon has little to excite the visitor, but is adjacent to the beautifully geometric **Chongsokjong** rocks that protrude from the sea like great teeth. Another 42km along is Kosong, the last major town before the glories of Mt Kumgang.

## WILDLIFE

Four hundred species of butterfly flit through the steep, forested slopes of Kumgang. Of the dozens of animal species in these mountains are musk deer, roe deer, antelope, bear, wild boar and flying squirrel. The area ranges from deciduous to lower alpine forests, in which are stashed some 1,200 plant species, from bamboo to fir, oak, chestnut, hawthorn and varieties of maple and pine, thuja, Sabina chinensis, mountain cranberry and blueberry. The mossy ground is shielded with azalea, yellow clematis, primulas and lilies; Japanese red pine and herbaceous fern protrude from the cracked cliffs. Local species to be spotted include Kumgang stephanandra and Kumgang bellflower. Indeed, botanists to these parts are warned by the local tourist information agency: 'There are some plants that will attract you. If you fail to see them, you will regret for your lifetime.' Flying in and around are kingfisher, yellow fisher, pied wagtail, pheasant, black-naped oriole, migratory grosbeak, Korean scops owl, cuckoo, wild geese, heron and gulls apuses. The streams hold carp, trout, salmon, and ten species of batrachians, including the bell-toad.

## MT KUMGANG

*38.45° north, 128.1° east, 108km south of Wonsan, Kangwon Province, near to the DMZ and East Korea Sea*

Mt Kumgang is situated in the northern part of the Thaebaek mountain range on Korea's central-eastern coast, and covers an area of some 40km east–west and 60km north–south. Mt Kumgang means 'diamond mountains', so called as the granite peaks and hillsides glitter in the sunlight, but they have had different names in each season, being the Pongnae Mountains ('spirits enjoy visiting') in summer, Phungak ('variety of views') in autumn and Kaegol Mountains ('snow sided') in winter. The highest is Piro Peak at 1,639m and another dozen touch over 1,500m, with a hundred or so over 1,000m and peaks as sharp as 'the tips of paint brushes' – although there may be fewer than the commonly cited 12,000 peaks.

Kumgang's been considered sacred for millennia. 'Buddhism,' wrote Isabella Bishop in *Korea and her Neighbours*, 'which possesses itself of the fairest spots of nature, fixed itself in this romantic seclusion as early as the 6th century.' Access was through Tan Pa Ryong (since renamed) that means 'cropped hair pass', a Rubicon for anyone seeking a life of Buddhist solace. In feudal Korea, bachelors had heavy braids of hair, married men's hair was coiled into a topknot, but monks, unencumbered by considerations of marital status, shaved all their hair off. The town of Choanjri once housed a great concentration of 16 temples and halls dating from the 6th century. Even by the late 19th century, when Buddhism had long fallen from official (and therefore financial) favour and most Koreans were succumbing to Christianity, 45 monasteries, nunneries and shrines were counted in the area. Thirty-two remained pre-World War II, but today fewer than a handful remain in any use.

However, tourists have long been filling out the space left by thinning pilgrims. Cavendish observed in 1887 that:

> The Koreans are great lovers of nature and admirers of scenery, and are also great pedestrians; they – that is, the men, who always seem to have plenty of time to kill – often make pilgrimages to places whence a fine view may be obtained … annually they [Diamond Mountains] are visited by hundreds of Koreans.

The Japanese turned the area into a park, and today Kumgang's spiritual splendour has allowed it to be the only place in the DPRK that ROK Koreans can visit relatively freely. Kumgang is divided into three areas, Inner, Outer and Sea of Kumgang, with 22 sub-divisions within it and so many different routes of peaks, pools, lakes, waterfalls and temples to follow that a serious walker would need a week to cover the place.

Kumgang's proximity to the border with ROK led to the area to being closed off for most of the Cold War, with its tourists and Buddhist pilgrims replaced with soldiers. Only in the last decade has the area become accessible to tourists, and initially this was restricted to Outer Kumgang and the Sea of Kumgang. Inner Kumgang was even more restricted. The gates to Inner Kumgang creaked open to Westerners for the first time in decades in 2002 and one man made a fleeting visit:

Taking the road in from the east coast, we were soon in a shallow valley, with sheer granite hillside either side, our Volvo grumbling along a grotty track hewn from a hillside with a stream trickling past the other way. The track alternated between dust, rubble and strips of asphalt as we climbed, passing the very occasional eave-sheltered bench.

We were the only passengers on this road, as it snaked into higher passes, tighter turns, thicker foliage and into breezier expanses. In three hours I only saw one single truck, laden with workers, hammer past us at a junction on a ridge where our car had decided to give up for a while, having shaken some important parts of itself loose.

As my driver and two guides got out for a breather and to fix the car, I spied nearby a thin dirt track, closely shielded with trees with interlocking branches clasping overhead, and atop the track, about 150m away, I could see a gateway to some kind of village. My guides being busy, I wandered up this track, waving my camera around as if photographing the butterflies. Only a few metres short of this village, one of my guides somehow had quickly but silently legged up behind me and strongly indicated with his hand that we should go back to the car. Noting his silence, I looked at him quizzically, trying to impart with my face a message of innocent 'what's the problem?' He nodded past me to the village gates, to where I looked and suddenly spied a good half-dozen big green army trucks shielded by foliage. I realised this was possibly the most inhospitable place on earth to a wandering foreigner with camera and I sped down the track with the guide.

We continued and came atop a kind of plateau, flanked by tall, more sheer rock formations rising sharply from the edges of flat fields with a few farmers here and there, where maize grew in ditches, and in the distance the higher peaks of Kumgang could be seen lazily lifting their noses up into the clouds. In these hillsides were many small triangular entrances which my guides said were mines – possibly gold, they weren't sure.

I lost count of the number of checkpoints we went through, the final one being amid a copse of pine trees (we were high up by then) and taking a good 15 minutes. Then it was a final climb up over a ridge and into a valley walled with sharp pointed pale grey granite festooned with lush greenery and breathing mist. My guides told me it was the first time a British man had been there in 60 years, and their first time there as well – we all cheered.

Still there was no-one else around.

I received some opprobrium from Nick Bonner for antagonising a cicada then swatting it with my hat in the presence of the Temple's chief monk, although my Korean guides found it hysterical.

Access to Inner Kumgang from the DPRK side has remained intermittent at best, but may yet change dramatically. In contrast to the megalithic tourist complex built to take in Outer Kumgang and Sea of Kumgang by the ROK behemoth, the Hyundai Asan corporation. And Inner Kumgang is on a multi-billion-dollar expansion plan to extend Hyundai's theme park into an area possibly going all the way up to, and including, Wonsan, with accompanying development of the beach and lake resorts along the road heading north.

However, for now, take it that out of Kumgangsan, Inner Kumgang is the only accessible area from the DPRK side, and that is not guaranteed. Coming from the ROK gains access to Outer Kumgang and Sea of Kumgang but no further into the north.

The following outlines of walks and tours in the three main areas of Kumgangsan are the most 'usual' but are not exhaustive, and not necessarily doable without guides, but are suggestions nonetheless.

**INNER KUMGANG** The long road towards Inner Kumgang from Kumgang town (Kumgang Province seat) is of goodish quality, hugging the hillside as it wiggles higher and higher up a very spacious valley marked by new pavilions to stop and admire the view from. A long, lush plateau stretches out, flanked by wall-vertical cliffs with mines burrowed into their bases. The road quality deteriorates as it descends from the plateau past the hamlet of Naegang-ri, 10km from Kumgang, into a copse of trees and the final checkpoint. Herein its dirt tracks crudely cut from the sheer cliffs battle to prevent the foliage from taking this exposed earth for its own. The final climb and descent is slow going and through thick greenery, but spectacular peaks flit into view, locked in frozen battle with the tentacles of tree roots and ivy. Eventually you pass the Naegumgang Resthouse, and the road forks. Right goes past the Okgyong Pond, for 2km to Monggyong Rock, like a great split mirror 90m high. In legend it read the minds and showed the sins of those who saw it. Two caves emerge further on, and then the path splits as the stream splits. The right fork goes to Ryongwon Hermitage, south of Jijang Peak, and continues for 4km to Paekma Peak. The left fork goes around Jijang Peak's north side and takes in a series of waterfalls en route to the Mun, Jungmyong and Tabu pagodas. However, this is quite a trek.

Back at the main road from Naegang-ri, the road snakes along, hugging the stream, past the three-storeyed, 7th-century pagoda of Jangan temple, one of the four major temples of Mt Kumgang. Continuing north past Ul Pond, 3.5km from Naegang-ri, is the Sambul Bridge which is the diversion of Sambul Rock. The latter is covered with three large and 60 small Buddhist images that date from the last century of the Koryo kingdom. Legend has it that the images were carved by two bitterly rivalling monks named Raio and Kinko, who challenged each other to carve the greatest Buddha. The loser would have to commit suicide, and the locals didn't consider Kinko's 60 small Buddhas as fine as Raio's three big ones, so Kinko threw himself into the river nearby. It's at this bridge that a track loops east-southeast to the paths around Sibwang and Jijang peaks.

Staying on the main track going north, you pass a monument erected in 1632 to the great Buddhist priest Sosan, a local who valiantly led monk-soldiers against Hideyoshi's invaders in the late 16th century. On the right is the Paekhwa Hermitage. Then, round a bend and over a bridge is Phyohun Temple, first built in the 670s under the Koguryo and was for centuries one of the largest temples in the area, with 50 monks. Its original buildings were destroyed in the 16th century by Hideyoshi's invaders, and the reconstructions were flattened during the Korean War, but the rebuilt temple is still technically active.

A hundred metres from here is the 'valley of ten thousand waterfalls', and – to make sure everyone knew where they were – a 16th-century calligrapher wrote 'Kumgang Mt and Manphok Valley' just below the large Kumgang rock. The Chinese graffiti are actually the names of visiting dignitaries carved in Chinese script by the monks in thanks for their patronage, and here the valley splits.

Strolling up the right valley, bathe your feet in the dark-blue Hukryong Pool and listen out for the mandolin sounds of Pipa Pond, if not for the hiss of the flaming dragon in Hwaryong Pool.

Beyond a flimsy-looking suspension bridge, the lowly turret of Podok Hermitage appears up on the right, seeming to hang off a cliff or perch precariously atop a brass pole. Podok was built in 627 under the Koguryo and solitary monks would inhabit the site for their monastic lives of devotion to Buddha, looking down onto the ravine through a hole in the floor. Be careful that you are not so overwhelmed by the beauty of the monks' solace that you kill yourself, as one foreign visitor is fabled to have done. At least see the Jinju Falls first, just beyond Podok.

Alternatively, back at the graffiti, take the left valley up past a series of ponds. Continuing north you come to Sumi Pagoda and Sumi Hermitage, nestled at the base

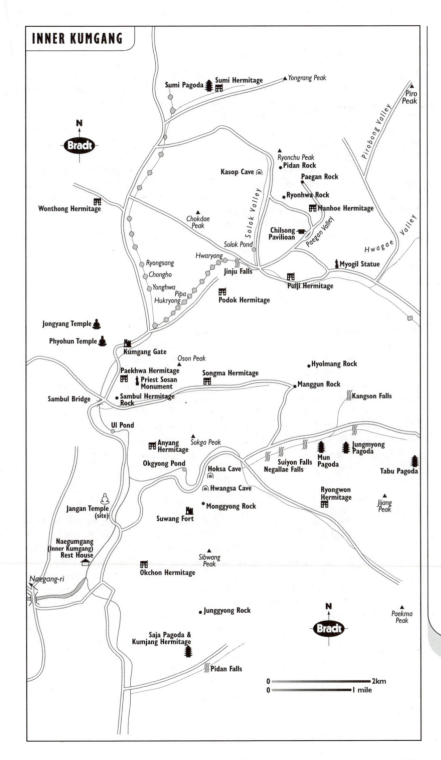

# INNER KUMGANG

Sumi Pagoda    Sumi Hermitage

*Yongrang Peak*

*Piro Peak*

N **Bradt**

*Pirobong Valley*

*Ryonchu Peak*
• Pidan Rock

Kasop Cave

Paegan Rock

• Ryonhwa Rock

Manhoe Hermitage

Wonthong Hermitage

*Chokdae Peak*

Solok Valley

*Paegan Valley*

Chilsong Pavilioan

*Hwagae Valley*

*Solok Pond*

*Hwaryong*

*Ryongsang*
*Chongho*
*Yonghwa*
*Hukryong*   *Pipa*

Myogil Statue

Jinju Falls

Pulji Hermitage

Podok Hermitage

Jongyang Temple
Phyohun Temple

Kumgang Gate

*Oson Peak*

Paekhwa Hermitage

Priest Sosan Monument

Songma Hermitage

• Hyolmang Rock

Sambul Bridge

• Sambul Hermitage Rock

• Manggun Rock

Kangson Falls

Ul Pond

Anyang Hermitage

*Sokga Peak*

Okgyong Pond

Hoksa Cave

Suiyon Falls
Negallae Falls

Mun Pagoda

Jungmyong Pagoda

Tabu Pagoda

Hwangsa Cave

Jangan Temple (site)

• Monggyong Rock

Ryongwon Hermitage

*Jijang Peak*

Naegumgang (Inner Kumgang) Rest House

Suwang Fort

*Naegang-ri*

*Sibwang Peak*

Okchon Hermitage

• Junggyong Rock

N **Bradt**

*Paekma Peak*

Saja Pagoda & Kumjang Hermitage

Pidan Falls

0        2km
0        1 mile

of Yongrang Peak. Before that, however, the path cuts right (east) to circle the Chokdae Peak. A complex network of converging valleys make the paths loop and double back to surround a wealth of rocks, peaks, pavilions and hermitage, known as **Paegundae District**. The path almost loops back to the Podok Hermitage. Paegun Valley has good views of Inner Kumgang, but its main attraction is the sliced buttresses of Paegun Rock. It's said that the clouds here scatter in the morning and return in the evening to play with the cranes. Pobki Peak along here is heavily inscribed, before Junghyangsong (rampart of smoke from a million incense). Here also is Kumgang's finest spring of water. Solok Valley has good views from Ryonhwa Rock, Ryonchu Peak with its cactus-shaped crown and the sensuously smooth Pidan Rock.

The final gulley in this knot of valleys is the fabulous **Hwagae Valley**, with its climbing, winding paths that pass the extraordinary Myogil Statue, a huge 15m Buddha carved onto a rock. It's thought that the victorious monk Raio completed it as a sculpture of honour in late Koryo. The 7th-century Manhoe monastery is nearby and it's 4km up through the Pirobong Valley to Kumgang's highest point, the 1,639m Piro Peak, where you're some 8km from your start point of Phyohun Temple.

**SEA OF KUMGANG** Just inland from the spectacular rock formations that dot this part of the coast is Samil Lagoon, or 'three-day' lagoon, where a king stopped for a rest and stayed three days, captivated by its beauty. The Tanphung (maple) restaurant and Chungsong Pavilion are on its shores.

**OUTER KUMGANG** The Kumgangsan Hotel is a juncture for many hikes. It's 300m from the **Kumgangsan Spa**, the silica-imbued water of which simmers nicely between 37° and 44°C and is good for hypertension and heart troubles. Nothing gets the blood going like a bit of revolutionary fervour, mind, and you could find yourself being lured into the **Kumgangsan Revolutionary Museum**. Alternatively, get your boots on and head for the hills.

**Sujong Peak** Sujong Peak, a good place to watch the sunrise casting its net of mist over the mountains, is 3km northwest from Kumgangsan Hotel. From the hotel, cross the Onjong stream towards the Kumgangsan hot springs, behind which is a track that's an hour's jaunt up the Sujong Valley to Sujong and Pari peaks. First is a small drinking spring, and then follow 30m and 100m 'seasonal' waterfalls. Beyond a stone gate is the roundish flat rock of Kangson where the fairies used to come. Look out for three rocks, shaped like a turtle, a flying pigeon and a man in bed.

The trail forks towards a suspension bridge that leads to an 'observatory' beneath the ridge on which sits Sunjong Peak, like a cluster of artichokes. From here can be seen the sea. The right fork goes to the hollows and water of Kumgang Cave, then the ridge goes right to the smooth dome of Pari Peak, like an upturned bowl.

The Onjong stream flows from west to east through Onjong-ri, flowing past the Kumgangsan and Onjong hotels on the way. A road follows the stream, sometimes referred to as Hanha stream. Following the road due west away from Onjongr-ri, the Sujong Peak area is on the right, Singye Valley is away on the left, and Hanha and Manmulsang valleys lie ahead. Hanha (cold fog) Valley is the broadest valley in Mt Kumgang and splits into many sub-valleys between peaks. Sanggwanum Peak (1,227m) aligns with the other oddly shaped peaks of Nunggot Rock, Kom Rock and Tol Gate.

On the left appears Kom Rock, a bear with its paw raised against the cliff. This bear once mistook the gemstones in the stream below for acorns, but got stuck on the way down to get them. It's near the Onjong's Munju Pond and Munju Bridge, a couple of hundred metres from the 43m-high Kwanum Falls also on the left or south of the stream.

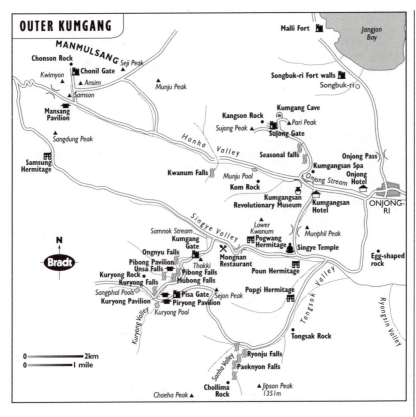

### OUTER KUMGANG

MANMULSANG

Chonson Rock
Kwimyon ▲
Chonil Gate 🏯
Seji Peak ▲
Ansim ▲
Munju Peak ▲
Samson ▲
Mansang Pavilion 🏯
Sangdung Peak ▲
Samsung Hermitage 🏯

Malli Fort 🏯
Jangjon Bay

Songbuk-ri Fort walls 🏯
Songbuk-ri ○

Kumgang Cave
Kangson Rock ■
Pari Peak ▲
Sujong Peak ▲
Sujong Gate

Hanha Valley

Seasonal falls

Kwanum Falls 〿
Munju Pool ●
Kom Rock ●

Kumgangsan Revolutionary Museum

Onjong Pass
Kumgangsan Spa
Onjong Stream
Onjong Hotel
Kumgangsan Hotel

ONJONG-RI

N
Bradt

Singye Valley

Samnok Stream
Kumgang Gate
Ongnyu Falls
Pibong Pavilion
Unsa Falls
Kuryong Rock ●
Kuryong Falls
Sangphal Pools ●
Kuryong Pavilion 🏯
Piryong Pavilion 🏯
Kuryong Valley
Kuryong Pool

Thokki
Pibong Falls
Mubong Falls
Pisa Gate 🏯
Sejon Peak ▲

Lower Kwanum
Pogwang Hermitage 🏯
Munphil Peak ▲
Singye Temple
Mongnan Restaurant ✕
Poun Hermitage 🏯
Popgi Hermitage 🏯

Egg-shaped rock

Tongsok Valley
Ryongsin Valley

Tongsak Rock ●

Sonha Valley
Ryonju Falls
Paeknyon Falls
Chollima Rock
Chaeha Peak ▲
Jipson Peak 1351m ▲

0 ▬▬▬ 2km
0 ▬▬▬ 1 mile

Continue west for about 10km from the hotel until you arrive at Mansang Pavilion, the start of an odd walk of curious boulders. First is Samson Rock, like three spirits, then Kwimyon Rock, the figure of a goblin or a massive petrified tree. Look out for the 'man on seven rocks', and those resembling eagles, bears and tortoises. It's a steep, sharp path up Jolbu (axe chop) rock to Ansim (saddle) rock.

Fork right 100m to the spring of 'Forget stick' (*mangjang*), whose rejuvenating waters are said to make the old forget their sticks. Then it's a climb to Kumgang's highest gate, Chonil (sky) Gate, to see over Chonson Rock, which doubled as an observatory. From here you can see the weird, smashed white glass face of Manmulsang. Look out for the Samsong Hermitage and the looming peak of Sandung. An off-shoot from the track goes northeast and then divides, the right fork looping back to the main road, the left continuing for a good few kilometres to Chonpok Valley, with its series of falls, odd rocks and caves.

**Sejon Peak** A different road heads due south of Onjong-ri and then bends westwards. Take this road through Sulginomi Pass where the egg-shaped rock appears on the left. About 1.5km beyond the bend in the road, a short cut from Kumgangsan Hotel appears, joining the road just where sits one of Kumgang's oldest temples, Singye, that dates from 519. The temple and its three-storey pagoda mark the entrance to Singye Valley. From this pagoda are brief excursions up to Munphil and Lower Kwanum peaks, flanking the path going north to the Kumgangsan. From the main road, two paths loop southwards and converge on Sejon Peak. The first route starts a few hundred metres east of Singye Temple, going up the shallow Tongsak Valley on a very pretty jaunt of mild exertion. Tongsak holds the shaking Tongsak Rock that weighs tonnes and shivers with the lightest prod. It leads into Sonha Valley with its Ryonju and Paeknyon waterfalls and where sits the Kobuk (turtle) Rock, a turtle that stretched its neck to drink water but was so captivated by the falls it turned to stone. From Ryonju, look southwards to the 1,351m Jipson Peak, Kumgang's sharpest point, high on the northern range with the cloud-shrouded Chaeha Peak to the west, and the Chollima Rock (like Pyongyang's statue) between them. The path from Ryonju carries on westwards along a ridge to Sejon Peak.

East of Jipson Peak is the 4km Ryongsin Valley, a track tacking round waterfalls and pools, with the 7m-deep Jonju Pool and 8m deep Ryongyon Pool. In south Ryongsin Valley is Palyon Valley with a stone-arch rainbow bridge, and the 8th-century Palyon Temple beside it.

The **second route** to Sejon Peak starts some 2km further west along Singye Valley from Singye Temple. Going west, Pogwang Hermitage appears on the right, and you cross a bridge where insam and deer antlers are dissolved, and come to Mongnan restaurant. The road, now a track, forks to the south, from whence Ongnyu and Kuryong valleys extend like a twig from a branch from a tree, each littered with waterfalls and pools going up to Sejon Peak, about 4km from the restaurant.

The Samnok Stream trickles from Ongnyu (clear water) Valley, so you follow it up and south, past the Thokki (tortoise) Rock on the left. Sliding through the eye of Kumgang Gate seals your presence in the valley. Look for the flower-like Chonha rock. Ongnyu Falls channel through flat-sided trenches to the 6m-deep Ongnyu Pond, over a bridge and 200m more past Ryonju Rock and Falls, then the spectacular Pibong Falls (Phoenix Falls, from the swirling mists) tumble 140m down a thousand broken dinner plates and past Mubung Falls.

From the Pibong Pavilion, Unsa (silver string) Falls are next as you continue upwards towards Kuryong (nine dragons) Pavilion, stacked onto the hillside of Kuryong Valley. Here's a fine view of the 74m-high Kuryong Falls, one of Korea's largest. Nine dragons reportedly lived in the 13m pool at the bottom, defending Kumgang from interlopers. About 100m up from the Kuryong Pavilion is Piryong Pavilion with grand vistas of all around.

From Kuryong Pool, cross Yondam Bridge and traverse 700m of rocky cliff and ladders to arrive at Kuryong rock, from where are visible the eight large green pools (the Sangphal Pools), noted as bathing spots for good spirits. Sneak through Pisa Gate and nothing but a ridge-hike remains until you get the grand overview from Sejon Peak, now reached from both sides.

**Further possibilities** Other areas to enquire about in Outer Kumgang include the Songrim District, which has Songrim Cave and Songrim Hermitage, but be careful! 'If you are enthralled by the views, you are liable to get behind from your companions.' Unsudae District is the site of the 9th-century Yujom Temple; Kumgang's largest temple, it was destroyed by US bombers and only the foundations remain. Chonbuldong District is in the Chonbul stream basin in east Manmulsang District, with the 1,000 Buddha-shaped rocks of Mt Chonbul, and Sonam, Chonpok and Conbul valleys.

**Hyundai cometh to Kumgang** The tourist complex built at Kumgang by Hyundai Asan, the firm also behind the Kaesong Industrial Park (see page 133), is like nothing seen in DPRK ever. The resort, called Onjeong gak, has taken the older facilities and spruced them up and then added a task force of sparklingly new developments of mostly first-class hotels, bungalows, chalets, yurts and caravan parks dotted amongst restaurants and facilities for all seasons, including cinemas and sledging (in winter) to jet-skiing (in summer). There is also a small hospital, a Family-Mart shop, and is a zone apart not just in looks and wealth but administratively, too, having been re-designated the Kumgangsan Tourist Region and set apart from its host Kangwon Province in 2002 to be largely self-administered. That said, the giant paintings, inscriptions, plaques and mosaics of the Great and Dear Leaders are there and will be paid homage to on tours. But there is a marked difference between these zones and Inner Kumgang, still under the control of the DPRK, and Outer and Sea of Kumgang, under effective ROK control. However, with tourists having to wear necklace tags at all times, which contain their identity details and 'debit cards' specially for the resort, they follow set itineraries and guides and endure other proscriptions to movement and photography. Hence ROK-run tours are not totally dissimilar to DPRK ones, or indeed those big group tours seen worldwide with gaggles of Japanese, and increasing numbers of Chinese, tourists milling around, gawping and flashing.

The scale and glitz of the Hyundai resort may be the shape of things to come should Hyundai's plans (as yet not fully disclosed) for Mt Myohyang and Mt Paektu come to fruition – probably more a question of when than if.

Tourists from ROK have been visiting Kumgangsan since 1998, when over 15,000 visited in the last two months of that year, an immediately high rate that has been growing since, with some 213,000 visiting in 2000 and an annual average of about 240,000 going north, with the million mark passed in mid-2005. Although hiccups in inter-Korean relations have seen numbers drop by up to 600 tourists a day, the plans and prospectus are for ever stronger growth and up to 400,000 visitors are planned to be catered for in 2007, all of course coming in on pre-arranged package guided tours.

The benefits are many-fold, as DPRK gets a levy out of the profits from the resort, in the region of US$40 per tourist. Since 2003 North Koreans have supplied the men and materials to build and run the resort with hundreds of millions of dollars in cash coming back the other way and some merry little 'private' enterprises being set up, from guides to hawkers of fruitmeats and teas to tourists, a prospect that has brought in sellers from an area beyond the mountains. That said the visitors are still able to see up close the more traditional existence of the DPRK population working the fields or standing by in uniforms from the other side of fences they cannot cross.

Tourists coming from the ROK by ship, from the port of Sokcho, alight at Kumgang through a port converted from use as a DPRK naval base, and a golf course has been converted from an artillery range, hence there is a tangible peace dividend from the development. Further, access to the resort by road has led to a breach in the world's most fortified border with bus trips now driving through the DMZ (the rail links await completion). Whereas buses would once ginger up to the border for passengers to disembark and put a foot over the demarcation line, now they sail on through. Seoul to Kumgang by road is now a seven-hour dawdle, including a break (if travelling with Asan, as is likely) at Hwajinpo resthouse and crossing the DMZ.

Tourists of all nationalities (barring Japanese and Americans) have been welcome on the Hyundai tours although no linguistic provisions have been made for them. However, that changed in 2006 when Hyundai Asan launched a 'Special Weekend Tour Package to Mt Kumgang for Foreigners only!' With two nights (it's a minimum of three days from Seoul to Kumgangsan and back by boat, Friday morning to Sunday evening, whereas the bus route can be a daytrip) and breakfast at the Hotel Oe-Kumgang, as well as entertainment from the Pyongyang Moranbong Acrobatic Troupe (US$25), the whole trip goes for around US$640 per person. Reservations are required at least two weeks in advance.

While Hyundai's Kumgangsan is like nothing else in DPRK, so is the Kumgang Tourist Development like nothing else in the DPRK – indeed in many respects it is not the DPRK any more. Developments like Hyundai's are harbingers of peace and prosperity and are as such good things, but invariably there is the loss of the 'local' with these outside flows of income and influence, and areas that were once pristine and gloriously empty are filling with people wishing to see the same. The Hyundai complex is almost like a gilded cage plonked onto a country deemed by many as a prison state. With the holiday camp and tourists replacing army camps and troops, some physical and cultural barriers are broken down, but also throw into sharp relief other more deep-seated barriers between the DPRK, it's southern brethren and the world beyond.

Restrictions on laptops, mobile phones, cameras, camcorders and binoculars are the same as for coming into Pyongyang (see page 87). Leaving the ROK at Goseong, Westerners go through the 'foreigner' queue and end up on a bus that is 'theirs' for the whole tour, so note the number. A re-entry permit to the ROK is not required for these excursions, because travellers haven't actually left Korea at all ... for the resort travellers get a temporary 'passport' containing their passport info, a debit card for use in the resort, and a filled embarkation card, all carried in a plastic sheath worn around the neck at all times and the loss or damage of such will incur a fine. Also, no photographs outside designated areas, in the bus, or of North Korean civilians or facilities; interference with a public official in the exercise of his duty; criticism about the North Korean government or leadership; and no pointing at or trying to buy the badges off of North Koreans.

**Getting there and away** If you are to access Kumgangsan from south Korea, tour reservations have to be made at least ten days in advance. Usual restrictions on what can and can't be taken into the DPRK apply. To come from the ROK by ferry, see www.hyundai-asan.com or try the general number ☎ +82 2 3669 3000. For short road tours to Kumgangsan specifically for non-Koreans, try ☎ +82 2 3669 4164 or e jjmariakim@hdasan.com. Hyundai also does the road tours and the www.mtkumgang.com website is very detailed albeit all in Korean, about the centre, and the number is ☎ +82 2 739 1090. Another company **Go'n'SeeKorea** (f *+82 2 732 7708;* e *info@gonseekorea.com; www.gonseekorea.com*) also organises these tours.

 **Where to stay** Alongside the chalet parks, caravan park and yurt park are numerous hotels, all having their own restaurants, shops and karaoke facilities.

🏠 **Hotel Haekumgang** (157 rooms) This is a floating hotel moored off Sea of Kumgang (lucky it floats then). Looks like a giant Connect 4 game. It has a nightclub & can arrange massages. $$$$

🏠 **Kumgang** (173 rooms) Previously the 'Kim Jung-Suk Recreational Centre', ie: it used to be 'luxurious' & has been refurbished to make it even more so. It lights up like a Christmas tree at night. $$$$

🏠 **Kumgangsan Hotel** (240 rooms) Onjong-ri, Kosong. Opened in 1958 but revamped. There are also a few bungalows. Facilities are a shop, dance room, bar & a bath-house that derives hot water from a spring. $$$

🏠 **Kumgang Family Beach Hotel** (97 rooms)

✗ **Where to eat** Aside from the eateries in the hotels the following are scattered across the resort:

✗ **Kosung Seafood Restaurant** Fresh *sashimi* amongst others, overlooking Kosung harbour. A platter of raw fish for 3–4 people is US$80, & is the top end of the range of foods. $$$$$

✗ **Kumgangwon** Traditional local cuisine. A spread of salad, dumplings, cold noodles, fish & pork goes for around US$25. $$$$$

✗ **Mokrangwan** A folk restaurant serving traditional North Korean specialities with a view of Kuryong Falls. Cold noodles, mixed vegetable rice & bean-curd is US$10. $$$$

✗ **Tanpung Restaurant** One of the original restaurants, shaped like a key, on Samil Lagoon.

# 9

# East Coast to Tanchon

*with Robin Paxton*

## MUNPYONG

*39.16° north, 127° east; Kangwon Province 12km, northwest of Wonsan*
Munpyong is famed for its lead smelter, a 1930s-built relic of the Japanese occupation. Slag heaps dominate the horizon: behind its imposing gateway, the ageing factory employs around 1,800 people and produces lead bullion for use in the local battery industry and for export to China.

From Wonsan, the town is reached along an attractive tree-lined road that runs for several kilometres without turning a corner. There is also some agriculture in the region, with farmers labouring under rows of fluttering red banners on the outskirts of town.

## HAMHUNG

*39.5° north, 127.35° east, 110km north of Wonsan, South Hamgyong Province*
Hamhung is North Korea's second city. The birthplace of the founder of Korea's Ri dynasty and the site of a famous battle during the Korean War, Hamhung has since developed into a spacious industrial city of around 750,000 inhabitants. The city is renowned as a heavy engineering centre and is also famed for the enormous Hungnam ammonium fertiliser plant, the largest in the DPRK.

Hamhung's whitewashed apartment buildings and tree-lined streets are best viewed from Mt Tonghung. The historic hill is home to several ancient temples and stands at the southern edge of town. The city is located close to the northern end of Hamhung Bay and is served by the nearby port of Hungnam, one of the country's largest export centres. A little further down the coast lies the Majon beach resort, reputedly eastern Korea's answer to Club Med.

Relative to other cities in the region, Hamhung is bustling with activity. Though there are few cars, cyclists tear along the pavements and pedestrians stroll past the grandiose theatre building. The occasional street vendor does a brisk trade by the roadside and there is some construction work in evidence in the medium- to low-rise residential areas.

Hamhung also boasts a proud academic tradition. The city's branch of the Academy of Sciences is particularly strong in the field of chemical research, developing a PVA, limestone and anthracite compound known as Vinalon, mass-produced for the textile industry at the February 8 Vinalon Complex. However, this well-publicised expertise has given rise to suspicions among Western intelligence sources that the city is also a potential centre for chemical weapons production.

The Majon resort at Hamhung is actually pretty good, with villas which can be taken whole or by the room – the rooms have their own bathrooms. Meals can be good, with local seafood. The aid agencies/NGOs work out of the resort, so there

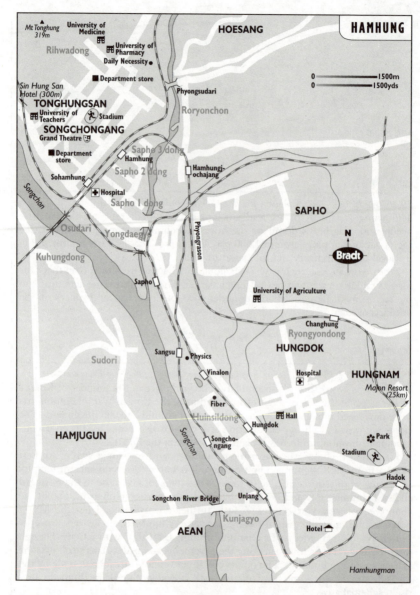

Map labels:

Mt Tonghung 319m
University of Medicine
Rihwadong
University of Pharmacy
Daily Necessity
Department store
Sin Hung San Hotel (300m)
TONGHUNGSAN
University of Teachers
Stadium
SONGCHONGANG
Grand Theatre
Department store
Hamhung
Sapho 3-dong
Sapho 2-dong
Hamhungi-ochajang
Sohamhung
Hospital
Sapho 1-dong
Songchon
Osudari
Yongdaegyo
Phyongrason
Kuhungdong
Sapho
HOESANG
Phyongsudari
Roryonchon
SAPHO
N
Bradt
University of Agriculture
Changhung
Ryongyondong
HUNGDOK
Sudori
Sangsu
Physics
Vinalon
Hospital
HUNGNAM
Majon Resort (25km)
Fiber
Huinsildong
Hall
HAMJUGUN
Songchon
Hungdok
Songcho-ngang
Park
Stadium
Hadok
Songchon River Bridge
Unjang
Kunjagyo
Hotel
AEAN
Hamhungman
0 ———— 1500m
0 ———— 1500yds

will probably be some foreign company if you stay there. The beaches are very good.

**HISTORY** A settlement at Hamhung dates from at least the 12th century AD. A walled city around Mount Tonghung is believed to have been built in 1108. The ancient city is possibly the birthplace of the founder of the Ri dynasty, which ruled Korea from the late 14th century until Japanese occupation in 1910.

The Hamhung/Hungnam area was also the site of a major battle during the Korean War. Twice in 1950, the city was evacuated, with the Songchon River Bridge destroyed several times over. US and South Korean troops took the city in

October 1950 before being driven out by advancing Chinese-backed North Korean troops in December of the same year.

Hamhung's subsequent development into a major industrial centre has occurred largely since the independence of the DPRK. Much of the architecture is post-war. Kim Il Sung was a frequent visitor to the city.

**GETTING THERE AND AWAY** Hamhung is accessible by train from Pyongyang. The east coast line from Wonsan to the Russian/Chinese border passes through the city.

By road, Hamhung is three hours' drive north of Wonsan. Vehicles are checked on entry to the city. The road surface deteriorates into a two-lane dust track a few kilometres north of Wonsan, winding across mountain terrain. The landscape to the immediate north of Hamhung is flatter, where the road traverses the Hamhung Plain.

**WHEN TO GO** The most favourable seasons are spring and autumn, when the climate is cool and dry. Summer can be hot and rainy.

### WHERE TO STAY AND EAT

⌂ **Sin Hung San Hotel** (76 rooms) Tonghungsan District, Hamhung. The hotel is located on Hamhung's main thoroughfare, close to Mt Tonghung. There is a large car park at the front. A 1st-floor restaurant serves basic Korean food & a smoke-filled billiard hall & bar on the ground floor. In true communist style, the corridors are wide & ostentatious with thin, well-worn carpets. The hotel is next door to a large restaurant built in traditional Korean style.

⌂ **Majon Resort** Majondong, Hungnam District. Located by the beach, around 25km from Hamhung itself, the resort is a self-styled tourist village offering sea views & bathing facilities.

### WHAT TO SEE

**Mount Tonghung** This 319m hill at the northern end of Hamhung offers good views of the city. It is home to several temples, including the Kuchon Temple and the Sonhwa Hall. The buildings and city walls are believed to date from the early 12th century, though most of what is standing today has been rebuilt more than once.

**Hamhung Theatre** The large grey theatre, fronted by an expansive square, was opened in April 1984. The building is said to contain around 800 rooms and its main hall hosts various cultural performances.

**Songchon River Bridge** Effectively the entrance to Hamhung from the south, the wide low-level bridge spans the Songchon River estuary. The droughts of recent years have taken their toll on the once-mighty river, now little more than a trickle as it drains towards Korea's East Sea.

## TANCHON

*40.28° north, 128.55° east, 150km northeast of Hamhung, capital of South Hamgyong Province*

When the river in Tanchon runs grey, say local residents, it's a sure sign that the lead and zinc mines further upstream are in full swing. This bodes ill for any remaining marine life, though is a boost to the industrial needs of the northeastern port city. Environmentalists balk at the metallic content of the Pukdae River as it drains into Korea's East Sea but Tanchon has taken a prominent position in the national economy following the construction of a zinc smelter and magnesia plant on the coast.

Tanchon is one of several major ports along the eastern Korean coastline. The city lies in the delta of the Pukdae River, below the imposing foothills of the Paektu mountain range. The city's uniform white apartment blocks give way to more ramshackle, rural housing closer to the coast, where oxen haul carts along the road from the nearby fields. Tanchon is also a regional agricultural centre though, like other parts of the country, has suffered from the droughts of recent years.

A long, straight road runs from the city centre across sandbanks and the river delta to the zinc smelter and magnesia works. The approach to the plants is marked by a string of prominent letters, proclaiming: 'Long Live the Dear Leader Kim Jong Il, Sun of the 21st Century!' At shift's beginning and end, the road is packed with workers in brown overalls cycling to and from the factories.

The city is also a useful stop-off point for travellers to the far northeast of the DPRK. World Food Programme convoys plying the Pyongyang–Chongjin aid route often spend the night in Tanchon, grateful for the respite from the treacherous, winding roads.

**HISTORY** Though an important eastern port of the DRPK, Tanchon is traditionally behind Wonsan, Hungnam, Chongjin and Rajin in the pecking order. Its prominence has grown since the flat stretch of land between the town and the coast was selected by Kim Il Sung himself as the site of a new zinc smelter in the early 1980s.

Smelting began in 1985, using ore from the Komdok mining complex some 80km inland. A brand-new magnesia plant followed in 1997, fed by magnesite ore from Ryongyang. There has been talk of a plan to expand the port's facilities to accommodate an increasing level of exports. The zinc plant's owners are proposing an overhaul that would cost as much as US$100 million. These plans are at an early stage, however.

**GETTING THERE AND AWAY** Tanchon is on the main rail route linking Wonsan with the Chinese/Russian border. A branch line runs the 80km inland to Komdok.

By road, the city is a five-hour drive from Hamhung and around eight hours from Wonsan. The road between Hamhung and Tanchon is a winding two-lane dust track, extremely scenic in parts as it flirts with the East Korea Sea before disappearing back into the mountains. The route is certainly not conducive to high-speed travel.

**WHEN TO GO** The most favourable seasons are spring and autumn, when the climate is cool and dry. Summer can be hot and rainy.

 **WHERE TO STAY AND EAT** Accommodation is available in a hilltop hostel, situated around 2km from Tanchon itself among well-tended gardens. The hostel's VIP suite offers a double room with desk, fridge, deckchairs and some startling colour schemes. The en-suite bathroom has running water only periodically and there is no hot water. Also attached to the suite is a spacious meeting room decorated with several photographic portraits of Kim Il Sung.

Meals are served in a cafeteria housed in an adjacent building. The range of food is substantial and the dining room boasts a fresco of the Tanchon shoreline across one entire wall.

## WHAT TO SEE
### Kim Il Sung and Kim Jong Il murals
Like every town in the DPRK, Tanchon displays extracts from Kim Il Sung's and Kim Jong Il's writings on large, stone walls. In Tanchon, the monuments can be found in a courtyard set slightly back from the main avenue through the town's modern housing.

**Tanchon Zinc Smelter** A huge, red gate and heroic picture of Kim Il Sung and his subjects welcome visitors to the plant. Though opened only in 1985, the smelter is already in need of a facelift. Positive steps are being taken to engage international investors. The factory employs around 2,300 people.

**Riwan** The attractive town of Riwon nestles at the end of a river valley, only 40km south of Tanchon. The town is a fishing centre and is home to a high concentration of naval officers. The town hugs the coastline of Riwon Bay, where the road from the south dips to sea level before climbing inland into the mountains again. The east coast railroad skirts the western edge of town.

## KOMDOK

*41.05° north, 128.55° east, South Hamgyong Province, 80km northwest of Tanchon*
Most Koreans associate the town of Komdok with one thing above all others: mining. The town, nestled around 600m above sea level at the end of a valley in the Paektu Mountains, is revered throughout the DPRK as the country's leading source of several metallurgical ores, primarily lead, zinc and silver.

Komdok translates roughly as 'Spider Plateau', a reference to the arachnid form apparent in maps of the area, which show seven major mine shafts scuttling outwards from the main body of the town. The eighth leg is now being developed.

Komdok also forms part of the 'Precious Mountain' area that encompasses the adjacent Ryongyang mining centre, the DPRK's primary source of magnesite ore. The name stems from an age-old eulogy attributed to President Kim Il Sung about the mineral wealth held within the mountain.

The Great Leader's words are everywhere. Enormous letters superimposed upon the hillside remind workers to 'move forward together under the red banner of socialism'. Colourful murals and stone-carved extracts of his writings dominate the town's central square, while piped instructions and reports on the day's production achievements are barked through speakers hung strategically around the town.

There are 7,000 lead and zinc miners living in Komdok, plus their families and many of the workers at the Ryongyang magnesite mine. The town's main institutions are built around the square, though the workers' houses cascade haphazardly across the hillside. A single-track tarmac road climbs up the valley side to an isolated ore processing plant at 1,200m above sea level, offering a breathtaking panorama of the valley and town below.

Komdok is also close to the source of the Pukdae River, though its waters often run milky-grey rather than blue. At times, up to 10% of the lead concentrate produced on site is believed to escape into the river. As the town seeks to improve its industrial base by engaging foreign investment, environmental considerations must be high on the agenda. Agriculture is limited, though potatoes are grown in small plots of land on the hillsides above the town.

Komdok suffered heavily in the floods of the mid-1990s, which caused widespread damage to the town, interrupted mining and severed transport links with the Korean coastline. However, in attempting an ambitious modernisation of its facilities, the town is entering a new era. Residents of Komdok exude pride in the mining achievements for which their town is renowned throughout the DPRK.

**HISTORY** The site was first mined in the 14th century, though silver was discovered in the area as early as the 10th century AD. There are two major mining complexes at Komdok: the first mine reached along the road from Tanchon, the Ryongyang mine, produces magnesite ore, while the second is the larger lead and zinc complex, which produces silver as a by-product. Komdok has operated as a fully-fledged mining complex since 1946, though has suffered periodic stoppages along the way.

The complex has grown in stages. The lead and zinc complex has seven operational mines and three processing plants, the latest of which was built in the early 1980s. One hundred million tonnes of ore have been mined since 1946 and another 300 million tonnes are estimated still to be underground.

The great leader and eternal president, Kim Il Sung, visited Komdok twice during his lifetime, in April 1961 and May 1984. During the second of these visits, he supervised the opening of the third ore processing plant high on the mountainside. Outside the main entrance, a red line on a billboard depiction of the plant traces his every step that day. His words, including the immortal line that the factory resembled a 'sea of machinery', are reproduced in large letters inside.

The most celebrated visit, however, was that of Kim Jong Il in July 1975. The younger Kim is reputed to have ventured inside the main mine shaft and expressed horror that workers were spending up to 14 consecutive days underground in order to surpass production targets by as much as 150%. (See *Underground Mining Museum*, opposite.)

Kim Jong Il made his second visit in June 2002. In the 27 years since his previous appearance, Komdok has endured some difficult times. For much of the late 1990s, chronic flooding caused widespread damage at the mine and knocked out vital road and rail routes linking Komdok with the coast. Rusting railway cars still protrude from the river further downstream in grim tribute to the succession of natural disasters.

However, things have recently taken a turn for the better. A new body with ministerial status, the Korea Zinc Industrial Group, has been established to revitalise the mine as part of its wider industrial remit. The eventual target is a US$200 million investment that would double mining output from just over seven million tonnes annually to around 14 million tonnes. Though cautious, there has been some interest from foreign investors.

The mines and associated infrastructure were built entirely by the North Koreans, though the last few years have seen some equipment imported from Europe.

**GETTING THERE AND AWAY** A dusty mountain road and railway traverse the spectacular 80km stretch between Komdok and Tanchon, both following the route of the Pukdae River. The road journey takes around three hours, less time than it would take to travel by train. Road travel is by private transport; there is no regular bus service. The rail route is used primarily, though not exclusively, for goods transportation.

The road surface is poor in places, making for a bumpy ride, but the scenery more than compensates for any mild discomfort. From Tanchon, the road ascends quickly, passing through rocky valleys. Around halfway, the route passes through a mountainside settlement producing phosphorus for use in the manufacture of fertiliser. The railroad spans the Great North River by way of two large iron bridges and runs along the valley floor to Komdok, while the road passes along the side of the valley, cutting through a succession of tunnels on the approach to Komdok.

The road is also notable for several cartoon stone sculptures. The most impressive, around 10km from Komdok, is that of a small bear carved underneath a rocky outcrop with arms aloft, in a manner that suggests he is lifting the enormous boulder with his tiny arms.

**WHEN TO GO** April–June and September–October are the best months to visit. Winter temperatures fall well below freezing; due to the altitude, night-time is cold all year round. Rain is common in the summer months.

**WHERE TO STAY AND EAT** Accommodation is available in the hostel that forms part of the Komdok Mining Complex's headquarters, overlooking the central square.

A single room has en-suite bathroom and living area with television and couch. Hot running water is available on request for one hour per morning. Hotel staff will fill the bath for the duration of your stay.

There's a sauna in the basement.

Meals are available on request in the en-suite dining area. The building has a canteen.

## WHAT TO SEE

**Central Square** The central square is the focus of the Komdok community. A huge fresco at one end depicts the visits of the two Kims to the town. Two pictures are mounted on a grey, craggy background: the smaller picture shows Kim Il Sung, in dark hat and trench coat, flocked by the enthusiastic womenfolk of the town, while the larger picture shows a young Kim Jong Il, in a dazzling white coat, holding court with the miners deep underground. A jagged mountain backdrop adds to the dramatic scene.

Along another side of the square, Kim Il Sung's writings are carved in red upon another large stone structure. Opposite stand the main company offices and hostel. A bridge leads off from the square towards the stone obelisk, again inscribed with the words of Kim Il Sung, that marks the centre of every North Korean town. From the obelisk, it is a small climb to the entrance of the main mine shaft.

The square is best viewed just before eight o'clock in the morning. Practically the entire adult male population makes the trek to the mine entrance to begin their shift. Their journey is illuminated by Komdok's wives and mothers, ranks of whom sway gently in time with their songs of Korean reunification and the fulfilment of daily production targets. The female choir and dancers are resplendent in national costume, each waving bouquets of bright pink Kimilsungia.

**Komdok Museum of Mining** The museum is housed in the lower storey of a medium-rise building near the central square. The building is easily recognisable by the two large Korean characters, reading 'Juche', out front.

In addition to the pictures of Kim Jong Il's reputed Mt Paektu birthplace, ubiquitous throughout the DPRK, the museum has painstakingly preserved memorabilia relating to the younger Kim's 1975 visit. His wicker helmet is displayed along with a host of black-and-white photographs. The centrepiece of the Kim Jong Il display, however, is the mining car in which he travelled into the mountainside. Everything, from the dark green exterior to the red-and-cream upholstery, has been preserved for posterity.

The museum also houses an interesting scaled-down model of the Komdok mining complex, viewed as a cross-section of the mountain. It is possible to trace the underground route of the miners. And with the flick of a switch, the curator can set a motorised train in motion, turning the model into a giant train set.

**Underground Mining Museum** The train journey into the main mining shaft takes around 35 minutes, barring any derailment (a not infrequent occurrence, though more inconvenient than perilous given the slow rattle at which the train travels). On disembarkation, it is a surprise to find a small shrine dedicated to the first visit of Kim Jong Il.

The room in which he sat, talked and wrote during his several hours underground is preserved as it was in 1975. The room is basic, with whitewashed walls and ceiling, and is lit by a single electric light bulb with no shade. Kim's small wooden desk and chair remain untouched, though miners can make use of the bench seating that runs either side of the office.

Directly outside the office, with a splurge of colour not seen anywhere else underground, billboards display an array of socialist artwork and reproductions of workers' bulletin boards of the time. One such placard relates the tale of the miner who worked a 14-day unbroken spell to exceed production targets by 150%; this poster reputedly prompted Kim's decree that all miners must return above ground at shift's end.

**Number 3 Ore Processing Plant** Built in the early 1980s at the behest of Kim Il Sung, the plant is the newest building within the mining complex. The journey is notable for the views along the road from Komdok town, which rises 600m in a series of wide twists and turns. Along the roadside, there are a number of small, attractive cartoon carvings: a cow heading a football, a bear drinking from a bottle and a rabbit downhill skiing.